A Girl Worth More

By **Joanne Phillips**
with **Shannon Kyle**

MIRROR BOOKS

MIRROR BOOKS

All of the events in this story are true,
but names and details have been changed to protect
the identities of individuals.

1

Published in Great Britain and Ireland in 2022 by
Mirror Books, a Reach PLC business.

www.mirrorbooks.co.uk
@TheMirrorBooks

Print ISBN 9781913406868
eBook ISBN 9781913406875

Page design and typesetting by Danny Lyle

Printed and bound in Great Britain by
CPI Group (UK) Ltd, Croydon, CR0 4YY

To my children – thank you for all your love and
for being the source of my strength.

Prologue

London, Edgware Road, 1994

This was a mistake nobody had noticed. I am left alone in a flat with money and a handgun. And I have minutes, possibly seconds, to make a decision about what to do next.

My trembling hands loosen the grip on the bankroll. One £20 note unfurls and drifts slowly to the carpet. I know very well what girls have to do to make twenty quid. The menu of what I should offer runs like a mantra in my head.

'£30 a blow job, £10 a hand job, £50 full sex.'

This was weeks' worth of work. Revolting, hideous, soul-destroying time spent.

Think, I tell myself with urgency. *You've got to think fast.*

I close my eyes and beg my thoughts to calm. After years of living in a high state of adrenalin this had become increasingly hard to do. This was the biggest chance to escape I'd ever had, there was no time to waste. I force myself to stand up. All I possess are the clothes on my back. Yet with this cash, I could afford a taxi and a ferry back to Northern Ireland. There was a way out of here alive. So what was I waiting for?

Out of nowhere a memory echoes in my mind. Words spoken by Catriona, one of the prostitutes I was forced to work with in a London sauna.

'Sounds like you're from a nice middle class family. So why are you here? Girls like you don't belong in this world. How did you end up in a place like this?'

She was right. How does a girl who used to be top of her class, who once dreamed of being an English teacher, whose graduate mum lived in a lovely big Victorian house, end up as a slave working in brothels across the country?

I didn't have an answer for Catriona then and I still don't now. But none of this matters because I face a stark choice: Escape with the money and my life before anyone gets back or leave later, in a body bag.

1

The sharp turn around the corner made the milk bottles tinkle tunefully together.

'Hold on tight,' Dad winked. Laughing, I grabbed the edge of my seat as our milk float whirred up to my school gates. A few of my classmates walking to school eyed up the bottles filled with red and orange fizz when we stopped.

'Hands off!' Dad laughed. 'I'd love to give you all a free drink but want to keep this job, thanks.'

I hopped off the ride, offered my cheek for dad's peck goodbye, then watched his float whirr away. Dad often had different jobs, but I liked this one the best so far.

My dad is a milkman often rolled proudly off my tongue in school but later back home that evening, Mum seemed less impressed.

'How long are you going to stick at this job?' I overheard her say to Dad in the kitchen. 'Longer than the last?'

Dad had had lots of jobs, including being a mechanic and a repair man. He wasn't like his dad, my granddad, who'd worked in the same accounts job for a supermarket all his life or mum's dad, who worked in the army.

What people did for a living was important to Mum. She said my dad's mum, my nanna, who was a part-time

1

cleaner, didn't have a good job either. But what Nanna did for a living didn't worry me. She and Grandad were always there for me and my brother Anthony, ushering us into their cosy living room to sink into her squishy sofa and watch the big colour TV.

Nanna cooked three courses every evening, including home-made soups, delicious steak pies or stews and she always made sure she had Arctic Roll in. Afterwards, I'd sit on Grandad's knee, holding his hand while we watched cartoons as we let our dinner go down. On Sundays sometimes we'd join them when they went to church, where Grandad was an elder. I'd proudly watch him join in, singing loudly, or taking part in the ceremonies at Christmas or Easter time.

Nanna was different from Mum in every way. She always wore lipstick, a smart twinset and a necklace, even while standing over a hot stove. 'It's important to make an effort,' she once winked when I said I liked her red lips.

Whereas Mum said makeup was unnecessary. To her, studying for her degree at Queen's University was far more important. She believed in what she called 'equality' for women and was always talking about education being a way out.

'One day we will escape our council estate,' Mum always promised us. I didn't know what we were supposed to be escaping from. I liked where we lived on the outskirts of Belfast. We were close enough to see Nanna and Grandad's house a few streets away and although we weren't as close to Mum's parents, they were also nearby.

Sometimes, Mum's younger sister Barbara came to babysit for us too. Divorced with a little boy called John, she did Tupperware parties to make extra money. I liked my auntie. She was younger than Mum but always had time to chat and play. All of my relatives did. As the first girl for a generation, my whole family spoiled me rotten.

It was when I was six years old that life changed. Mum told us Dad was moving out.

'Where to?' I asked, feeling worried.

'Near us. You can still see him. But we don't get along anymore,' she explained.

I didn't understand. I'd never heard them rowing. But I'd overheard Gran say things about Mum sometimes. I understood Mum and Dad had me when they were both 16, which meant Mum had to get married quick, even though she was about to start a new job. Nanna and Grandad strongly believed married people should stick together and make the best of it. So why did my dad have to go?

I hardly had time for the news to sink in before Dad was packing a bag and saying goodbye.

'Don't you worry Joanne,' he promised, crouching down to look me in the eye. 'I will be seeing you and Anthony every single weekend.' He gently used a thumb to wipe away a tear that rolled down my cheek.

'You'll hardly notice I am gone,' he said, planting a kiss on my forehead.

True to his word, Dad saw us that weekend. And the next. And the next. And every single weekend without fail. He took us both swimming and to watch football, then when I started Majorettes, he stood proudly on the side of the street cheering me on while I proudly twizzled my baton in sync with the other girls. He never had much money but always tried to spoil us whenever he could. During school holidays he took me and Anthony camping in the woods at Crawfordsburn, in-between Belfast and Bangor. Sitting around the crackling log fire, our faces aglow, munching on a sausage butty, we told each other stories before settling down together in sleeping bags, to listen to owls hooting. Warm and cosy in the tent, listening to rain patter on the canvas, I couldn't have been happier. I loved being outside in nature.

Turned out that life with divorced parents wasn't so bad. In fact, we seemed to have even more fun with Dad than ever before.

Meanwhile, Nanna's house became like a second home. With Mum busy studying we went there every weekend while, during the week, if I wasn't at Brownies or gymnastics, we waited in the university grounds for Mum to finish.

We loved racing through the buildings playing chase or hide and seek outside in the university grounds. I learned the names of the different grasses and trees and dreamed one day of working in a job outdoors. Then we'd run back inside the atrium, where the lecturers got to know our names and looked out for us, allowing Mum extra time to finish her essays. One afternoon a lecturer asked me what I wanted to do for a living so I announced I'd like to be a zoo keeper.

The lecturer laughed but Mum didn't. 'No, Joanne can be a vet instead,' Mum said quickly. 'She can study at university and go into training. Can't you Jo?'

I don't want to cut up animals, I thought. *I want to cuddle them.* But I knew better than to argue with Mum, so shyly agreed.

A few months after my parents split, Dad took us to a pub called The Morning Star. It was a hectic place, filled with people banging pints on the tables but Dad seemed more keen on chatting to a particular barmaid than drinking.

The next day, when I told Mum where we'd been the previous night, her face dropped.

'Your dad has taken you *where?*' she gasped.

Apparently The Morning Star was a terrible place full of terrible people, she said crossly. I tried to explain it wasn't like this, but Mum was convinced. She grabbed the phone, asking to speak to solicitors and talked about seeing Dad in court. We were not to see Dad until a judge decided what to do.

*

The next weekend, I missed Dad and overheard Nanna whispering in the kitchen. Something told me Nanna and Grandad didn't like Mum anymore but they were careful not to speak badly of her. Instead Nanna tried to cheer us up with extra helpings of her steam pudding with hot Bird's Eye custard poured on top. 'I know your mum doesn't have much time to cook at home,' she said, handing me a dessert spoon. 'You need fattening up if you want to grow tall, so tuck in,' she winked.

By the time I was ten years old, we'd long settled into a routine.

Weeks were spent at school and evenings waiting for Mum and then at weekends, we saw Dad briefly over Sunday roasts at Nanna's house. By then, the barmaid from The Morning Star, Jude, was his girlfriend and they seemed happy, although he always told us how much he missed us. He had a new job working for an engineer and said one day we could come and stay at their new council house.

*

From a young age, Mum told us how important our own education was, so she taught us both to read early on. In primary school, I devoured books like Black Beauty and Stig of the Dump but my favourite story was The Secret Garden by

Frances Hodgson Burnett. The idea of having a secret garden all to yourself which nobody knew about was so exciting. The friendship between Mary and the boy intrigued me too. How wonderful to have a secret friend if you were feeling lonely.

Luckily, I didn't have to imagine making friends like Mary in the story. Often after school, I played traditional games like skipping or hopscotch on the cobbled streets with my friends. Sometimes I would meet my friend Sam, who lived across the road from Nanna's at the weekend. Sam's mum was also a single parent, who worked in a factory doing night shifts, so she spent a lot of time home alone. I sensed Nanna didn't like Sam but she still made her a place at the kitchen table.

While Dad's life had moved on, Mum kept telling us our lives would change soon too. She'd secured a new student placement in a town called Telford in England.

'It's going to be amazing,' she beamed over breakfast one day. 'We're moving to a new house with a big garden.'

I pictured a chocolate-box cottage with roses around the door, and playing with my dolls in a pink-painted bedroom without my annoying little brother around. 'Sounds amazing Mum,' I smiled. 'I can't wait.'

Over the next few months Mum started clearing out our house, while we were at Nanna's. One Sunday, I came home to find most of my toys in bin bags.

'I've chucked out all your teddies from your bed,' Mum announced. 'You're too old for them anyway.'

Upset, I began to root through one bag but she snatched it away.

'You won't miss any of it Joanne,' she said. Anthony began looking for his Lego so Mum quickly reassured him none of it had been touched.

'I know my boy loves building,' she smiled, ruffling his hair. 'Don't worry, I've kept most of yours.'

As moving day approached, I noticed Nanna spent longer gazing sadly out of the kitchen window when she prepared dinner.

'Are you okay?' I asked her.

'Now you listen,' she said gently. 'I am going to miss you and your brother but a bed will always be made up for you here.'

I slid my arms around her waist. I was almost as tall as her now. 'Of course,' I said.

The night before we left for England, I went to bed dreaming of our new life ahead. Although I'd never heard of Telford before, this sounded like one big adventure!

*

After the ferry to England, the train journey to Telford was the longest one we'd ever been on. I took my books to read, including a copy of my favourite story The Secret Garden, but in excitement couldn't focus. Instead, I pressed my nose to the window watching scenery whizz by, changing from lush green to red brick houses and then terraces built with darker bricks, then factories and main roads. Absorbing the new scenes, I couldn't wait to arrive.

We walked from Telford station, down a series of small grey streets, to a council estate. The houses were back to back and were nothing like the streets of Belfast. Ten minutes later, we arrived at The Meadows, a street of small, square-fronted houses halfway up a hill. I couldn't see any kids playing out here. Nobody was skipping in the streets and the only sign of any kids around were broken toys on the front lawns.

Mum unlocked the door to one of the houses and let us in. It was a three-bedroom place, with no carpets and peeling walls. The layout of the rooms was strange, with a living room on the first floor and the master bedroom downstairs.

'All this place needs is a lick of paint and lots of books to make it feel like home. Go on, go and look in your bedrooms,' said Mum.

Anthony had first choice and chose the biggest room at the back, so I got the box room at the front overlooking the backyard of the neighbour's house. I stood by the window staring at twisted overgrown brambles and knee-high grass, thinking this house wasn't what I'd imagined. We'd hurt ourselves on the thorns if we tried to play games outside. I looked further over the wall, and could see the other gardens, filled with discarded bike wheels and dog poo. The cobbled streets of Belfast felt very far away.

That night I fell asleep staring at the bare lightbulb above my head. Tomorrow, I decided, I'll take my skipping rope into school to help me make friends.

2

Mum's face was flushed as she quickly packed her bag with her books and notepads.

'Right, this is your new routine. For this week I am going to collect you at lunchtime. Then I have organised a child-minder for after school. She will give you tea and make sure you do your homework. Meantime, today I will meet you by the shops near the school this lunchtime. Okay?'

We nodded. I was nervous about starting school, but I was also excited about the prospect of making new friends. Mum walked us to the gates, where I took a deep breath and put a smile on my face. Nanna told me smiling at people made you more approachable. 'Remember to meet by the shops near the school,' Mum said over her shoulder.

She seemed distracted, but then she often was. I knew she always had essays to write or a lecture to attend. She often complained how tough it was fitting everything in and often blamed Dad for not helping enough, especially with money. Not wanting to make a fuss, I said goodbye cheerfully and went in.

I had to ask a passing pupil where my new classroom was. After I spoke they stifled a giggle behind a hand. I had no idea what they were laughing at and continued down the corridor. Finally, I found my classroom and was introduced as the new girl by the teacher.

Thirty pairs of eyes swivelled around to look. Suddenly I felt very self-conscious. I'd never been the new girl before.

At break, a few girls were whispering when I walked past and then one of them came up to me.

'Where you from then?' she asked.

'Northern Ireland,' I said, proudly. I was about to tell them all about my family but thought better of it when the girls burst into giggles.

'Alright, Paddy,' someone shouted when they walked past. I joined in their laughter because I wasn't sure what else to do.

At lunchtime, I left the school gates to meet Mum by the shops, like she'd asked. But I mistakenly turned left instead of right and couldn't see any shops, so kept walking, hoping I'd come to them. After about ten minutes I found myself surrounded by an unfamiliar housing estate. In panic, I quickened my pace.

Back at my old school in Belfast we'd had several lessons about Stranger Danger. A police officer with a kind face came in to warn us about talking to strangers or venturing into places we didn't know. I was way less than five foot tall and everyone always told me I looked young for my age. My heart began thudding as I turned each corner, fearing bumping into a child snatcher on the way.

Suddenly a man's head popped up above a fence and I stopped in my tracks. He didn't look like a child abductor but dare I ask him the way?

'Are you okay?' he asked, switching off a lawnmower.

'I am lost,' I stammered. 'Do you know where The Meadows is?'

He rubbed his chin. 'That's a long way from here, love. You are very lost aren't you?'

Tears sparked in my eyes. 'We have just moved here,' I blurted out. 'Me and Mum and my brother are from Northern Ireland. It's my first day at school and I am lost but meant to be meeting Mum.' Panic rose in my voice, so the man held up his hands to calm me down.

'I'll drive you back,' he said gently. 'Come on.'

He unlocked a side gate and I followed him in silence to a car near his house. He unlocked the car door and I climbed in. *Should I be doing this?* I thought. But then again, how else was I going to get home?

Thankfully, within minutes, we pulled up by the shops and he cheerily told me where to go. I thanked him, relief washing over me. The man hadn't been dangerous after all, he was just a lovely neighbour.

Moments later, I saw Mum. I was so happy to see her, but her face clouded like thunder when she clocked me.

'What the hell do you think you're playing at?' she spat, grabbing my arm. 'I've been waiting for an hour and a half. Lunchtime is finished. What happened?'

I tried to explain but her grip at my elbow tightened. 'How stupid you are to get into a car with a stranger. You're just asking for trouble. I can't trust you to do anything can I?'

'You can!' I sobbed, tears streaming down my face.

Mum marched me back to school in silent anger. Just as we reached the gates, she narrowed her eyes. 'You're just like your dad, Joanne. Always causing problems. Never doing what he said he'd do. He was a waste of space, like you.' Her words landed like shards in my chest but quickly I wiped away my tears because crying also annoyed her sometimes too.

*

Over the next week, I learned a lot about my new way of life here in England. While kids found my accent funny, their quirky habits like rolling their skirts up to make them shorter and rolling down their socks were strange. But I was determined to make friends and copied the dress code. Then I produced a skipping rope from my bag.

'Fancy a go at this?' I asked.

One girl, a tall blonde called Tracey pulled the rope from my hands. She started spinning it around like a lasso while the others erupted with more laughter.

'Ah, you haven't quite got the hang of it,' I giggled, trying to reach for it, but she was taller than me. 'Here, let me show you.'

She threw me the rope.

'Turn the rope and jump in,' I explained, handing her one end. After a moment, they all joined in, laughing and giggling. But after a few minutes, I heard my name being shouted.

'What do you think you're doing?'

It was a teacher.

'I was showing the girls how to play skipping, sir,' I stammered. He snatched the rope from my hands.

'This is a hazard in the playground and is now confiscated,' he snapped. 'Any more of this nonsense and I will have you in detention.' He stalked off, twisting the rope in his hands like it was a piece of rubbish.

'Never mind,' said one of the girls. 'We were on our way to watch the boys playing footie anyway.'

Feeling deflated, I followed them to the football field while they chatted about makeup and who they fancied. I didn't own any makeup and couldn't see why they found a boring game of football fascinating.

Within minutes I began picking at the daisies, wondering if anyone wanted to help me make a daisy chain. For some reason, I guessed they didn't do this for fun either.

'Hey, have you got a boyfriend?' asked Becky.

It was my turn to laugh then. 'Nah,' I said. 'I find boys really annoying if I am honest.'

They all laughed. Then Becky picked up a discarded daisy and threw it at me, so I pretended to join in the laughter too.

Over the next couple of weeks, I didn't give up trying to make playtime more fun but the teachers kept confiscating my games. They said my juggling balls might smash a window and the elastic to play Chinese ropes might hurt someone. After about a month or so, I'd started to gain a reputation as a troublemaker, but I was only trying to have fun.

Despite break times being boring, I enjoyed lessons. I was in the top sets of all my classes and my favourite subject was English. One day, I told the teacher I wanted to write a book.

By the end of the first term, I couldn't be happier. I had made friends who seemed nice enough, even if I didn't understand why they talked about boys all the time and Mum was pleased how well I was doing. There was only one thing I wanted to change. I no longer needed a child-minder.

By the end of the school year, my last in primary school, I begged Mum to stop making us stay with a child-minder after school.

'I'm 11 now, Mum,' I begged. Mum frowned. 'But who will make you do your homework?' she sighed.

'I'll do it, I promise,' I shrugged. 'I am top of the class aren't I?'

That weekend, we cleared out the garden. There was an old outhouse at the bottom, so I made a suggestion to Mum.

'We could hang out in here after school,' I said. I even found some old cushions and a chair to help make a den. Eventually Mum relented. 'Quite honestly, I am too tired to argue,' she said.

The next morning Mum explained our new routine.

'Right. I will make a stew in the pressure cooker and it'll be ready by the time you two get back. Joanne, you can walk your brother home and you're to come in, do your homework and then spoon out dinner on plates, then wash up afterwards. I will be back by the evening. Okay?'

I wrinkled my nose. I didn't like Mum's stew much and eating it every day, all week, would be rank but it was still better than having to go to a child-minder.

3

My new secondary school was a sprawling comprehensive in an old village in the middle of Telford. The imposing red brick building, a sign of the town's industrial past, stood out against the other ugly prefab 1970s buildings. Standing in front of it, looking up, my heart jangled with nerves and excitement.

Kids from all walks of life attended, and although I had managed to soften my broad Belfast accent, I still attracted strange stares when I spoke. But I hoped I could make even more friends here.

Within minutes of entering my new class, I got chatting to a group of girls – Becky, Sharon, and two girls called Alison. Although straight away I realised these girls appeared much older than me, they invited me to join them at break time. Not only did they roll their skirts up and socks down, they wore heavy makeup and didn't only talk about boys, but hung out with them. Sharon seemed especially mature for her age, thanks to her long, womanly nails. She often spent break meticulously painting them bright colours. I was mesmerised, watching each brush stroke while she mused over who fancied who in the playground.

One thing we did all have in common was our love of pop icon Madonna. It was 1987 and Madonna had just released her new film Who's That Girl. We were all massive fans, miming to hits such as Like a Virgin and Papa Don't Preach when we went around to each other's houses. My new girlfriends all started to dress like Madonna too, with little belly tops and scrunched up perms and one dangly earring. I was desperate to fit in, but Mum wasn't having any of it.

'That Madonna is talentless,' she said. 'That's why she has to flounce around with few clothes on to get the attention.'

But I loved her music and the way she danced. Madonna looked so happy and comfortable in her own skin. On the verge of puberty myself, I longed to feel the same way.

Luckily my Auntie Barbara came to my rescue when it came to my dowdy wardrobe. Still in her 20s, she kept up with what was fashionable and made sure to give me her cast-offs, fashionable jumpers and skirts from shops like Tammy Girl.

I started wearing short cut T-shirts under my hand-knitted jumpers so I could fit in with the girls when I left the house.

We all wanted to be like Madonna when we grew up. Here was a woman in control who seemed to enjoy life in a way nobody, including our mums, seemed to do.

*

In my new routine, I either got the bus or walked with my friends along a disused railway line through the woods to my estate and then Anthony made his own way.

Then, I'd slop dinner onto our plates and we'd hang about waiting for Mum to get home. Often she didn't make it until late evening, but I didn't mind. Anthony never caused much trouble, he often spent hours on his own playing with his Lego while I watched TV or did homework.

After a year or so in Telford, I appreciated our trips back to Belfast to see Nanna, Dad and my Auntie Barbara, even more. During the week we only saw Mum briefly before she went to bed, and at weekends she kept herself busy shopping for the week or catching up on studying. Sometimes I felt really lonely or spent Saturdays knocking the doors of friends to find someone to hang out with.

My relationship with Mum had soured too. The older I got, the less she seemed able to hide her annoyance around me. Although she'd always made her frustration with single motherhood clear, now her anger often bubbled over.

One day, I was late meeting Mum to go shopping after school, after losing track of time with my friends. By the time I arrived, she was furious.

'Who do you think you are, keeping me waiting?' she spat.

I opened my mouth to say sorry but never had the chance.

'You're nothing but trouble,' she said, her face twisted. 'You know when I got pregnant with you, people warned me I'd be trapped. They told me to get an abortion and you know what? I wish to God, I had!'

I blinked rapidly to stop tears spilling over my eyelashes. Mum's words took my breath away. I trailed after her as she stormed off to the shop, my heart broken because I knew she meant every single sentence.

The next morning, Sharon was sitting on the classroom table, feet on the chair, painting her nails as usual, when she told us about a group of lads she'd started hanging around with. 'They're older,' she smiled. 'One even drives a car.'

We all looked at each other with excitement. This was big news! I'd never met a boy who was old enough to drive.

'Who is he?' I asked.

Sharon tapped her nose. 'You'll all find out soon enough,' she said.

Since I'd started secondary school, I'd noticed a rivalry between other schools. Lads often met outside for fights. I'd also spotted groups of lads sauntering around our estate from other estates, looking for trouble. They all looked rough, none of them remotely attractive. I always avoided them, but Sharon's announcement intrigued me too. I wondered which boy she was seeing?

Fitting into this friendship circle was hard work. I was always careful to keep myself updated about the latest Madonna lyrics or steal a glance at the teenage magazines I couldn't afford to buy. Mum never bought me anything and I had no makeup, so it was a struggle to keep up.

I never bought my friends back to the house either. Mum made it clear this wasn't allowed. Besides, our house wasn't exactly a welcoming place. Mum always kept it immaculate and only picked the best furniture to have in the house but she hated anyone touching anything. There was talk of Mum buying the council house and she kept saying she had to save hard for it. She blamed Dad for not providing, so often we went without new clothes, although thankfully Nanna often sent us items of clothing or pocket money.

*

In the Easter holidays of 1987, I was staying at Nanna's house when my friend Sam knocked for me one Saturday.

Nanna's face fell when I said I wanted to go with her into town. But she pecked me on the cheek anyway and told me not to get into mischief. She always said Sam looked like she was looking for trouble.

'Don't worry Nanna,' I said. 'I'll be back before tea.'

We walked off together to get the bus when Sam suggested we went to the local supermarket, Fine Fare.

'Come on,' she said. 'We're going to get some makeup.'

I still didn't wear makeup and didn't have any money, so mentioned this.

'Oh, that's not a problem,' winked Sam

We browsed the makeup counter when Sam suddenly told me to steal a black eyeliner.

'It's easy,' she whispered. 'I do this every weekend.'

I watched with horror as she lightly picked up a small black pencil and dropped it into her coat pocket.

A slick of sweat formed above my lip. This wasn't how I'd been brought up. Nanna would have been devastated.

Sam's voice urged me on, as I stared hard at the shelf. *Could I really do this? Be a thief?*

'Now or never,' Sam hissed.

I didn't want my friend to think less of me, so I quickly slipped the pencil into my pocket. With my heart banging in my throat, we dashed out of the shop. Stopping at the street corner, Sam was laughing and I joined in but my laughter was fake. Already the pencil felt like a log burning a hole in my pocket.

'You did it!' smiled Sam. 'Well done.' But this was the worst thing I had ever done in my life.

Months later, when we waited for Mum to come home from university there was a knock at the door. Anthony looked at me. 'Who's that?' he said.

Convinced police had somehow followed me over from Northern Ireland to arrest me for stealing the eyeliner, I ran upstairs, grabbed the offending item and chucked it out of the window into the long grass. My heart pounding, I ran back downstairs to open the door. It was a postman with a late delivery and I could have hugged him with relief.

*

Mum got a mortgage to buy our council house, so worked extra hours during the day to pay for it. Now when we got home from school, she often didn't come home until around 8pm.

I grew bored of trying to look after Anthony and let him do what he wanted. Often he'd go wild, running around the house so I ignored what he got up to, even when he began climbing onto the roof. When he found other friends to hang out with and came back later, just before Mum did, I felt relieved.

I didn't blame my little brother for disappearing to spend time with friends. Life at home alone was very boring. I only came home to eat. Doing homework wasn't a priority anymore either. Keeping up with my friends and the latest music and fashion were way more interesting.

One week, my Auntie Barbara came to stay. For the entire week, Mum was barely around. At the weekend she also stayed out for most of the day because she had met a new boyfriend called William. Mum said William was a much more successful guy than Dad, who owned his own art shop and lived in a big house in Wem, a posh village. 'William's well known for this work,' Mum said proudly. I couldn't care less about art. All it meant was we saw even less of Mum.

My auntie was appalled when I told her later in a phone call.

'It's not right your mum is leaving her two kids home alone as much as this,' she said. 'You're good kids but you still need caring for.' But it was what we'd grown used to.

One day, I was walking home from school with Becky, Sharon and a few other girls through the woodland when we spotted a shadowy figure in the distance. It was a man in his late 30s wearing a tracksuit. Becky had told me his name was Roberts and he was the local flasher.

I didn't understand what a flasher was, but not wanting to appear stupid, I laughed. Then, feeling mischievous, opened my gob to yell at him.

'Hey Roberts, you flasher you!' I yelled. The others dissolved into giggling. I had a bit of a reputation now for being the loud-mouth joker of our group. The shadowy figure paused and then started running full pelt towards us.

'Come here, you slags!' he yelled. 'I'll fucking have you.'

All of a sudden the joke wasn't funny. In complete panic we began running away. Two of the girls split off into another pathway and one of them even wet herself with fear, while Becky and I were the fastest in PE and felt confident we could outrun him. Then, at the woodland exit, we reached an unexpected fence with barbed wire on the top.

'Shit!' cursed Becky. 'Quick, this way.'

We could hear twigs snapping under Roberts's feet not far behind and my legs felt like jelly as we sped up. Finally, we made it to a clearing and convinced we'd lost him, collapsed on a mound of grass.

'Bloody hell, that was scary,' I admitted to Becky.

She looked pale too. 'He's a horrible man,' she said. 'My boyfriend would soon see him off if anything like that happens again.'

Becky had started mentioning a boyfriend more and more. Nobody had met him but she said she was going to go 'all the way' with him one day.

Sharon said she'd already lost her virginity but gave us no more details. I was so intrigued. I didn't really understand sex, aside from the few basics I'd read about in magazines. I hadn't even started my periods but didn't want to admit that either. My friends were growing up faster than me and I didn't like being left behind.

Following that afternoon, the girls stopped walking down that disused path home. One of the girls said her parents thought I was a trouble-maker because I was home alone a lot, so she couldn't walk home with me anymore. This hurt. It wasn't my fault Mum was always studying but I tried to brush it off.

So I only walked home via the woodland alone if I wanted to save my bus money to buy sweets. I was a bit scared and always looked over my shoulder, but imagined I could look after myself. Not only was I a fast runner, I was used to looking after myself.

A few weeks later, Sharon invited me and Becky to hang out with her after school in a nearby field with the lads. I couldn't believe how cool she looked, standing with an older teen boy in a leather jacket, his arm slung casually around her shoulder, smoking, she reminded me of Sandra Dee with Danny in the film Grease.

I found myself feeling very shy. The boys all seemed so sophisticated, puffing on their fags, eyeballing us. I was glad none of them tried to speak to me.

I wandered home with Becky that day.

'You know Sharon goes all the way with her boyfriend don't you?' she said, nudging me. 'What about you, Jo? Are you going to try and meet up with someone soon? You're still a virgin aren't you?'

My mouth went dry. She was right, I was a virgin. I'd never even considered kissing a boy let alone having sex with one. But I smiled in what I hoped was a knowing way.

'Oh, loads of boys fancy me,' I lied. 'I just can't decide who to go out with.'

Becky pushed her arm through mine.

'Well, maybe it's time you made up your mind,' she giggled.

4

During my next trip back to Belfast, I quizzed Sam about boyfriends. She too had started hanging out with boys and said I should at least try kissing one. I pulled a face at this advice. The idea was horrible. Although I was nearly 13 and had small boobs, people still said I looked about ten and I felt like it. I still loved skipping, reading and watching cartoons occasionally. But deep down, I worried about being left behind. I didn't wear makeup and never styled my long hair. Maybe I just wasn't pretty enough?

When a few months later, a boy in my class called Steven started chatting to me I was relieved. He was a sweet kid, with large brown eyes and a mop of unruly dark hair. At break times he looked for me and we chatted about things we liked on TV and the latest Madonna songs.

Days later, he was joined by a much taller boy called Darren, who had manky teeth and a Jason Donovan-style hairdo. Darren was 17 and I'd heard all about him because he was a kid who had been kept behind a year. It turned out he was a cousin of Steven.

When Steven sat nearby on the school bench, Darren rudely sat the other side, squashing me, but I didn't want to offend him by shuffling away.

'I think my little cousin might have a crush on you,' he teased. 'I can see he has good taste.'

I recoiled when he snaked an arm around me but Steven looked apologetic and I didn't want to make a fuss. Darren was one of the biggest kids in the school and he frightened me.

The next break time, the same thing happened. And the next. Until it became the new routine. Steven came to find me with his cousin in tow. Then the pair began joining me on my walk home from school. Darren said the woodland was the same way he walked, even though his estate was on the other side of town.

On one walk home, Darren kept his arm around my shoulders all the way.

He doesn't mean any harm, I assured myself. Besides, I didn't want to get called 'Frigid'. That was the worst insult for any girl at school.

One afternoon, Darren was on his own outside the school gates waiting for me.

'Where's Steven?' I asked, looking for him, panicking at the idea of being alone with Darren.

'He's gone,' he smirked. 'Guess it's just you and me Jo.'

As we walked our usual route, Darren chatted about what films he watched last night. I tried to keep up with what he was saying, even though I'd not seen half of them. We never had the money for a video recorder, but I didn't want him to think I wasn't cool.

When we arrived in the woodland area, Darren slowed his pace. There was a disused windmill and a clearing with litter strewn around at the edge of the woods. It was clearly a place where people sometimes came to get drunk.

'Hey you're a virgin still, aren't you?' Darren sniggered, pushing me lightly on the shoulder.

'No, I am not!' I shot back loudly. I didn't want anyone thinking that. I'd heard other kids being teased for being a virgin. They never heard the end of it.

'Oh right, really! Well, guess you need to prove it then,' he said.

A shiver ran down my neck. *Prove it'? What did he mean?* Instinctively I clutched the top of my school shirt tighter.

'Prove it,' he repeated. His eyes turned hard and glittery. His gaze slid like liquid over my body in a way that made me tremble with fear.

He moved his face towards mine and kissed me hard on the lips. His breath smelt foul but I stopped myself from showing disgust. Quickly he pulled up the hem of my skirt with one hand while unbuckling his jeans with the other. My back was now against a tree trunk.

'Prove. It,' he repeated, his teeth clenched together. Before I had a chance to react, he pushed me onto the ground and was on top of me. I heard a crinkle of plastic and saw him snap on a condom with one hand.

I twisted my face to the side. Then felt something sharp and just as suddenly he was pulling himself out of me.

He laughed.

'Get up. Yeah. I can see you're no virgin Jo. Little slag.'

Shakily, I pulled my underwear back on, feeling embarrassed. I couldn't believe how fast that had happened. But yes, I was no longer a virgin. I let out a nervous giggle. It's better to try and laugh it off, I thought.

'See ya,' he winked before running away.

Feeling sore and confused, I walked quickly over to Becky's house nearby, blinking away tears. I needed to tell someone. Although that had been horrible, I tried to persuade myself this was, in fact, exciting. I was like one of the older girls now. Finally, I fitted in with my friends. Becky's mum opened the door and invited me upstairs to her room where Becky was on her bed, doing homework.

'You'll never guess what,' I said smiling. 'I've had sex. Literally, just now, a few minutes ago, in the woods. Can you believe it!'

Becky's face dropped into a mask of disgust.

'You what?' she said. She didn't need to say anymore. I realised then she must have been lying about her boyfriend and having sex. Feeling embarrassed, I shrugged. 'It's no big deal really,' I said airily. But I wasn't sure if I was trying to convince her or myself.

*

The next morning, Darren leered at me in the playground. I tried to walk past him but he gave me a hard stare and then whispered to his friends who all broke into laughter.

I tried to shrug it off. I hadn't done anything wrong, I told myself. Loads of people had sex. Sharon definitely had. Attention from boys was just part of being a teenager…wasn't it?

That afternoon, Darren was waiting for me by the gates. This time, to my relief, with Steven.

'Walking home?' he winked.

I didn't want him to join us, but he marched along, close to my side. Once we reached the woodland area again, he caught the sleeve of my school cardigan.

'Hey, where do you think you're going?' he smirked. 'Remember, this is our special place?'

I looked around at the empty windmill and mud floor, littered with fag butts and used condoms, something I'd not noticed before. Clearly this was a 'special place' for lots of people. I forced myself to smile but felt trapped. I really didn't want sex with Darren again but how could I say no? And Steven? What would he think? Did he even know what I'd done?

27

'This time, Steven is having a turn after me. Okay?' Darren insisted. He wasn't asking. He was telling me. I didn't want this, I really didn't. I glanced around in panic. The woods were empty. Should I just grin and bear it? But Steven actually was my boyfriend wasn't he? Before I had a chance to decide what to do, Steven pulled off his trousers to reveal a huge hole in the back of his boxers. Suddenly I realised these lads were probably from really poor families. I froze as Darren approached me, lifted up my skirt and all of a sudden was on top of me.

When he was finished, Steven looked more nervous, but did the same thing. Afterwards, I scrabbled to pull my skirt down.

'See ya tomorrow,' grinned Darren and they both disappeared. I felt sick and empty inside. I walked the remainder of the way home, my mind racing. I didn't know what this all meant. Did I have two boyfriends now? Would I have to do this again?

The next day, I decided to get the bus home to avoid Darren and Steven. But when I sat down, I could tell people were whispering about me.

The following day, I came across Darren in the corridor near a vending machine. I could feel the heat of his hard stare on the side of my face.

Becky and Sharon were with me and whispered, 'ignore him', so I walked past.

'Hey Jo,' Darren yelled.

I turned to feel hot liquid splashing over my face and hair. Darren had thrown his hot chocolate at me.

'Look at me when I talk to you,' Darren snapped.

Tears of humiliation welled up as chocolate dripped off my chin.

'Come on,' said Sharon. 'Let's get you cleaned up.'

The next day, I decided to walk home alone again because I couldn't stand the whispers on the bus. I knew what people were saying.

You're a slag.

A slut.

The local bike.

Darren and Steven had obviously gone around telling everyone. I hung back, waiting to make sure Darren and Steven had already left, but they jumped out at me.

'Come on,' they said, linking arms through mine. 'We'll go together.'

By the time we reached the woodland, another lad with ginger hair and freckles was waiting. His pink tongue darted over his lips when he saw me.

'Yeah, so it's not just me and Steven this time for sex,' Darren grinned, beginning to unbuckle his trousers. 'My other mate is having a turn with you too.'

'No way,' I said, recoiling.

'What the fuck?' snarled Darren. He grabbed my sleeve again and stood over me. The look on his face was so menacing, my arms and legs turned to water.

'No,' I yelled, shaking off his hand. 'I am not doing this.'

I ran as fast as I could, hearing their laughter at me echoing through the trees.

After this, I avoided Darren and Steven at all costs. But they didn't make it easy. Every time he saw me, Darren would shout rude things, or push me with his shoulder so I crashed into a wall. I began to skip lessons if I thought he'd be nearby. At the end of school, I tried to disguise myself in the crowd of pupils, or hide under a coat, but they often managed to find me.

A couple more times, I had sex quickly with them both just so they'd stop harassing me. Every second I hated it, but quickly it was over, so I could run home and be free of them. One time, after they'd finished, I heard voices from the bridge overlooking the woodland. Lads from a different estate had spotted us. Burning with shame and embarrassment, I ran all the way home, hoping they hadn't seen everything.

I began to have trouble sleeping, dreading the next day at school. I knew I couldn't tell any of my teachers in case Darren hurt me afterwards. None of the staff noticed what was happening in the corridors and by the school gates anyway. And Mum was always too busy and tired to talk. Besides, what would Darren do if I told anyone? It felt easier just to go along with what they wanted or, I discovered, to skip school completely.

At the time, I didn't know what the word 'rape' meant or that sex should be between consenting adults. I was completely confused over what boyfriends and girlfriends did together.

To avoid the boys, I started to hang out with Sharon in the local shopping centres or in the nearby field, waiting until classes were over. Sharon also hated school and seemed quite troubled, although she never spoke about her personal life anymore. She seemed to want to keep her boyfriend private and I never told her about Darren and Steven either. I didn't want my friend to think I was a slag too.

By the end of the school year, I'd missed most of my lessons, even English, my favourite subject. Mum didn't know and the teachers never followed up my absences. So I got dressed in my uniform and pretended to go into school every day to keep the peace at home and then skived off to keep safe from the boys.

*

One afternoon, around 5pm, there was a knock at our door. Mum was out as usual, and Anthony was at a friend's house. I opened the door to find four older lads I vaguely recognised from the other estate when I was with Darren and Steven.

'My mate fancies you,' said one with blond hair, smirking. He was about a foot taller than me and chewing gum. 'You wanna go out with him?'

I shook my head. I didn't like the way their hard eyes slid towards my chest.

'No thanks,' I said, folding my arms.

'Wanna come out with us?' one with dark hair asked.

'No thanks,' I said. 'Got to stay in, Mum's told me.'

'What accent is that?' one laughed.

'Irish,' I said.

'Ha ha, like a Shamrock?'

'Where's your mum?' another said, cocking his head, peering into the hallway behind me.

'At work,' I said. 'I'd better go.' I quickly pushed the door shut before they had a chance to react.

'Why do you have to stay in if your mum isn't at home?' one shouted through the door.

I stood with my back to the wall, waiting until their shadows disappeared from the doorway.

The next afternoon they were back, peering through the letter box asking where Mum was. I turned up the TV and tried to ignore them. The next afternoon, they arrived again, this time their voices louder and more persistent.

'We know you're in there. C'mon little Shamrock, we want a little chat. What's up with you?' one said.

I still didn't want to let them in, so shouted back. 'My mum won't be long.'

The following afternoon, they returned again, this time only one was at the door.

'We just want to make friends. Is that so bad?'

I opened the door a bit. I wasn't planning on letting him in but didn't want to upset them either. Besides, I was actually quite lonely. *Maybe they might be okay to hang about with?*

'I reckon we'd get on,' he said. The boy was about 17, with mousy brown hair. 'My name is Kevin.'

I tried to smile and look friendly even if I didn't know what to say.

Then suddenly, I heard a noise. A side door, connecting our house to the bin area, was creaking open. I turned and suddenly there were three more lads standing like giants in our hallway.

'Nice gaff,' said one, eyeing Mum's china she had laid out on a shelf in the lounge. Recently she'd taken to buying more antique knick-knacks. I guessed it was to impress her new boyfriend.

'My mum will be back really soon,' I said weakly. I followed their backs, feeling like a lost sheep, while they wandered from room to room, eyeing up Mum's books and cassette tapes. One flopped onto the sofa.

'Comfy,' he grinned. They all introduced themselves. Paul was the blond one, Brian and Matt had dark hair and Kevin had mousy brown. I smiled politely.

Then Brian went into the kitchen and I could hear him rifling through drawers and opening the back door. My heart began thudding in my chest. I forced myself to smile to keep things calm. Matt then picked up an antique china figure. Terrified he would break one, I stepped in.

'Um, please stop,' I begged, in panic. 'Do you want to come to my room instead?' It seemed better to get them away from Mum's things in case they broke something. Their faces lit up.

I opened my bedroom door and moved a few dollies from the duvet so there was more room. I sat on the bed, staring up at them. The boys' B.O. and bad breath filled the air.

'Mum will be home soon,' I repeated, trying to sound confident. 'Do you want a cup of tea or something?'

Brian licked his lips. Paul sniggered.

'We'd rather you showed us your bits,' Paul said. They all stared at me. I wanted to scream.

'What do you mean?' I said, weakly. I couldn't believe this was happening. Tears smarted in my eyes.

'Go on. Just a tit, Shamrock. That's all we want.'

The room fell silent. I prayed Mum or Anthony would come home now, but there was no sound of a key. One boy glared at me, with a look in his eye that scared me. Very shyly, I moved down my school shirt a few inches to show the top of my boob.

'More,' Matt snapped. I moved it down to show the whole boob with my eyes shut.

'Lovely,' Brian laughed. 'What about your other bits?'

I reasoned if I did it, they would leave, so very fast, I pulled down my skirt and pants, stood up and pulled them up again like lightning. Blinking at tears, I asked them to go now. Laughing, they all suddenly ran out of my room down the hallway and out the front door, leaving it wide open. I raced to close it, then stood with my back to it, breathing fast. I never wanted to see them again.

Mum came back about an hour later. Straight away she noticed something was wrong. 'Why have my things been moved?' she demanded. 'Who has been touching the cassette tapes?' She walked from room to room, then into the garden.

'Oh my God,' she cried when she saw a kitchen knife embedded in the fence.

'What the heck has been going on here, Joanne? Have you been having a party or something?'

I started to protest but Mum was so angry there was little point. I just helped her put things back in their places and returned to my room.

I lay on my bed worrying relentlessly about the side door. I knew we couldn't lock it from the inside, so what was I going to do?

5

The next afternoon, I asked Sharon and Becky if I could go home to their house to avoid any more knocks at my door. But both of them were busy. I had no choice but to go home. Thankfully, Mum was dropped back by William early and nobody came. I wondered if the boys were watching the house to see if she was in.

A week later, home alone after school, there was another knock on the door. This time I ignored it and ran into my room to hide under the duvet, but they knew how to gain access through another door at the back of the house.

'Find her!'

It was Paul's voice.

I pulled my cover off, scared they would find me trying to hide. I didn't want to make them angry.

I ran into the hallway to see the boys rampaging all through the house, pulling things off the wall. One picked up a china figure and threw it to his mate. Another put on the TV and sat on the sofa with his feet up. Terrified again of them breaking something, I told them to come to my room once more. Immediately they dropped what they were doing and followed me.

Once again I found myself alone with them. I sat on the corner of the bed, my knees to my chest, while they all stood over me.

'You had any boyfriends before Shamrock?' Kevin asked.

I half nodded.

'Give us a kiss,' Paul said. I tried not to control my face as he pushed his lips onto mine.

'Okay, you need to go,' I said in a sing-song voice. They all sat down next to me. Paul put his arm around my shoulder.

'All of us want a kiss,' he winked.

I sat numbly as I felt hands all over me. Then I closed my eyes, as my clothes were removed and I was pushed backwards on top of one of my dollies.

I knew what was going to happen next but was powerless. I went limp and twisted my head to the side to stare into the eyes of my doll.

One by one, they forced themselves onto me. While they pawed at me, I felt as if my body no longer belonged to me. Hot tears gathered while I lay still, listening to them groan then laugh.

'Same time tomorrow?' Paul laughed. And as fast as they arrived, they left.

I lay still on my bed, my private parts throbbed with pain. I couldn't believe what had just happened. What did this mean? Did I have four boyfriends now?

Mum came home about an hour later. Straight away she was fuming. She could tell people had been over. She barged into my room to find me lying on the bed.

'I've been hard at work while you're having friends over for parties and now look at you. Lying around in bed like lady of the manor,' she snapped. 'Get up and get this place tidied up. I can't trust you, can I?'

I stood up, ignoring the pain and helped put Mum's china back while she ranted at me.

'You're such a waste of space,' she said. At that moment, feeling hurt and empty, I couldn't have agreed more with her.

That evening when Mum went to bed, I sneaked into the hallway to look at the phone directory. More than ever, I desperately wanted to return to Belfast. I wondered if I could find a school listed. But the directory was only for the local areas, so I found other schools in Telford. But maybe if I changed school, things would improve? I made a list of phone numbers.

In the morning I touted the idea to Mum but she made a snorting sound. 'You just need to get on with the school you have,' she said. 'Stop making such a fuss about everything.' She had no idea how much I'd been bunking off because I still got dressed in my uniform and left the house at the same time every day.

'Oh, by the way,' Mum said. 'You're grounded for the rest of the month. And if I see any evidence you've had people back to the house I'll extend it further.'

*

So now I was grounded in the very place I was under attack. Every day the boys waited to see if William's car was there and if it wasn't, they barged straight into my bedroom, then raped me one by one. Except I didn't understand what rape was. It wasn't something I knew about. I never argued. I never fought back. I let them do what they wanted, then quietly sobbed as they left. To try and make things better, I reassured myself they were my boyfriends. I told myself not to make a fuss. I had no choice in the matter anyway.

One afternoon, the door knocked with a different sound. I opened it to find a girl about 17 looking red-faced.

'Stop sleeping with my boyfriend,' she yelled. 'You're a slag, that's what.'

I didn't ask her which one was her bloke, I just mumbled sorry and shut the door before the neighbours heard and told Mum.

The following day I decided to try and avoid an attack by laying face down on my bed. When I heard the back door opening, I got into position. I lay on my front, dollies either side of me, face in the pillow. I kept my legs tightly shut and my arms clamped by my sides.

'They'll leave me alone now,' I thought with relief. 'They'll see me lying down like this and know I don't want anything.'

I heard the door open and Brian and Paul sniggering.

'Oh right, Shamrock, I see,' jeered Paul. 'We're doing it in this position today are we?' He pulled up my skirt and began touching my bum. I twisted around sharply, full of embarrassment.

They laughed as they lined up by the bed, one of them kicking my dolly on the floor out of the way.

'Ah, so usual position after all is it then?' Brian joked.

After they finished I raced to the loo to wash myself, a habit I'd developed. While sitting on the loo, I found myself zoning out, staring at the tatty last piece of loo roll hanging on the holder. What had my life become?

*

By the end of my third year at school, I spent more time skiving off with Becky and Sharon than going to lessons. We whiled away the days hiding in the park, belting out Madonna songs or giggling over magazines. It was my only escape from the relentless worry of the knock on the door at home.

While I still loved Madonna, I now only ever wore the belly top with my big thick coat over it. I'd also started wearing shorts on under my trousers, anything to help me feel more secure and protected. I hated attracting any kind of attention to my body.

I never told the girls what happened, especially about the boys who kept entering the house. Occasionally I made a joke about having lots of boyfriends and Sharon occasionally mentioned going off to meet her lad on his bike, but we never spoke about our feelings about sex or the blokes. I felt too ashamed and besides, I knew Becky was disgusted by the idea of sex.

I'd even begun fantasising about being taken into care. I'd heard if you were fostered, you often went to nice homes where foster carers were in after school. I wondered if I phoned social services they might help me, but was too scared they'd say no or tell Mum.

One afternoon, while we sat on swings in our local park, Sharon suddenly suggested we all ran away together.

'I am sick of Telford,' she said. 'Where could we go?'

I couldn't have been happier about this idea. I hated being at home. I was either being raped in my bed or moaned at by Mum. Then I had an idea.

'Mum has a four-man tent under the stairs,' I suggested. 'Tomorrow I'll grab it and we'll set up a new home together.'

Sharon's red-stained lips moved into the biggest smile I'd ever seen.

The next day, I put on my uniform to pretend to Mum I was going to school as usual then met the girls at the end of my road. The tent was heavy, so we took it in turns lugging it down the street. I hadn't been able to escape to Northern Ireland for ages but this was the next best thing. After about half an hour we were tired, so chose the nearest field without any farm animals in it. Giggling, we pitched the tent and then all sat inside only realising then we hadn't bought enough food.

'We haven't thought this through,' I laughed. But still, it was better to sit in a tent with nothing than go home. I loved being outside, in nature again. Instantly I felt better about life. We lasted until nightfall, when we heard shouts of my name. I felt a prickle of dread when I realised it was Mum's voice.

'What the blazes do you think you're doing,' she said, unzipping the tent. 'Get out of there. Stealing my tent now? I can't get over your behaviour.'

Back home, I lay in bed and sobbed uncontrollably. I had been grounded again, this time for two months. That meant I'd never get away from the lads.

*

After another week of visits from the boys, I felt so desperate I knew I had to do something, so decided to tell Mum. My private parts hurt so much, every time I went to the loo. I had love bites on my neck I had to hide from Mum. It was a nightmare.

I waited until Mum got home then sat at the dining table. My tummy churned with nerves, so I focused on flipping a drinks coaster around and around my fingers. It was unusual for me not to be in my room, and Mum spotted something was wrong.

'Why are you sitting there like that?' she asked.

What was I supposed to say? Mum never talked about the facts of life. She wouldn't even buy me a bra. I'd asked her years ago but she looked embarrassed and made an excuse.

I swallowed.

'Mum,' I began. 'I am having trouble at…at…school. Kids call me things like 'Shamrock'.'

My mind scrambled for words. To find the words to describe the attacks, the lads, the fear. Why couldn't I just come out with it?

'I am getting badly picked on,' I blurted out. I flipped the coaster again.

'What do you mean?' she frowned. I heard her sigh. A small impatient sound so familiar in this house. Something inside of me was screaming to tell her but every time I flipped the coaster, words failed me.

'I am actually having trouble with boys, Mum,' I cried.

The words hung in the air for a split second, before she let out another sigh, louder and more exasperated.

'Oh, for goodness sake, Joanne? Trouble with boys? Is that it? You young lady should be focusing on your school work not messing around with silly boys. There. Problem solved.'

With that, she stood up to show the conversation was over. I left a coaster spinning on the table and went back to my room.

Days later, Mum looked at me tight-lipped over breakfast.

'You best get yourself to the doctors and go on the pill if you're getting attention from boys,' she said. 'The last thing you want is a teen pregnancy like I had.'

I felt embarrassed, so didn't reply. But I did what she told me and made an appointment to see the GP. Days later a male doctor peered at me over his glasses while taking notes.

'So, you're 14 and sexually active?' He asked.

Embarrassed, I nodded. Then he told me the pill could cause breast cancer and told me to sit on the examining table.

'Remove all your clothes from the top half of your body,' he said.

My cheeks reddened with humiliation as I did as I was told. Then he stood over me and pawed my boobs, rubbing his hands all over them.

'Okay,' he said briskly. 'Get dressed.'

I had no idea what the point of that was, but felt sick to my stomach getting dressed again.

He handed me packets of the pill and also the morning after pill.

'Sounds like you might need both,' he said.

Things got worse at home. Mum started bringing back her boyfriend William to stay over. He was a tall guy, friendly enough, but I could tell Mum wasn't keen for us to hang around when he was there.

Around this time, William bought a dog home for us. He was a lovely little Jack Russell he'd bought for his mum, but she couldn't cope with it. Both me and Anthony fell in love with the dog straight away and loved taking him on walks.

I half hoped he might offer some protection from the boys, but he was too much of a softie. I didn't mind though, I just wanted him to feel loved in his new home. He was a stray, a bit like how I felt.

Meanwhile, the boys continued monitoring my house, and breaking in when the coast was clear. Once William accused me of touching his UB40 cassette. I knew it was one of the lads who'd pinched it, but I couldn't explain this. The lads also worked out how to use the phone which Mum had put a lock on. It meant they ran up a huge bill and Mum blamed me.

So, in desperation, I suggested I went to Kevin's house on his estate instead to stop them from coming to mine.

'You don't have to keep coming here,' I said weakly after they'd all forced themselves onto me one Tuesday afternoon.

Kevin's eyes lit up. 'Yeah, why not,' he said, and he gave me his address.

The next afternoon, I turned up at a dingy two bedroomed council house where Kevin lived with his dad, who was never there. Kevin offered to make me a Pot Noodle and a cup of tea when I arrived, a tiny act of kindness that made me feel grateful. This was before they all attacked me again. I went home feeling numb and sore, wishing I didn't have to do this but, over the next few weeks, I continued. At least it meant Mum stopped shouting at me for spoiling things in her house. Within a month or two, the lads gradually stopped trying to grope and attack me. Instead they let me sit on the sofa and watch TV. I never knew why. I guessed it was because they'd found other girlfriends or got bored.

Around this time, my meetings with Sharon and Becky tailed off. Sharon spent all her time with her boyfriends and Becky said her mum wanted her home, so I had nobody to hang out with. I felt really lonely. Paul and his lads were some of the few people I knew in the area, so when I was offered lunch, I felt unable to turn it down. We never had much food in, I was always hungry and had little money.

Then Kevin and the boys let me sit while they watched Neighbours and Home and Away on TV. I didn't like them much but now they'd stopped attacking me, their company was better than being alone constantly.

Fed up of being skint, I looked for a job and found one in a local café as a waitress. For the first time ever, I had a feeling of control in my life. Getting a wage packet made me feel proud of myself. When I told Nanna in one of our rare phone calls, she was made up too.

'My little girl, growing up so fast,' she said. I blinked away tears. I wanted to tell her how awful things had been, but didn't want to upset her. And besides, what could she do from Belfast?

Even Mum acknowledged it was good to see me helping bring in a wage. She often talked about the importance of working your way up the ladder.

'I'm not ending up like your dad. You know he's still in a council house and always will be.'

I didn't mind what kind of house Dad lived in, as long as we could still see him. Which we did, but only once a year now. He was busy getting ready to marry his girlfriend, who also had a daughter, a bit younger than me.

In the spring time of 1989, Anthony and I were invited to Dad's wedding. We were excited to go along, but as I sat down in the pews I noticed unfamiliar faces staring at us.

After the ceremony, guests came up to us and all asked the same question: Who are you two? And I had to explain we were the groom's children.

Some of them didn't know my dad had kids or didn't recognise us because we were grown up. By the end of the evening, I felt like a guest at the wedding rather than family.

An Irish Ceilidh band played long into the night and when Dad spotted me, he pulled me to my feet.

'I don't know how to dance Dad,' I laughed shyly. But he spun me around anyway. For a few minutes, I felt all my cares in the world melt away with the sound of the fiddles.

When we said goodbye, Dad promised to keep in touch before we left to return to Telford. But I knew he would be busy with his new family. I hugged him tightly, not wanting to let go.

*

Soon after finding my job, I was asked out by a handsome lad called Edward. We'd first met at school, but our paths crossed again in the High Street and he asked me on a date.

I was nervous at first. I'd avoided boys in a romantic way for months, but when Edward pecked me politely on the cheek and bought me a milkshake in the café, I knew he was different from the others.

When I found myself alone with him he didn't try anything on either. He wanted to talk and hold hands. He even told me I was beautiful. Despite my fears around boys and men, I found myself falling in love. It was a bonus that Edward was also a successful bodybuilder. He walked around with big biceps and an air of confidence. For the first time since moving to Telford, I felt safe.

When he asked me over to meet his parents, I was scared of what they would think of me, but my worries soon melted away. His mother worked in a old people's home and was very welcoming. She sensed I didn't have a good relationship with my own mum and invited me over for a Sunday roast every weekend. His dad was also always happy to chat to me. He said we made a lovely couple.

The only person who didn't like Edward or his family was Mum. When she met Edward, she thought I could 'do better.'

'He's a nobody from a common family Joanne,' she scolded. 'Why are you wasting time on him?'

She completely ignored the fact Edward was a talented sportsman who had won championships or that I adored him and he adored me.

Some days, I had to sneak Edward into my house in order to see him. Once Mum caught him climbing into my bedroom window and chased him out of the house, even though it was after midnight.

'I can't trust you any more Jo,' she screamed. 'You're nothing but a troublemaker.'

I was still skiving off school and started to encourage Edward to do the same. Once, we took a train to the seaside with some sandwiches for a day out. He made me very happy, although I often found myself teasing him, asking for a 'fight'. He'd laugh it off but suddenly the urge to punch him would take over like a red mist.

I didn't have a clue what was wrong with me. It was as if I had a ball of fury inside of me and I wanted to lash out at my lovely boyfriend. But even when I goaded him, Edward never raised so much as a little finger. He laughed off my strange behaviour, something neither of us really understood.

6

Teachers never reported my absences to Mum until she asked me where my mock GCSE timetable was. When I looked at her blankly she immediately called the school, where it was confirmed I'd not attended classes for almost a whole year.

Mum completely lost it.

'How could you do this to me? Wasting your life like this. You've had every good opportunity and squandered it.'

An appointment had previously been made for a truant officer to come for a home visit. I knew they wanted me back in school but it was the last place I wanted to be. The kids would start teasing me again and Steven was still there.

An hour before the visit, Mum cleaned and polished all her new china and sorted all her bookcases. Then she carefully put a copy of the glossy magazine Country Homes on the coffee table.

'What are you doing?' I asked.

'I don't want them thinking we're like other council house people. Even if you behave like one,' she tutted. 'Now go to your room and wait there. When they come I'll tell them you're bright and not stimulated enough in the classroom. Hopefully they'll give you another chance.'

I lay on my bed, feeling really tired. I often slept badly thanks to shadowy dreams of people chasing me down the hallway waking me up with a start at night.

An hour later, I opened my drowsy eyes to a woman with a smiley face walking into my bedroom. Mum followed her with a gentle-looking expression, one she used when she spoke to people outside the house.

I sat up feeling disorientated as the woman perched herself on the end of my bed.

'I'm the truant officer. I've had a lovely chat with your mum,' she said, eyeing the dollies in the corner of my bed. 'You've not been going to school have you Jo?'

I shrugged.

'Why aren't you going to school?' she asked, cocking her head to the side.

I shrugged again and picked at a loose thread on my duvet.

'Well,' she said breezily. 'How about we all agree you'll go in tomorrow?'

I gave a slight nod. The woman seemed relieved the conversation had been that easy. 'Good girl. Well, that was a helpful chat wasn't it?'

Mum showed the woman out, apologising for wasting her time. Then she marched back.

'Dozing in your bed when she arrived was not the impression I was hoping for. Now make sure you go in tomorrow or else.'

The next morning, I got ready as usual, sliding into my uniform. I didn't roll my skirt up or socks down. I hated anyone noticing my legs and didn't have any friends left to fit in with anyway.

Miserably, I walked in. By the time I reached the gate, my breath was fast and thick. The sight of crowds of kids made me feel panicky. Keeping my head down, I ducked in and walked straight to my first class. It was history in Mr Dawson's class, a sour-faced middle-aged teacher who nobody liked. If I hoped I could sneak in unnoticed, I was wrong.

'So the stranger Joanne Phillips returns,' he said angrily.

Faces gawped at me while I tried to find a seat. I slid onto the nearest chair, head bowed, but Mr Dawson wasn't finished.

'You're just wasting my time aren't you Joanne? I've not seen you for months then you stroll in here like nothing has happened.' I shrank in my seat.

'It's a waste of your time being here,' he shouted. I closed my eyes, wishing I could disappear.

Finally, Mr Dawson turned his attention back to the lesson. I pulled out a notebook I'd brought. It was blank, but I needed to make an effort to catch up.

The lesson was a role play with Hitler and his enemies. Mr Dawson's eyes landed on me.

'Joanne. You, girl, can be Hitler.'

I stood up, to a mutter of laughter and walked slowly to the front of the class.

Mr Dawson passed me a sheet to read off but I didn't have a clue about any of it. The other kids spoke loudly, playing their role, while I stood mute, unable to join in.

By the time the bell went, I moved so fast I left the notebook behind on the desk. My legs took over like a wheel, churning down the corridor, across the playground, and out of the school gates. Mr Dawson's words were ringing in my ears. I was a waste of time. A waste of space.

Waste, waste, waste.

I ran all the way home without stopping but by the time I reached the door I didn't want to be there either.

*

That evening, Mum didn't notice my puffy face from crying. When she asked how school went, I replied 'fine' and she went upstairs for a shower. Then I continued the lie over the next few weeks, pretending to go in. Nobody chased me up when I didn't turn up for my GCSE mock exams.

I continued working as a waitress while seeing Edward at weekends and the evenings. Meanwhile, Mum finally finished her course and signed up for a post-graduate management course at the polytechnic. William also started taking Anthony to taekwondo classes, which Edward also joined. Sometimes I would go and watch them or help in William's shop. Although William and I didn't really have much of a relationship, I helped with stock takes, tidying and working the tills. He seemed nice enough, although he made me miss Dad more.

Our visits to Northern Ireland had dwindled every year, but that summer, I was looking forward to the next trip back to my Nanna's more than ever. Like always, Nanna welcomed me with open arms. Here, my bed was always made up and there was no risk of unwanted knocks at the front door.

Later, I met with Sam who had an idea to try something different.

'Why don't we sneak out of our houses at midnight and have a wander around the town?' she said.

I'd never been out that late at night. It would be fun to see all the stars and quiet streets.

'You're on!' I laughed.

That night, as usual, I watched TV with Nanna.

We loved watching soap operas together, although Nanna always changed channels during the adverts. She knew some of them had scared me, like the AIDS campaign from a few years previously, that said: 'Don't Die of Ignorance.' The Grange

Hill campaign called: 'Just Say No' against hard drugs like heroin, also left a lasting impression on me. While most girls my age smoked, I never did and I didn't drink either, even if Sam tried to tempt me with a bottle of Lambrini sometimes.

After our usual routine of dinner and TV, Nanna told me to go up to bed before I fell asleep on the sofa.

Nanna wasn't the affectionate sort, but whenever I slid in between the fresh clean sheets and soft eiderdown, I felt cared for. I always slept more soundly here. But tonight, I giggled to myself because I was going on a midnight adventure.

I waited until the house was silent, then got dressed and pulled up the window to shimmy down the drainpipe. Sam was waiting at the bottom, in the street.

'What now?' I said.

'Dunno,' she smiled. 'Let's just go for a wander.'

We walked some way down to the town, taking in the silent and still streets. There was something peaceful about the dead of night with bright stars above us. I loved the feeling of rebellion too. While everyone was in their beds we were awake, walking the streets like policemen. After about an hour, I let out a yawn.

'Think it's best we get back,' I said to Sam. But by the time I reached my house, I saw the lounge light was on. Immediately I felt full of guilt.

The door opened to find Nanna, brows twisted with worry. When she saw me unharmed and sheepish-looking, they contracted to anger.

'How could you do this Joanne?' she cried. 'Running away like that. Making me worried sick. I can't believe you would pull something like this.'

I looked down in shame.

'Sorry Nanna,' I began.

'Don't you like staying here with me?' she cried.

'Of course I do,' I began.

'Then why would you want to run away?'

Nanna sent me to bed and told me my dad would come for me in the morning. The next day, I went downstairs to find them both ashen-faced over cups of tea.

'I think it's best if you don't stay here any more,' said Nanna, sadly. 'If I can't trust you not to run off in the middle of night, I can't keep you safe can I?'

I opened my mouth to protest but Dad stepped in.

'Come on love, I'll take you back to the train station. I think you've caused enough upset for one visit.'

Eyes filled with tears, I packed my bag. I'd never seen Nanna so upset and hoped she would change her mind. But something told me I'd given her such a shock, she couldn't cope with this at her age.

Full of guilt, I came home to find Mum wasn't happy to see me either.

That evening I cried myself to sleep, deeply ashamed of how I'd behaved. Maybe Mum was right all along. I was a waste of space and didn't deserve anyone as lovely as Nanna looking after me.

*

A few months before I turned 16, Mum asked where my GCSE timetable was.

'What timetable?' I said.

The look on her face told me she'd guessed I'd been bunking off school again. She immediately rang them. After a short conversation, she came off the phone, pale and furious.

'How dare you pretend to go into school like last time,' she spat. 'I will never trust you again.'

Straight away she started looking for colleges for me to attend. Quickly she found one in Dudley. I was to travel there by myself and sign up to complete my exams. Because I'd missed my mock exams, the college asked me to do an entrance exam.

'How will I know where to get off the bus?' I said, anxiously.

'Ask the driver,' she said.

That evening, a feeling of excitement washed over me when I began to wonder if this college would be like the college on my favourite American TV show Beverley Hills 90210? I closed my eyes that night, dreaming of meeting a friend like Brenda Walsh played by Shannen Doherty.

The stale smell of fags clung to the dusty tartan coach seats and empty cans of cider rolled around my feet, but I couldn't have been happier to be on a coach to Dudley. I was travelling to a new life. Away from the horrible boys and my miserable school. I was determined to make new friends and start afresh. Maybe I'd start enjoying my lessons in English again? I had missed reading books.

But the further away from Telford we drove, the more anxiety grew in my stomach. I hadn't mixed with other kids for many months. My last memory of being shouted at in Mr Dawson's class suddenly sprung to mind and my forehead began to sweat. To calm myself, I tried to focus on the street names, trying to take in my new surroundings so I didn't get lost. The driver called for my stop and waved down the road.

'College is at the bottom, love,' he said.

I hopped off by a pub called The Tavern, checking for the change in my pocket to buy the ticket home. I had a bit extra to buy lunch too. I checked my watch. I was an hour early, so decided to wander down past the college to find a shop to get sweets, for a sugar boost.

As I walked past the college, a huge, looming, glass-fronted 1960s building, dreams of bouncing in like the new girl in Beverley Hills 90210 evaporated. I'd missed so much school, how would I ever catch up? Truth was, I hated myself. I often had bad dreams about the boys and sometimes flashbacks. What if more boys picked on me here? Feeling despondent, I carried on past the college. I didn't want to get lost, so checked for landmarks. It was then I noticed two people, a man and a woman, walking along the street in front of me. Moments later, the man jumped out at me.

'Hello lovely lady, you're looking a bit lost! You're not from around here are you?'

I inhaled sharply in shock as the man emerged. He was a black man, about six foot two and had a strikingly handsome face. Well-dressed and wearing jeans with a pressed crease down the legs, I was struck by how immaculate he looked. His soft brown eyes gazed down, waiting for an answer. I half laughed, relieved to speak to someone with a friendly face.

'No, actually I am from Telford. I've never been to Dudley before,' I admitted.

'What are you doing here, may I ask?' he said, cocking his head to the side. I noticed how defined his cheek bones were.

'Well, I totally messed up school,' I blurted out. 'I have to take my exams at college now. But I need to do a test first. Feeling a bit nervous to be honest. Had a few issues at school you see, with lads hassling me, but yeah, hoping this will be a fresh start. I am just looking for a corner shop for some sweets. Know of anywhere?'

I paused, feeling embarrassed for saying so much. But the man gave an encouraging smile. 'I'll show you where the shop is.'

He chatted in a friendly way, telling me he was called Gerald and lived nearby.

'Don't you worry about dropping out of school,' he assured me. 'Education is not for everyone and doesn't make you a failure in life. God loves all us, you know.'

I grinned up at him. I'd never spoken to a black person before or met someone who spoke in a religious way like this.

When we arrived at the shop, I picked up Trebor mints and Lucozade and then offered to get him something. He looked taken aback then asked for a Ribena. Gerald walked me back to the college, sucking on his drink. He said he lived in a room in an annexe of his auntie's house and was 21. His auntie was first generation Jamaican and was elderly, so he helped her out.

'Don't worry about exams, everything will work out okay Joanne,' he assured me with a confident wink when we reached the college entrance. Then he paused before heading off.

'I have the day off. Why don't I meet you afterwards? We could have a celebratory drink.'

His brown eyes searched my face when I paused. I didn't really want to. I had to get home and was meeting Edward later. I didn't know this man. But I didn't want to offend him after he'd been kind to me. What harm could one drink do? I looked at his shoes, which were very clean and shiny.

'Okay,' I said shyly.

During the exam, I managed to sneak in a Collins English Dictionary to help me along. By the end of the test, I knew I'd passed and emerged from college feeling more confident. For once I could make Mum feel proud of me too. When I left the college gates, Gerald was waiting for me on the wall opposite.

'Hey Joanne, how did it go?' he grinned.

I told him and he high-fived me. 'You deserve a drink,' he beamed, leading us to a nearby pub, where we sat in the beer garden.

'What do you want?' he smiled.

'Um, cider?' I suggested. Cider was the only drink I knew of and thought I could just sip it.

Moments later, Gerald slid onto the bench seat opposite me with the drinks. Quickly I realised how much I liked listening to this guy, who was charismatic and fizzed with energy and ideas. I was so intrigued by the cultural differences too as he talked about what he liked to cook and books he'd read. He mentioned the Bible and told me stories I'd never heard of.

Then suddenly he asked me a question. 'Do you have any babies?' he asked.

I laughed. 'No!' I said. 'I am only 16. Why?'

'Oh, some your age do,' he smiled. 'But have you had boyfriends?'

I took a sip of drink.

'Yeah I've had boyfriends,' I shrugged.

Then another black man appeared by his side. He was older, in his 30s, with a lovely warm smile.

'This is Neil, my cousin,' said Gerald. 'This is my friend Joanne.'

I was flattered to be called his friend, even if I never expected to see him again. Gerald suggested we get another drink, but then checked his pockets and had no money.

'Oh, I have some,' I blurted out. 'Ah, but it's for my bus fare home.'

'Okay,' smiled Gerald. 'How about Neil drives you home then we get one more drink for the road?'

I was worried now. But they both smiled in such a friendly manner, I told myself not to be silly. Neil had mentioned having a wife and kids, so I thought he must be okay. What harm could this do? I handed over the money.

An hour or two later, I found myself climbing into Neil's car. Only once we set off did I realise how I had put myself at risk, allowing two strange guys to drive me home. All the way, I held onto the seatbelt strap, praying no harm would come to me. When I saw a sign for Telford, I felt a huge sigh of relief. I had made a good judgement of their characters after all. I asked them to drop me off at a bus station, because I didn't want anyone to spot me. Gerald opened the door for me and quickly lent down to kiss my lips goodbye before I knew what was happening.

'Bye then,' I said, turning my head so he grazed my cheek. I didn't want to be unfaithful to Edward. I waved them off, filled with hope. Perhaps I would be able to make new friends in Dudley after all.

With a spring in my step, I made it to Edward's house. He was excited for me, although his enthusiasm was tinged with worry about our relationship. He was off to do a YTS course in a factory and with me commuting to Dudley every day, we were going to see far less of each other. That evening, after his mum made us dinner, I sat on the sofa with his arms around me, for once feeling hopeful about the future. If people in Dudley were as friendly as Gerald and Neil, it might not be that hard after all.

7

Towards the end of 1990, Mum had news of her own. She'd sold our council house and bought a four bedroomed Victorian house on Doris Drive in Dudley.

'It's right near your college Joanne,' she beamed. 'So no excuses about not going in, eh?'

I could see she was as pleased as punch. Mum had dreamed of 'doing better' for so long. A big house was her middle class dream.

Mum hadn't exaggerated when she'd warned us it needed 'work doing'. Although it had beautiful original fireplaces and a huge bathroom, every single floorboard needed replacing.

'I want to keep all the original features,' Mum said proudly. We were to live alongside builders while it happened.

We were moving within weeks. Meanwhile, I began my daily commute to college, doing courses in English, Maths, Law and Sociology GCSEs. Straight away old anxieties nibbled at the edges every time I took my seat in class. I found myself sweating if anyone spoke to me, or feeling light-headed if the teacher asked me a question. Unable to face it some days, I began to skip classes and the vicious circle of falling behind and then struggling to catch up began.

Although I chatted to a few girls, nobody ever asked me to join them for lunch. Many of the students had known each other since primary school and talked about holidays, driving lessons, and wore fashionable clothes. Mum never spent any money on us kids and the idea of a holiday was a pipe dream. I felt like the new girl who was also the loser from a very different background.

On the day of our house move, I was amazed to discover we lived around the corner from Gerald's house. I wondered if I would see him again, he seemed such a nice guy.

Over the first few weeks I carried on going to college, trying to get back on track, but found settling in was a struggle. Although Edward often came down to see me, a few times we cancelled on each other and I feared things were fizzling out.

*

About a month after our move, I spotted a familiar face near our house. I recognised the way Gerald walked like a peacock. 'Hey, remember me? I'm Gerald,' he waved.

'Yes,' I said, suddenly feeling shy.

'How are you doing?'

'My mum bought this house,' I said, pointing down the road. Gerald's face lit up like a Christmas tree.

'Wow, how cool is that? Why don't we meet up? I'll come and meet you outside college tomorrow.'

He was the first person who had offered this, so I couldn't have been happier.

'Yes please!' I agreed.

The next day I found myself sitting with a glass of Cola, listening to Gerald chatting in a pub garden. He was so charismatic and had opinions on many subjects, especially about oppressed people in the world. When he invited me back to his house, I didn't hesitate to say yes.

'My auntie will be in,' he winked, as if to reassure me.

Gerald's annexe was at the side of the house with a separate entrance. He briefly introduced me to his auntie, who scowled from her chair.

'Don't worry,' whispered Gerald. 'She's just not keen on white girls.'

In Gerald's annexe, the smell of cannabis hung in the air. By the time Gerald opened his bedroom door, I knew where it was coming from. In the corner of his neat and tidy bedroom was a huge ornamental bong sat on a wooden carved stand. Next to it was a Technics desk and a big record collection of Reggae music.

'Sit down, make yourself at home,' Gerald said.

I was so happy to be made to feel welcome. I sat on his bed, while he put a vinyl record on. He told me all about his love of imported Jamaican music. Tapping to the beat, he lit up the bong and offered me a toke.

I'd never tried to smoke cannabis before and after a lungful of thick smoke, I immediately began coughing.

'Urgh,' I choked.

Gerald threw his head back laughing.

'Can't take it, little girl, can you?'

My eyes streaming with irritation, I tried to join in his laughter.

'No,' I admitted.

Feeling embarrassed, I left soon afterwards. I didn't want Gerald to think I was too young to smoke weed, even if I didn't like it.

The next day, Gerald was waiting for me outside the college again. He stood out from the crowd wearing a V-neck lamb's wool jumper and iron-pressed jeans, his hair slicked back with gel. After a miserable day where few people had spoken to me, I was relieved to see his friendly face.

'Come on, let's go for a walk,' he smiled. We wandered around the town and then went to the pub.

There was a place called The Cider House where I noticed lots of BMWs were parked up outside with scantily-clad young women and girls hanging around them. Gerald ignored them, so I didn't mention them either. Gerald was in the mood to talk and told me lots about his background. He grew up in care because his mum had mental health problems and was unable to provide for him.

I felt so sorry for him. Life in care was even worse for him. They used the 'pin down' method to punish kids and many were harmed by it. He was physically and sexually abused too, he told me. I felt guilty for wanting to be put into care myself.

'I am a victim of the white middle class system,' he said angrily. 'Thankfully I am close to my dad's parents and his side of the family. Thanks to them and God, I have survived.'

Not only was Gerald religious but he was clearly smart too. He believed we lived in a police state and had a strong sense of injustice.

'We cannot do anything without being watched Joanne,' he said. I stared at my reflection in his brown eyes, almost hypnotised. Although I didn't have strong, or indeed, any opinions about a lot of things, I soaked up everything he said. When I asked what he did for a living he told me he was a wheeler dealer.

'I do runnings,' he shrugged, indicating the conversation was closed. Not wanting to seem stupid, I never asked him to explain what 'runnings' meant. I just knew he must be doing well for himself, considering how well he dressed and how he could afford Technics stuff. I'd never met anyone quite like Gerald before and found myself falling in love.

That weekend, I returned to see Edward but before he saw me, I spotted him chatting to some girls. My heart sank. I believed he was faithful but clearly his eye was drawn elsewhere. He quickly stopped the conversation when he saw me and we went for a date to a burger bar, yet we had little to talk about and had clearly drifted apart. I left that weekend, knowing in my heart things were over between us.

*

By now, I had a job working as a waitress at a hotel in town. I needed one because money was always tight and Nanna didn't send much over for us any more and when I suggested I came to stay at hers, she said no.

'Sorry Joanne,' she sighed. 'You know I love seeing you but it's best I think for both of us if you don't. I want to avoid any more shenanigans like last time.'

I was hurt. I hadn't meant to cause so much upset. But I had to respect Nanna's decision, which was final. So when I went up to Northern Ireland on the next holiday, I stayed with Dad.

I had to sleep in my eleven-year-old stepsister Victoria's bed while she was at a relative's. That night while I lay awake, I gazed around her room at the giant Sindy and Barbie house. I was too old for toys like this, but I felt a stab of envy anyway. We could never afford fancy ones like this.

When I got home, for once, I was pleased to be back. I had grown close to Gerald and missed him. He was nothing like the horrible lads who had attacked me in Telford. Older, more sophisticated and worldly-wise, I adored hanging around with him. I couldn't quite believe how lucky I was that he wanted me to. Gerald introduced me to other members of his family, he seemed to have so many cousins it was hard to keep up. Darryl was one cousin, a huge broad-shouldered guy who reminded me of a rhino, although he seemed quiet and friendly. I got to know Leanne, Neil's wife, and through her, met other girlfriends. They were all older than me, but bright, positive women who all wore lovely clothes and were devoted to their boyfriends, who they called 'my man'. I appreciated this female company after losing touch with my school friends.

By then, Gerald had kissed me a few times. Then, one day, while invited back to his room after college, we slept together for the first time.

'I'm 'your man' now right?' he whispered afterwards. I was overcome with happiness. I'd fallen for this beautiful man and couldn't believe how lucky I was. I still had no idea why he liked me so much, often he'd tease me for being gullible, but it was official: we were an item.

I never smoked nor drank but often joined Gerald, his cousins and the women in the pub. I started staying out later, coming home at midnight and then the early hours. Mum was furious and asked me who I was with. So one day, I bought Gerald home.

Proudly, I watched as my boyfriend with his immaculate clothes and hair shook hands with my mum. I could tell by the look on her face she was impressed by him.

'Good afternoon Mrs Phillips, ma'am,' Gerald said, offering a firm handshake.

Mum's face lit up with pleasure at his politeness. With his arm around me, Gerald told mum what a great girl I was. Hearing someone else say it gave me goosebumps. When he left, Mum turned to me in surprise.

'Well, he is very well spoken,' she said. 'I wasn't expecting that.'

For once in my life it didn't matter if I didn't feel like I belonged in my family. I had Gerald now.

*

About a month or so after we first slept together, Gerald didn't turn up on a date when he'd arranged to meet me. Worried something had happened, I went to his annexe to find him listening to music and smoking weed.

'Why didn't you show up?' I asked.

He shrugged and invited me in. We slept together, which reassured me everything was fine, but the next time we arranged to meet he wasn't there again. Once again I found myself roaming the streets, my heart in my mouth, like a love sick puppy looking for him. My biggest fear was him ditching me, I knew I couldn't handle the heartbreak.

But thankfully he never seemed to turn me down when I knocked on his door at home. He always welcomed me in and we often slept together. One afternoon, while we lay in bed, Gerald stared at me for longer than usual.

'You need to start paying me for sex Jo,' he said slowly.

'What?' I giggled.

'You should be paying me for sleeping with you.'

I sat up leaning on my elbow, smiling at this silly joke. 'Why?' I asked.

'Because I am a good looking man. Lots of women would like to sleep with me you know. You're lucky.'

He poked me teasingly in my side and I laughed aloud. But I could see a seriousness in his eyes. I felt a lurch in my tummy.

I had no reason to believe he wasn't faithful to me but I knew he was a handsome guy who attracted a lot of attention. Once again, my fear of losing him ignited.

'It's all about give and take Jo,' he said, seriously again. 'You give. I take.'

I pretended I understood when really I didn't at all.

Although Gerald encouraged me to attend college initially, I began to skive off. When Mum was at work, I'd sneak home and watch TV, waiting for the evening to go around to Gerald's.

Then around this time in January 1991, I noticed my periods had stopped. I had been on and off the pill for years now. Gerald wasn't keen on condoms and keen to keep him happy meant I went along with what he wanted. By now, Gerald often disappeared for days, sometimes even weeks at a time. I was always so anxious when he wasn't around, but Neil and Leanne always waved away my fears. 'He's just doing his runnings,' they'd say. Then Gerald would return and behave as if he'd never been anywhere. Instinctively I knew I wasn't allowed to ask where he'd been or what he'd been doing.

Anxiously, I took a pregnancy test. Staring at the line appearing in the window, a thousand feelings raced through my mind. What would Gerald think? How would Mum react? Gently I touched my tummy. Already, I knew I wanted this baby. After all, Gerald had told me many times how we would one day get married and have a place of our own.

I shoved the test in the bin and rushed off to work. I was late. The last thing I needed was to lose this job. Later that evening, I went over to see Gerald and told him. His face barely moved a muscle.

'You have to eat properly now girl,' he said. 'With my baby inside of you, you need to look after it.'

I nodded eagerly. I was relieved Gerald wasn't angry. But I didn't expect the same reaction from Mum and daren't tell her. Already I knew I was keeping this baby and would somehow hide the pregnancy for as long as possible, and then work out what to do.

8

A few months passed where I successfully hid the pregnancy from Mum, and spent as much time as possible out of the house working in my job. It was easy to do, especially because Mum was tied up with her house renovation and studying.

When I was three months pregnant, I was busy in the hotel kitchen when I heard shouting. The chef was always in a bad mood, and had been racing around like a bluebottle, getting extra breakfasts sorted. Suddenly, I felt a hard shove in my back, as he bustled past. 'Move, will you,' he snapped. My stomach, already growing and hardening with the baby, was pushed into the sharp edge of the kitchen counter.

Breath whipped in my chest. I pushed my hands out to regain balance.

'Eugh,' I gasped, winded for a moment. Instantly I feared the worst when a pain shot across my tummy.

An hour later, I was staring at spots of blood in my underwear in the loo. Tears welled up in my eyes. I rushed back to the kitchen to say I had to go home and walked miserably back feeling more blood gush from between my legs. On route, I found a phone box and rang Gerald.

'I think I am having a miscarriage,' I sobbed.

'Maybe you should go and see a doctor?' he said.

I didn't know if Mum had registered us with a doctor in Dudley, so I rang a surgery. They told me to go to hospital.

'Do you need an ambulance to your house?' the voice asked.

'No,' I cried. 'I don't want my mum to find out.'

I put down the phone and walked slowly home. Gerald called when I got there.

'Why don't you come over?' he asked.

When I arrived he kissed me on the lips, saying nothing. I was in pain now, but filled with relief he was behaving in a loving way. By now I was used to Gerald's moods being up and down. He always became angry very quickly, especially in phone calls, I'd noticed. I never asked why though, I sensed it would be a bad idea. He led me into the kitchen where he began kissing me like he wanted to have sex. This was the last thing I wanted, but I could see he was turned on and didn't want to disappoint him. His passionate kiss became more aggressive, as he pulled me onto the floor. There, he had sex with me in a forceful way, far more than usual. I winced, turning my head as blood seeped through my clothes. I prayed for it to be over and when he'd finally finished, I slowly got up. At that moment, a waterfall of blood left my body.

'Oh my God,' I cried, trying to catch what was falling out of me. I staggered to the bathroom. Thick red blood now coated my hands and the floor like someone had been murdered. The plughole became blocked so I started to prod it and tried to wash whatever was emerging down the sink. It was then I realised it was the remains of the baby.

Gerald dashed out and returned with big sanitary towels. I thanked him while he tried to help clean up. Shaking from the loss of blood, I was grateful not to be alone.

Hours later, after a shower and a change of clothes, I needed to go home. Gerald didn't say anything about what happened, he simply kissed me again and said he'd see me later.

Back home, Mum caught me coming in, looking pale and shaken.

'I've just had a miscarriage,' I whispered. She looked shocked briefly then her mouth fell into a hard line.

'Well, guess if you were pregnant then that's for the best,' she said coldly. She turned away, with nothing else to say on the matter.

The next day, I was due in work again but made an excuse to say I couldn't come in. An unsympathetic manager answered the phone and sacked me. I sat in the hallway in disbelief. I had lost my baby and now my job. Miserably I stared at the phone when it rang again. It was Gerald so I told him what had happened.

'Come over tomorrow,' he suggested.

The next day, once the bleeding had stopped, I collected the last of my wages from the hotel and walked over to Gerald's. Recently he had started to ask for money to help pay for food at his house so I gave him the last of my wages.

'Look, you need a proper job,' he said, fingering the notes I'd given him. 'And I can get you one.'

I had already been thinking about looking at adverts in the papers, but Gerald didn't seem interested in this.

'Listen, there is a guy I know who wants to have sex with you. He will pay me for you to do it,' he said.

I gaped at him.

'Don't worry. He's not a dirty old man or anything. He's quite young and okay actually,' he said.

'But Gerald, why would you want me to sleep with another man?' I breathed. I'd hate it if he slept with other women, wasn't it the same the other way around?

Gerald kissed his teeth. 'Look at it this way Jo. You've had boyfriends before me, right?'

I nodded. Unwanted thoughts of Darren and Steven and the lads, Paul and Kevin and Brian, flashed into my mind and quickly I batted them away.

'Then this is no different is it?' Gerald said.

I wanted to tell him no, it wasn't the same. But he started preparing his bong for a smoke, as if the subject was now closed and it all made perfect sense. I didn't want to anger him or seem stupid, so wondered whether him saying it was okay meant it would be okay.

'Don't worry,' he said, after relaxing with a big toke. 'I'll take you around to his house. You have sex. Then he'll pay up. And you don't have to worry about not paying your way. Okay?'

'Okay,' I agreed reluctantly.

*

That night I could hardly sleep, worrying about what I'd agreed to. But I told myself, this would be a one-off. I'd get another job soon. Besides, I didn't want to upset Gerald. Keeping him happy felt like the most important thing in my world.

A few days later, Gerald walked me over to a run down looking house where he pressed the buzzer for a ground floor flat. He took me inside and a young guy with a Morrissey-style hairdo opened the door. Gerald ushered me in and told me he'd wait outside. Nervously I followed the guy down the corridor of his house, into his bedroom. He didn't say anything to me, and looked very depressed. He didn't make a move to kiss me or anything. In fact, he looked as awkward as I felt. Thinking of Gerald waiting impatiently outside, I took a deep breath, took off all my clothes and asked him to get undressed too. It was all over so fast, I barely knew what had happened. I guessed he might be a virgin. With lightning speed, I put my clothes back on and left. Gerald was waiting around the corner. He looked pleased to see me. I hadn't been given any money but assumed Gerald had been paid upfront.

'Good girl,' Gerald said.

That night I tried to block out what I'd done. Although it had been over quick, I vowed never to do it again.

*

One day, I was at home watching lunchtime TV when the phone rang. It was Gerald.

'What are you doing at home?' he asked. I was puzzled. Why was he ringing the house when I was supposed to be at college?

'Skiving off for the afternoon,' I said shyly.

'Oh. Fancy coming for a walk?' he asked.

I agreed and met him outside half an hour later. Gerald was with Darryl but when they walked towards me they looked deep in conversation. Darryl didn't even acknowledge me, and stalked off in the other direction.

Gerald held my hand and we wandered off, not going any-where in particular, then he suggested a cousin's house nearby. We had a cup of tea and then he announced he'd walk me home.

While putting the key into my door, suddenly Gerald looked up.

'Whoa, stop right there,' he said. 'Something isn't quite right here. Look, the window is smashed.'

I looked up and the arched stained glass window above the door was broken. I opened the door and walked inside. Nothing seemed to be moved, but then, I spotted the video recorder had gone.

'Oh no!' I said, confused.

Gerald held his forehead with his hand. 'You need to call the police Joanne,' he said. 'You've been burgled.'

'No, I will wait until Mum gets home,' I said, flustered. I didn't have the confidence to deal with police officers.

'Joanne,' Gerald snapped. 'You need to call them now. And also say I was with you when you found this out.'

I looked at him in confusion but reached for the phone. I didn't know why he was being so insistent.

'I'd like to report a burglary please,' I said. Gerald watched me carefully. 'Oh yes. I've come home with my boyfriend and the video recorder is gone.'

The police said they would come home later, after Mum got back from work. We left to go back to Gerald's house and by the time I returned, alone, Mum was sitting on our sofa looking upset.

'What have I done?' I asked, knowing somehow I was to blame.

'Your 'friend' Gerald,' Mum spat, 'is in fact the local criminal and spent his entire life involved in crime.'

The policeman took evidence but advised my mum to do one thing: 'Keep your daughter as far away from Gerald as possible.'

I gawped at Mum in disbelief. Gerald? With his lovely clothes and clever opinions? I couldn't believe that he would do things like burgle houses.

'You're to stop seeing him,' Mum declared.

A feeling of panic rose in my chest. The idea of not having Gerald and all my friends and family in my life was unbearable. I didn't know anyone else in Dudley. How would I cope? Besides, I was deeply in love. No, I couldn't believe he was as bad as she said.

'Not a chance,' I cried. 'Gerald means everything to me.'

Mum's lips clenched into a tight line. 'If you don't get rid of him. Then you move out,' she snapped.

'Fine,' I replied. 'I will then.'

Sobbing, I ran out of the house to find Gerald. I wanted him to reassure me everything would be okay. Thankfully he was at home, listening to his decks, smoking and looking as cool as ever. I told him all about how horrible Mum was being to me and he quickly turned to comfort me. I'd bought a newspaper with me, hoping to find a bedsit or something to get away. When I mentioned this idea a grin spread across his face and we began circling available places.

'Oh, but how will I afford it?' I said suddenly.

'Don't worry about that,' said Gerald. 'I can find you lots of work.'

Gerald told me all about one of his cousin's girlfriends who worked in a sauna, earning hundreds of pounds per day. My mouth dropped open. I'd never been in a sauna before but had seen steamy pine boxes on TV shows. I imagined they must be working like the girls in the toilets in nightclubs who hand out perfume, makeup and sweets.

I smiled, not wanting to ask why the wage was so high. I hated it when he teased me for being naïve.

'Leanne also works for Neil,' he went on. 'She's good to her man.'

I stared at him. I wanted to be good to my man too.

'Besides, you'll need to keep working to afford your own place. And to keep me,' he grinned. 'But look, don't worry. I'm going to introduce you to a girl called Tonia. She's a working girl and has been for years. She can take you out. Show you the ropes.'

I didn't know what 'working girl' meant or why she would need to show me the ropes. But the conversation seemed to have perked up Gerald and I wanted nothing more than to keep him happy. Besides, I liked the idea of making a new female friend. Although I saw Neil's wife and her friends, they were all older than me and Gerald assured me Tonia was around my own age.

I wasn't disappointed. Hours later, Tonia walked into Gerald's annexe and her sunny smile made everything seem better.

'Hey Joanne,' she said, pulling me into a cuddle. She had blonde permed hair and was wearing a tight fitting dress and killer heels that she walked confidently in. Her bust and hair jiggled in unison when she laughed, which she did all the time.

'Tiger is my man and a cousin of Gerald's,' she said, breathlessly telling me about her life. 'I am 19 but going on 25 and I can show you everything you need to know.'

I didn't know what she meant exactly, but nodded along. I'd met Tiger briefly before and he was married. I wondered if they were breaking up if Tonia was with him.

It only took a few minutes to fall in love with Tonia. She asked me about myself, listening intently, making me feel so special.

'I am going to go out with you tonight Jo,' she said. 'Show you how things work on the street.'

I looked down at myself. I was wearing a black skirt, the same one I wore to work. It had once been my school uniform too and had been washed so many times the colour had faded. I had flat pump shoes on and a cardigan my mum had hand-knitted to save money. In comparison to Tonia I looked so dowdy. As if she read my mind, Tonia told me not to worry about a thing.

'Nobody minds what clothes you wear,' she winked. 'It's what's inside the clothes they want.'

I still didn't understand what Tonia was going to 'show me' but it couldn't be that bad if someone as lovely as her was involved, surely?

After a cup of tea, Tiger pulled up in a car outside. Gerald said he was coming with us, which was a relief. Tonia gave me a reassuring wink as I climbed in on the back seat with Gerald, while she sat in the front. Inside the car, the atmosphere grew thick and quiet. Gerald said nothing and Tonia and Tiger talked using innuendoes that went over my head.

We drove to a working man's club car park in Stoke-on-Trent, around 40 miles away. It had grown dark by now and it was 6pm. I was rather tired but daren't yawn. I still didn't know exactly what was going on or what I was expected to do. I guessed it had something to do with the young girls who hung around the BMWs near the local pub. Tonia stepped out of the car first and Gerald indicated I should join her.

'Oh,' he said, before I left the car. 'You need to think of another name for yourself. Choose one.'

I was confused. Why couldn't I use my real name? Then they drove off.

Nearby was a crossroads on this busy junction. Car headlights flashed past, lighting up Tonia's face while she spoke.

'Okay Honey. Well here we are. The area we work in is called the 'beat'' she said. 'We call the guys who come up to us, 'punters'. You need to go to the window and ask them what they want. Don't ask: 'Do you want sex?' because if it's a copper undercover you could be done for soliciting. You following?'

I nodded along but inside a voice started screaming. I didn't want to do this. How could I have been so stupid? How had I ended up here? Was I really supposed to go and have sex with random men in cars? This was so gross.

I didn't have a clue what 'soliciting' meant. When Tonia spoke, it was like I was mesmerised by her, without really taking in what she was saying.

Tonia reached into her bag to give me condoms. 'Right. You need to know the prices. It's fifteen for a hand job. Twenty for a blow job. Twenty-five for full sex. Do you think you can remember that Sweetie?'

By now when she spoke, my head swam. Was I really going to have sex for money? I couldn't believe this was actually happening to me. It was surreal.

I couldn't imagine how horrible it would be to give a stranger oral sex. I wanted to be sick. Then I thought of Gerald and his face if I told him I couldn't do it. I had to do this, for him. For the money to leave home and set up a place by myself.

'You okay Honey?' she asked, concerned. I didn't like seeing her smile fade, so nodded quickly.

'You a bit nervous?'

Tears formed in my eyes, I blinked to try and get rid of them. Tonia didn't seem fazed by this.

'Listen. When cars pull up I will ask the punter if you can come with me, yeah? When I do business you can always step out of the car but it means you're not left alone tonight, alright?' she said gently.

She reached down and took my hand, squeezing it. Her eyes were so full of compassion, I had to sniff loudly.

'Thank you,' I said gratefully.

'Oh and have you picked your new name?' Tonia said. 'Gerald is keen you use a different one.'

I thought of the first name that popped into my head. 'Nicky?' I said.

Tonia smiled. 'Nicky is lovely!'

We turned to face the traffic. Cars began slowing down within minutes. Standing in silence, I could tell Tonia was staring intently into the car windows, trying to catch a man's eye. She moved towards the kerb, her hand on her hip, setting the toe of her high heel to the kerb. Up until this moment, I couldn't believe this would actually happen. Involuntary trembles of fear rippled over my knees. The idea of being alone with a man, or any stranger and made to have sex was utterly terrifying. I'd done it once for Gerald but it was over so fast I hadn't time to think about it.

Close to tears, my limbs felt heavy, like they were filled with concrete. I stood with my back pressed against the wall, too scared to lift my head in case I attracted a punter's attention.

Suddenly, headlights beamed like a spotlight onto us. Tonia twisted her head. 'Time to go.' I followed her, watching her curly hair stoop to the window. Her giggle rang out into the night air, then she turned, nodded, and beckoned me into the car.

9

On the passenger seat, Tonia chatted away amiably, like she worked behind a bar and this man was a regular. It seemed such a strange idea that in a few minutes she'd be having sex with him. I couldn't see the man's face but he had short greying hair. His car, a Mondeo, was littered with takeaway boxes and the smell of cigs hung in the air.

'Yeah, my friend will get out while we get down to it,' Tonia assured him pleasantly. 'New to this lark, aren't you Nicky?'

She turned to grin at me and I forced myself to smile back.

The man turned the car into an industrial area so I took my cue when we stopped. I stood at the rear of the car, not knowing where to look or what to do with myself. Or even how long I should wait. I could see the car shuddering from the corner of my eye, so turned my back to stare at a brick wall. Minutes later I heard a door open.

'Nicky?'

I almost didn't recognise who she was asking for, but got back in the car. It smelled of rubber from the condom and sweat. Tonia continued to chat as he drove us back. Once the man dropped us on the dimly lit pavement, Tonia's lovely smile returned to her face.

'See Honey? Easy peasy.' She flashed some notes in the palm of her hand.

Over the course of the next couple of hours Tonia and I chatted. She was so sweet, eager to ask about my life and where I was from.

'I can see you're such a young 'un,' she teased. 'But I am sure you're going to be just fine out here.'

I found myself blushing, glad of the poor street lighting so she didn't notice how inadequate I felt. I told her all about Nanna, although I squashed any thoughts of what Nanna would think if she saw me standing here.

'Me and Mum are not getting on at the moment,' I said sadly, playing things down.

'Well, not all mums are meant to be mums,' Tonia sighed, throwing her arm protectively around me. I rested my head on her shoulder. I couldn't believe I'd only known her for less than a day, and yet already she felt like my big sister.

Tonia confided in me how she'd been on the streets since the age of 12 and had been in care for a few months aged 14.

'But they don't really care much about you,' she half laughed. 'I started working the streets afterwards to get some money behind me. Then I met Tiger and he became my man when he realised what I did for a living, and the rest is history as they say..'

I didn't pry about how their relationship worked, or tell her at one point I wished I could go into care instead of living at home with Mum because another car was already pulling up.

Over the next hour, I joined Tonia inside another two cars. Each time, just before she began, I stepped outside then spent half an hour trying to stop my body trembling from cold or looking anywhere near the steamed-up windows. Then she called me and I climbed back inside so the punter could drop us back to our beat.

The fourth time when Tonia politely asked if I could sit in the back, the punter shook his head.

'Sorry love, he says no this time,' Tonia whispered. 'But don't worry it's only a blow job. I'll be back in two shakes.'

Before I had a chance to say anything she slid back into the passenger seat and I watched the tail lights disappear, wanting to be sick. It was now the early hours of the morning and a cold mist had collected around the orange glow of street lamps. Fewer cars were driving past, but I stood rigid against the wall, desperate to melt into the shadows.

Minutes felt like hours. I couldn't get rid of the lump in my throat. When would Tonia be back? Then headlights filled my view and I heard tyres slow down. Eager to spot Tonia, I glanced up. When her bouncy curly head emerged from the car, I almost ran to hug her in relief.

'You okay my Honey? See, it's not so bad out here on your own is it?' she said, rubbing my arm.

We picked up the conversation where we left off but it wasn't long before another slowing car interrupted us. Instead of rushing towards the kerb, Tonia took a clean step backwards.

'Shit. Fucking vice,' she hissed.

'What's 'vice'?' I asked, alarmed.

'The old bill,' she sighed.

My face dropped to match hers when two policemen stepped neatly out.

'Please get in the car,' one said in a clipped voice. We did as we were told. I was so tense, I thought I'd be sick, but sensed Tonia relax in the back seat.

'You been busy tonight?' she asked the copper driving.

'Not too bad. Got my break after this,' he replied. 'We've got a new chef in the canteen too.'

Tonia chatted amiably all the way to the station. I listened, amazed. Why did Tonia know the police so well?

We were taken around the back of the station. Tonia clearly knew the way. She even said a cheery 'hi' to a few of the coppers behind the desk. I stood behind her, pulling the sleeves of my cardigan over my hands as we were asked to sit in a waiting area. A hush fell over the place and we were left alone.

'Now listen,' whispered Tonia urgently. 'You need to think of a fake name, fake date of birth and fake address. Got that? Just go along with this because I have a warrant out for my arrest now.'

'You what?' I cried.

'If they find out exactly who I am, I will go to the clink,' she said simply.

'What's the clink?' I gulped.

'Prison,' she said, shooting me a straight look in the eye. 'I've already done time there and let me say I wouldn't recommend it to anyone.'

A look of genuine fear flashed across her face before she settled her features back to her sunny smile. I wiped a tear from my cheek. She spotted this and her voice softened again.

'Listen Honey,' she said. 'I'll explain what will happen, so no need for tears. It's not that scary really. When you get arrested, you'll get a sheet of paper with a court date on it. You sign the sheet of paper and they will keep a copy and you get a copy. That's called your 'charge sheet'. You get cautions at first. Then you get a court date where you'll be fined. If you don't pay your fine, they will issue a warrant and you could go to prison. I have to get the money soon or I will go to prison. Means there's a lot of work to do. But look, they will arrest you loads of times before a court date happens.' By 'work', we both knew exactly what she meant.

'Don't worry,' she said again, squeezing my hand. 'This is the first time you've been arrested, so you won't have to go to court or anything. It's only then things get tricky.'

We fell silent again when the custody sergeant returned to the desk.

'Right-o,' he said. 'Come here please and we can get the ball rolling.'

In a small faltering voice, I recited my friend Becky's full name and address. I felt terrible doing it, but could only hope she wouldn't get into any trouble.

By this point, Becky had already turned 18. I was still underage and was desperately scared of getting into trouble with either the police or Mum. I knew what I was doing was illegal now, but surely if they knew I was a child too, I'd end up in even more trouble. While I gave details from someone in Telford, Tonia gave her address as Walsall. The copper didn't blink or ask us how we ended up in Stoke.

After the paper work was done, Tonia asked the quickest way back to the beat. The sergeant pleasantly gave the fastest directions.

'Mind how you go,' he said, when we left.

I was pale with shock because I now had an official police caution to my name.

'Don't worry Honey,' Tonia soothed. 'They can only arrest us once a night so we're free for the rest of the evening.'

She hooked her arm through mine to step out into the night together. Almost like we were going clubbing and not back to the red light district.

It took us over an hour to walk back. I had a hundred questions about what prison life was like. Prisoner Cell Block

H used to be one of my favourite programmes and I'd never met anyone who'd been to a real jail before.

Tonia wrinkled her nose at the memories.

'You have to wear prison clothes,' she said. 'Including prison knickers which get swapped around with other prisoners in between washes. It's so horrible, especially if someone has crabs.' I stared at her in sympathy.

'Sounds awful,' I said, shuddering.

'Nah, well, if you do end up in prison for soliciting it's only for a few weeks,' she shrugged.

The closer we got back to Stoke town centre, the quieter I grew. I was exhausted. I wanted to go to bed, but also, I knew I'd not earned any money at all. What would Gerald say? As if she'd read my mind, Tonia gave me my charge sheet she'd stashed in her bag.

'When you get home, give your man this,' she said. 'Proves we were arrested and explains why you've come back empty handed this time.'

I took it from her gratefully to fold and put in my pocket.

I didn't like the way she said 'this time' because I knew it would be mean I'd be doing this another time. Right at that moment, I couldn't think beyond the following day.

Back at Gerald's flat, I immediately showed him the charge sheet. I thought he'd be shocked or worried for me, but his face remained blank. He'd already got food in, his favourite doner from the local kebab shop and a big bottle of cider.

He nodded to invite me to sit and eat with him and nothing else was said, so I didn't say anything either. After half an hour, I knew I'd better get home. 'Make sure you're back tomorrow night,' Gerald said.

*

I tip-toed to my bedroom, but Mum's bedroom light flicked on. 'Joanne?' she hissed. I knew I was for it. She opened the door, her face red with fury.

'You're grounded,' she spat.

The next morning, I woke early. Mum didn't know I had lost my job, so I told her I needed to go out and get some things for work. She couldn't argue with that. Then instead, I went straight round to Gerald's. He was still half asleep and making up a bong when I arrived.

'I am so sorry but Mum's grounded me so I can't come out tonight,' I began. His jaw clenched.

'You fucking what?' he snarled.

I swallowed. I hated seeing him angry, usually it was only with people on the phone about his 'runnings' he lost his temper. He'd never directed it at me like this before.

'You fucking little bitch,' he shouted. 'Think you can come and go and do as you please? Let others pay for you, eh? Who pays for the food? Who pays for your man?'

I sat on his bed, my head in my hands. A rising feeling of having done something terrible washed over my stomach and chest.

'I am sorry,' I said, crying. Tonia, Tiger and Gerald's other cousins including Neil were in the living room of the annexe and I was filled with shame they were overhearing this.

'You know you're a bitch too, don't you. Yet this is how you fucking treat me?'

He was yelling, standing over me. I stood up to leave, his words ringing in my ears. I ran outside, tears pouring down my face, not knowing what to do.

For the rest of the day, I miserably stayed in my bedroom. Gerald didn't call the house. By that evening, I missed him so much and wondered what would happen. Would he dump me now? I had to try and apologise. While it was true I didn't want to work the streets, maybe I could get another job and contribute that way?

The next day, when Mum was at work, I sneaked back to Gerald's house. This time, I begged for forgiveness.

'Please, please, don't be angry,' I said. 'Give me another chance.'

As soon as the words left my mouth, I wondered what I was asking for another chance to do but Gerald smirked, to my relief.

'Okay,' he said slowly. 'We're going to Stoke tonight, just like before okay?'

I stared at him as he waited a moment for my response.

I breathed out. 'Okay.'

Tonia was already up and about, her face of full makeup. When she saw me, she smiled.

'Oh, I've missed you Jo,' she said, pulling me into a hug. 'It wasn't the same without you last night.' She smelled of perfume and hairspray and a flood of warmth overcame me. Having her as a friend meant everything.

That night, I got ready. I still didn't have any makeup, so Tonia let me borrow some. I had the same mini-skirt I always wore for my waitressing job and ballet pumps on. I didn't bother doing my hair, I always wore it down and long anyway. Looking at me like I was her younger sister, Tonia affectionately pinched my chin. 'It's all going to be fine,' she reassured me.

Like last time, Tiger drove us down there and Gerald said he wanted to see me coming back wedged up. I swallowed, wondering what I'd have to do to get a decent amount of money.

Once they'd gone Tonia encouraged me to go for it.

'Honestly, you'll soon get into the swing of it,' she said breezily. 'Have more belief in yourself. The men all roll into one by the end of the night. It's not hard.'

Out of nowhere she started singing 'I am the one and only...' by Chesney Hawkes and I couldn't help but join in. I loved that song and belting out the tune into the street lightened my mood. Afterwards, we fell about laughing and I'd almost forgotten why we were here.

But I didn't have long to wait for the fear to return. When the next car pulled up, Tonia stepped aside and nodded. I swallowed hard, trembling, forcing myself to walk over.

'Now or never,' I told myself like a mantra. Knowing Tonia was coaxing me on, and Gerald needed money, I bent down when the man opened his window.

'Handjob please,' he said.

To my surprise, he sounded quite well-spoken so I tried to reassure myself he wasn't a serial killer, took a deep breath and opened his car door.

The man drove off at speed. He barely spoke, just asked me if I was busy. I said yes. I didn't want him to know this was my first time.

Adrenalin made my arms and legs feel jerky when he pulled into a dark side road. Smoothly, like he'd done this a thousand times before, he unzipped his flies. Before I had a chance to think, I held my breath and did what I had to do. Inside I felt revolted and counted in my head to pass the time. Minutes later, he handed me a ten-pound note.

Within half an hour, I was standing back on the street next to Tonia.

'I can't believe I earned ten pounds that fast,' I said, relieved it was over. Tonia looked at me proudly.

'Gerald will be pleased,' she said, squeezing my shoulders.

Minutes later, Tonia went off on her own, so I stood back against the wall in the shadows waiting for her. I avoided looking at any other drivers. I'd made some money. I didn't want to do it again.

Tonia was back and forth many times and by midnight had a fist of notes in her hand. Then suddenly a familiar face was winding down a car window. The vice officer.

'Come on ladies, jump in,' he sighed.

Once again the officer amiably chatted to Tonia and she replied with her usual infectious enthusiasm. This time I knew what to expect and didn't panic so much when I calmly gave Becky's details. I got my charge sheet and we were sent on our way.

Back at Gerald's, I was buzzing with relief. Not only had I done what Gerald asked, nothing bad had happened – but he didn't look impressed.

'Is this all you made?' he said, eyeing the tenner.

'What do you mean?' I asked. 'It's ten quid. That's good, right?'

He put it in his pocket. I didn't realise he was taking all of it. Thankfully Tonia giggled her way into the room, relieving the tension.

'Come and have a bath Joanne,' she said.

I followed her into the bathroom where bubbles were filling under the taps. 'Always have a bath straight away after work,' she advised me. Then she poured a cap of disinfectant in it, filling the room with a pungent smell of pine. 'This always helps too.'

With no embarrassment, she stripped off, and climbed in. I was in awe of how comfortable she was in her own skin.

'Sit on the loo and chat to me!' she giggled, while she scrubbed herself. We talked about our favourite tunes in the charts, perfumes we loved and what films we wanted to watch. Much needed girlie chit-chat, after a terrifying night. Then she had something else to say.

'Before I forget Jo,' she said. 'Even when you're on your period it can't stop you from working.'

'Eh?' I said. I assumed at the very least when I was on a period I wouldn't have to do anything that night.

Tonia pulled herself from the bath, wrapped a towel around her and opened the bathroom cabinet to show a washing up sponge. Using nail scissors she snipped off the scrubby part and cut it into a cube and made it wet under the tap.

'You put it inside you like a tampon,' she explained. I looked at her in horror.

'That way, punters don't know you're on a period and whatever time of the month it is you can still work see?' she smiled, like it was some sort of amazing invention. I wanted to be sick.

After I had a quick bath, we shared a towel. Only then did Tonia's smile fade.

'Listen babe,' she said. 'Gerald is actually getting really pissed off. You need to start making serious money or you'll be in trouble.'

I giggled nervously. 'What are you on about? I made a tenner!' It would take me hours at work waitressing to make the same amount.

'Please listen to me,' she said, shaking her wet curls. 'There'll be trouble if not.'

Afterwards, I went to find Gerald in his small kitchen, ironing creases into his jeans.

'Have I done something wrong?' I asked. He put the iron down, steam rising between us. He leaned over the ironing board to place his forehead right up against mine. I stared deep into his dark eyes.

'You need to be scared of two people Jo,' he said in a menacing voice. 'Me and God.' The black of his pupils expanded so I could see my own reflection in them. I stepped back and he picked up the iron again, which let out a huge hiss of steam.

10

The next morning, Mum quizzed me again about what time I had got back. I lied and said I missed the bus home after going to the pub.

'You're grounded again,' she screamed at me. So I stayed in my room until she went to work and then went over to Gerald's. After what he'd said, I was scared he would lose his temper with me, or even ditch me. I didn't know what was worse. The fear of losing him or the fear of being on the streets again.

Gerald was cooking a delicious dinner, a Jamaican recipe of fried beans, butter and onions when I arrived. By now he had introduced me to lots of Jamaican cuisine, including fried plantain and salt fish. I'd offered to cook a few times but he always refused, telling me I wasn't 'clean' enough.

I didn't understand what he meant. I had a bath every day and always tried to wear clean clothes, even if I didn't have many. But I knew Gerald was obsessed with cleanliness which he said was next to Godliness. He spent hours cleaning the kitchen after every meal and if I ever washed up, criticised me for not doing it properly. However hard I tried, I could never quite get things right. Maybe Mum was right, I was useless.

Once again, I told myself everything would be okay, as long as I kept my man happy. And after we ate, Gerald told me of his next plan.

'I have this counterfeit money,' he said. Then he sighed, realising I didn't know what he meant. 'Fake money to you,' he said. 'You need to go to the shop to make sure it works.'

He handed me a few twenty-pound notes. 'Don't try a shop where they have a fake money scanner,' he winked.

I walked out into the street, trembling. This was illegal. The last thing I wanted to do was get into any more trouble. But equally I didn't want Gerald to dump me. Things at home were awful. Mum did nothing but scream at me or didn't want me around while she was with William. I had to get back into Gerald's good books.

In a panic, I walked into the first shop I saw which was a branch of WH Smith. I tried to buy a bottle of water but the cashier immediately asked me to go into the back room of the shop while police were called.

'It's okay,' I said, trying to stand taller. 'The police know who I am. They'll let me off.' I had no idea if this was true but had to pretend it was.

I waited at the back of the shop, my heart banging. The police did turn up but after running checks on me, to my amazement, let me go. My bravado about being 'known' to police had worked and the shop attendant looked furious. Gerald would be pleased, I hoped.

But back at his annexe, Gerald was furious and rolled his eyes at me.

'Typical of you,' he spat. 'You're too honest for crime.'

It was true. I didn't know if this was a compliment or not. Then Gerald slowly smiled and wrapped me in his arms. 'But the good news is, I can trust you can't I, Jo?' he said.

I assured him he could completely trust me. I was also anxious to let Gerald know I'd never tell police about him or his address.

'I won't ever get you into trouble,' I murmured into his chest.

*

Days later, on a warm night in July 1991, I found myself standing with my back against the wall with Tonia by my side again. Tonight she didn't crack as many jokes, focusing instead on catching the eye of drivers. I could tell she was under pressure to make more money. So was I. Before we left, Gerald said I wasn't to let him down like last time. A car pulled up and Tonia strutted over to the driver's window.

'I'll be back soon,' she whispered over her shoulder. 'Just go for it. You can do it Jo, or should I say Nicky?'

I swallowed hard, watching the red tail lights of her punter's car disappear into the darkness. I knew I had to attract a driver soon or else. I stepped to the edge of the kerb and a car soon pulled over. This time, the man asked me in. 'Full sex,' he said simply.

My stomach lurched with nausea, but I opened the door and climbed in. I tried not to look, but had clocked he was a middle-aged man with greying temples, similar to most of the punters so far. His car smelled freshly valeted but I could smell alcohol on his breath. He skidded off, driving to a side road, and then pulled down his seat to a lying position.

Do what you need to do and get out of his fast, I told myself. I rummaged in my bag for condoms and undressed. While I pulled my cardigan off, I realised my body felt numb. It was as though someone else was doing this, not me.

We went through the motions. Relieved it was over, I was soon standing back at my wall. This time, my body wasn't trembling. All I could think of was the three ten pound notes in my pocket and how I had to make more. I had the fine to pay. Gerald to pay. And probably my own place to pay for. Gerald kept mentioning the need for my own address. I had no idea how I'd pay for that either.

Four more times punters came and asked for sex. Four more times I did it. Each time was gross in a different way. The smell of someone's BO. The choking fug of cigarette smoke hanging in the car. The feel of a bristly beard. The stench of pongy feet. Each time, I turned my head to look out of the window, into the street lights to think of something else.

One punter parked up near a side street. While he got what he wanted from my body, I focused on the blur of orange street light through the windscreen. It became a flickering campfire back in Northern Ireland. Dad was laughing with me and I was sharing a sausage butty with Anthony. The lovely memories flooded through my mind and my heart. I was safe, warm, happy.

'Get dressed,' the man's voice barked. Suddenly I was back in the stranger's car, half naked with someone who had no respect for me.

After more hours, more cars, more horrible men, I had money in my pocket. I was so relieved it was over and it was time to find Tonia.

I wandered around for an hour before finding her. She appeared from nowhere, giggling her head off. 'Oh, it's home time,' she said, linking her arm through mine. For the next few weeks, I became trapped in a routine where I slept in the day, then sneaked out at night to Gerald's where he took us to work the streets in Stoke. Afterwards, he dropped me back at Mum's or asked me to stay over at his. Mum often grounded me, but Gerald would beg me to stay so I'd end up in more trouble in the morning when I returned home.

I was arrested several more times too. Each time the fine jumped up in cost. They started at £15 and went to £50 and then £150. That meant even more punters were needed and so the vicious cycle I was in had begun.

I was absolutely filled with intense shame about what I was doing. I wanted it to stop, but had nobody to tell. Nobody to help me. I couldn't admit to anyone what was happening, and feared what would happen with Gerald if I didn't do what he wanted. Although I had learned to completely switch off during the sex, I knew I didn't want this life. A few of the girls I met on the streets had been doing it for years and I noticed in their eyes how broken they were. Many had bruises or cut lips. Some of them were in their 40s. I couldn't see beyond the following week but knew I didn't want this for myself but had no way of stopping it.

Then after getting back late one night and another huge row with Mum, she told me to leave. 'If you can't abide by my rules, you cannot be here,' she snapped. I grabbed a bin bag, and threw my clothes into it.

'Okay. Bye then,' I yelled.

Deep down, I wanted to confess what was happening to me, but I knew she wouldn't believe me or would judge me. I feared she might tell my Nanna or my Auntie Barbara. Or worse, Gerald might burgle her again. I knew deep down he had done it but luckily the police never pressed charges. I was scared but also, feared losing my boyfriend. Everything was such a mess, I had no idea how to get out of it.

*

After arriving on Gerald's doorstep again he didn't look surprised when he saw the bags. He told me to go and get another newspaper and this time we'd definitely find me a place to live.

Eventually we found one nearby, a room to let, part-furnished with a single bed and a chest of drawers, a little desk and a shared kitchen. The rent was £50 a week. A huge amount to me. When the landlady gave me the keys, I was scared. How would I manage the responsibility? How much would the bills be? But Gerald kissed me on the lips.

'You will have to work hard to pay for this,' he said. 'But don't worry about that. Now what would you like for dinner?' I had no pots or pans, so Gerald bought some from his place to cook with. Then he made a delicious goat stew and cleaned up afterwards.

That night in September, he drove me back to the street with Tonia. When the first car pulled up, a man with yellow teeth asked for full sex. I felt tears spring into my eyes but blinked them away. I needed to switch off again. I had no choice but to get through this. Hours later, shivering under the lamppost, I waited for Tonia to come back. It had been hours since I'd last seen her so I wandered around the corner to look down the other streets. After turning one corner on a dark road, all of a sudden two angry women in their 20s came charging like bulls at me.

'Get the fuck off our corner,' one blonde girl screamed. Her eyes were bulging with rage and her fists were clenched.

She was dressed in trackies and trainers, so I guessed she had planned this attack.

In panic, I ran into the centre of the main road, believing nobody would attack me in public. But I was wrong, the women caught up with me and dragged me back to the side street. Punches and blows came from all directions. I fell to the floor, kicking at their legs.

'Stop, I don't have any money,' I shouted, but nobody was listening. I looked up to see a sign for a fish and chip shop nearby. In the window, customers were standing waiting for their chips, clearly pretending the commotion outside wasn't happening. I scrambled to my feet, swapping blows with two of the girls. One blonde girl pushed me hard so I landed on my back, then the glint of a knife caught my eye.

'Give us your money,' she spat, crouching down holding the knife to my neck. I could smell the scent of chewing gum on her breath. The other girl was trying to pull at my feet, but I kicked out.

'No, please,' I begged.

'Hand it over,' she snarled, moving the blade closer. I closed my eyes, imagining her cutting my flesh, blood spurting everywhere. I wondered why nobody in the shop was coming to help. I felt someone tugging at my feet, where many girls kept their money safely stashed and within seconds they were gone. I sat up, dazed, feeling for my notes in my shoes but found only fluff.

Shaken up, I walked back to the street corner near the working men's club car park. Aching all over, I strained to look for Tonia but there was no sign of her. Then, simultaneously, Tiger's car pulled up and Tonia appeared behind me.

'Where were you?' I asked. I realise I could taste blood in my mouth. 'I got beaten up.'

'So sorry my Honey, I didn't see you. It's been such a busy night. Oh, you poor love!'

She gently touched my face, wincing. 'Oh no,' she went on. 'You know it's because people are jealous, don't you? You're the fresh, young face. The punters all want you. It's competition for the other girls see?'

Gerald got out of the car to open the door for Tonia and then glanced at me.

'Where's my fucking money?' he asked, holding out his palm.

The ridiculousness of the situation hit me. I couldn't help the nervous giggle emerging from my mouth.

'Some girls took it all,' I giggled. 'I made a hundred quid too!'

Completely off guard, the first punch landed straight on my nose. Instantly I hit the tarmac so instinctively I curled into a ball. Effortlessly, Gerald picked me up by an arm and leg and slung me into the back of the car. I felt closed knuckle punches all over my back, shoulders, legs and arms. Each blow made a groaning sound happen, and then I realised I was making the noise.

All of a sudden the punches stopped, the engine revved up and we were going home. All the way, I daren't even look at Tonia.

I staggered over the threshold of Gerald's house, hurting all over. I couldn't believe my boyfriend had hurt me so badly. Tonia shot me a look of sympathy then went into the bathroom while Gerald chatted to Tiger in the lounge like nothing had happened.

A voice inside screamed at me to leave.

Go. Now.

Save yourself.

Get the fuck out.

My legs appeared to act independently, running out of the door, down the road and didn't stop until I reached my bedsit. Gasping for breath, I shut and locked the door. Feeling disorientated, the room spun around. I'd escaped. I was safe. I closed the curtains and went to bed and cried. From now on, I was putting this all behind me.

*

The next morning, I woke up, imagining it was all a bad dream. I didn't know what to be more upset about. Losing the money, having to have sex for money or Gerald beating me badly. Stumbling into the bathroom, I looked at the face staring back. My lip was split, I had two shiners and a big bruise on the side of my cheek. Gently, I touched the areas. Then, for several seconds, I stared at myself. What would Nanna and Grandad think of me now? Since Dad's wedding, I'd barely heard from my family.

After splashing water on my face, I took a deep breath. I had nothing in the bedsit, only the sparse furniture the place came with and no money for food. I ate the last of what Gerald had left and then made a cup of tea from a few bags he'd brought around. I needed energy to think. I needed to go into town and find a new job and rebuild my life somehow. Maybe I could find another waitressing job? Maybe I could even go back to Northern Ireland? But quickly I dismissed this idea. There was no room at Dad's, Nanna didn't want me at hers and, besides, I had fines to pay. What if the police followed me to Northern Ireland? Unable to face going into hotels or bars to look for work, I decided to wait until my wounds had healed. I couldn't face going home to Mum's either so stayed in the bedsit, whiling away the lonely hours by sleeping.

The next day, a knock came on my door. It was my landlord who lived in the flat above.

'There's a girl at the front door asking for you,' she said. 'And she looks terribly upset.'

I rushed to the front door to find Tonia, her face puffy with crying, eyes blood shot with no sign of her usual smile. Even her curls were motionless.

'Joanne, please can you come back?' she said weakly. Her voice was flat but her eyes stared with desperation.

My heart squeezed for her. I stepped forward, wanting to hug her like we usually did. But something stopped me. I didn't want this life. I didn't want to be a working girl, a prostitute and live in fear.

'I can't Tonia,' I sobbed. 'Gerald beat me up. I have to get away,' I said. Tears welled in my eyes obscuring my vision.

Tonia's body stiffened. She was wearing a big coat, even though it was a warm day. Then I noticed, through her makeup, signs of new bruising.

'Jo,' she said shakily, clearing her throat. I could tell she was choosing her words carefully.

'Gerald promises he will never ever hit you again. Please, please come back.'

Her eyes locked onto mine, pleading in a silent way I had never seen anyone do before. Unable to stop myself, I reached out to cuddle her. Her shoulders trembled through her coat. 'Please,' she whispered.

I understood then. Tonia was terrified. They had not only beaten her up but God knows what they would do to her if I didn't go back. I loved Tonia, she was my best friend. How could I leave her to face the consequences of my actions?

'Yes okay, I will,' I said quickly. I had to save her. I just had to.

Tonia kissed my cheek gratefully. I had barely time to get my things ready upstairs before Gerald was outside in the car, waiting. He'd started taking driving lessons recently but Tiger was driving and Gerald was in the back so I sat next to him. Tonia slid onto the front seat when suddenly I felt a slap so hard my head bounced off the window. I started crying.

'I want you to count all the cat's eyes on the road on the way to Stoke,' he snarled.

'What are cat's eyes?' I asked in a small voice. Already I was filled with regret at the choice I'd made.

'Little lights on the road. Just count them. Okay?'

I lent my head against the window, counting as we set off. I lost count after about 200, an exhaustion and feeling of emptiness had set in.

Once we arrived, Gerald asked me how many I'd counted.

'1571,' I said, making up a number.

He reached over to open my side of the door then pushed me out of the car so I fell onto the pavement. 'Now go and make some fucking money, bitch.'

11

Just two weeks after moving into my bedsit, I lost the tenancy because I couldn't keep up with the weekly rent, fines and Gerald's demands. I only spent a couple of nights there anyway. For the next couple of weeks, I slept on Gerald's sofa in his annexe.

One night, I was dozing with Tonia spooning me in a cuddle. While watching TV, we heard the door and voices. It was Gerald and one of his friends. They were laughing and joking, talking about beating up a woman who was nine months pregnant. My heart lurched with fear.

'What did they say?' I whispered to Tonia, wondering if I had misheard them. She stroked my hair and told me not to worry.

'Just lay still and pretend you're asleep,' she soothed. But the conversation worried me. Were Gerald and his cousins really that violent?

The next day, we woke to find Gerald whistling in the kitchen, making us breakfast. 'I have a new place for you to stay,' he said. 'It's a flat belonging to a girl called Nicola who's gone away for a while.'

Hours later, he took us to an empty place on the first floor of a Victorian terrace. There were bars on the windows and little furniture, no bed or sofa, just an old wardrobe and a few cupboards with a few bits and bobs left behind on moving day. Gerald said he wasn't going to pay for the electricity or gas meter unless he was over to make dinner. 'But if you work hard you'll be able to afford furniture,' he winked.

I was worried. I didn't want to stay in a place with nothing in it. But Gerald was adamant it could make a decent home if I worked hard enough. He brought around a mattress and a few sheets, telling me this was a start and it was up to me to do the rest.

That night, he left me in the flat alone for the first time. I had to sleep on a bare mattress, shivering. I was scared but also scared to complain. Gerald's temper appeared to worsen, and whenever we were alone, he often thumped me around the head or slapped my face for something I'd said or done. Occasionally he'd lose the plot completely and give me a good beating, then afterwards make me dinner like nothing had happened.

The next morning Gerald woke me up, made food, then Tonia came over and we got ready and they drove us to the beat. We had sex with lots of men and then came home to give Gerald and Tiger the money. This was the routine that continued for weeks and I often made around £500 per week, all of which Gerald got.

I still didn't understand what Gerald did for a living. I could never quite work out exactly what was going on. He often disappeared for a few hours or even days at a time. Neil, Darryl, Tiger and another one or two others were involved, but in what capacity I didn't know. Gerald was keen to keep me separate from all his 'runnings', whatever they were. Tonia often disappeared during the day too. She never explained where she'd been or what she'd been doing either. I knew I was not allowed out, or if I did go, Gerald would quiz me nastily on the way back. Besides, I had no money or friends or anywhere to go anyway, so I just waited in the bare flat for Tonia to return. She never failed to make me smile or cheer me up. Without her, I knew I couldn't survive this.

*

Gerald's words warning me to make money rang in my ears when I found myself back on my beat, standing by a wall. I knew I should step closer to the kerb, catch drivers' eyes and tempt them, but I hated this. Now I was also fearful of bumping into those girls again. God knows what they'd do to me if they spotted me back here.

A man stopped in his car. He didn't say what he wanted, but nodded, so I got in. Unlike the usual middle-aged men, he was younger.

'For somewhere quiet, go to the industrial estate,' I suggested. There was something hesitant about him, so I assumed it might be his first time, but he turned off at speed in a different direction, ignoring me. My hand tightened on my seatbelt.

'I know somewhere else,' he said quietly. He took a turning out of town, heading towards the countryside. My insides turned icy. I guessed this guy was something to do with the two girls who had beaten me up.

'Can you just take me back?' I asked, hating how meek my voice sounded.

He ignored me again and kept driving. Desperate panic rose in my guts, and when I saw a lorry driver coming past, I grabbed the steering wheel. I wanted the driver to notice our car being driven erratically and hopefully try and intervene. Seizing the chance, I stared up through the windscreen and even made eye contact with the lorry driver in his cab, but he didn't notice anything was wrong.

'What the fuck are you doing?' the man snapped, shoving me away and quickly regaining control of the wheel. The lorry passed by, my chance gone.

We quickly reached a small area of woodland. I had missed several road signs and had no idea where we were or how to get back. Tears smarted in my eyes. *What was he going to do to me?* I steeled myself, fearing the worse.

He turned the engine off and made me get out of the car.

'Right, take your clothes off,' he ordered. I began taking off my top, limbs trembling.

'Are you going to rape me?' I asked quietly. Wet mud covered the ground. I didn't know what to do, whether to lay down in the cold mud or stand up. 'I don't want to do it here.'

He stared at me. There was a softness in his blue eyes. Not the usual animalistic look I recognised in the eye of a man who is about to rape. Confused, I offered to have sex with him. But he didn't move. I felt like prey to a cat, playing a game before dinner time.

Within moments, I guessed he didn't actually want to hurt me, even if someone had asked him to. Like he could read my mind, he suddenly ordered me back into the car. He couldn't go through with whatever he had been asked to do, we both knew it. On the way back, he began turning another way so panic returned to my throat.

'Where are we going?' I begged. 'Please take me back. Please.'

He put his foot down, and the car sped over a ring road, then a flyover and a dual carriageway. The speedometer showed he was doing 60mph. I spotted nightclub buildings nearby, wondering if

Gerald was there, waiting me to finish for the night. How I wished he was here.

'Let me out of this car,' I demanded in a louder voice. The guy kept his eyes on the road and pressed on. 'Please. Let me out.'

Unbearable panic expanded inside so I grappled at my seatbelt.

'I am getting out,' I said breathlessly. The man shot me a startled look. We both knew how fast he was going. I could be seriously injured or killed.

'Stop it. What are you doing? Don't be stupid,' he snapped.

I could see thoughts flash in his mind. Police would be involved if I jumped. Witnesses would see, especially in such a populated, well-lit area. I knew he didn't believe I'd really chuck myself out of a car. But he didn't know how much by now I didn't care whether I lived or died, got killed or injured. Nobody cared about me. So why should I?

Before I had any more time to think, in one smooth movement I undid the seat belt, threw open the door and launched myself onto the rushing gravel below. Car horns beeped, engines whined and I felt a painfully sickening skid then, momentarily, everything stopped.

*

I opened my eyes. Headlights were flashing towards me. I was on my hands and knees. Painful grit in my eyes, hands, legs, but somehow... I was alive.

Totally disorientated, I stood up shakily and, in between hoots and shouts, staggered towards the metal central reservation. I shuffled along the same side of the road where the cars faced when a beat-up Fiesta pulled over. With two girls in the back and one driving, they pulled me inside the vehicle.

'We saw what you did!'

'Oh, poor thing. Where can we take you?'

My top was half ripped. Shivering, I pulled it around me.

'I need to find my boyfriend,' I mumbled. There was no way I was telling them the truth. Every instinct told me to cover up for Gerald, who I expected would be furious about what had happened.

'I lost him in a nightclub,' I lied. 'I need to get home to Dudley.'

Feeling dazed, the girls instantly agreed to drive me all the way home. They knew I was lying but didn't press further. An hour later, I asked to be dropped on Gerald's road. 'Thanks for your help,' I said. I tried to smile, look normal, but all I saw were their worried expressions.

I sat on Gerald's doorstep, shivering for an hour, waiting for him to come home. I wondered if I should try and run away but I was in too much pain and had nowhere to go. Soon the sound of a car pulling up and an angry voice told me it was too late anyway.

'Where the fuck have you been?'

Gerald grabbed my arm and frogmarched me into Nicola's flat. Before I had a chance to react, he grabbed a fist of my hair at the roots, and dragged me up the stairs.

'No, no,' I screamed, but he slapped me over and over.

'Get into that bedroom!'

He punched me all over my body, until I collapsed into a tight ball, sobbing.

'Think you can go off with anyone you like?' he spat.

'No!' I yelled. 'It wasn't like that.'

He disappeared briefly and then returned. I peered through my fingers, wondering why he was untangling a wire coat hanger. He spotted me looking, his face twisted in fury.

Raising the piece of wire high over his head, he whipped it down with full force across my bare arms, thigh and legs.

Whack!

I yelped out in pain.

'Please, no,' I yelled.

Whack!

The more I cried, the more riled up he became. The wire cut through my skin like a knife through cheese. Next he dragged me by the hair back into the living room. I waited, sobbing when he briefly disappeared to return with a broom. He pulled off the brush end and with full force brought the handle down all over my body. The blows merged into one as my eyes closed. I heard a snapping sound when he hit my knee. Breathing hard with all the exertion, he suddenly stopped. I lay still, pretending, wishing I was dead. I heard him leave, lock the door and was left in silence. For several minutes, I couldn't move. The pain was too unbearable. I wondered if anything was broken but part of me didn't care.

I waited for several minutes before staggering into the hallway. The kitchen and bathroom are at the back of the flat, overlooking wasteland but the window was covered in metal bars. I was completely locked in. Limping, I went into the bathroom to run a bath. The water was freezing, because the gas wasn't connected. But I was covered in blood and mud and it had become my routine, like Tonia suggested.

I eased myself into the water, wincing with pain. Lumps and bruising alongside the cuts from the wire criss-crossed my skin. Sobbing, I pulled myself out again and walked over to the sink. I lent onto it and peered into the bathroom mirror. The eyes that stared back were unrecognisably puffy and bloodshot. There was something dead behind them.

These were the eyes of a girl who felt worthless.

*

I shuffled back into the bedroom. Gerald had recently taken the sheets away for a wash, so I opened the fitted wardrobe, and luckily found a discarded old duvet cover. Wrapping it around myself, I shivered and lay on the mattress. Hours passed. I woke up thirsty and hungry.

Knowing there was nothing, all I could do was drink water from the tap. And, for the next two days, that's all I had. By day two, I was still in pain, weak and very hungry. I'd lost track of time, but began to panic that Gerald wouldn't ever come back. Maybe I would starve here? Every now and again I rattled the door handle of the flat, hoping someone might hear or by some miracle it would open. But nothing worked. I curled back into my ball, praying Gerald would come back.

By the evening, a key twisted in the lock. Gerald came in with rustling plastic bags. He glanced at me, still wrapped in the duvet cover while he pulled out pots and pans and food.

'Hey, I'll make dinner,' he said, breezily. Like nothing had happened. I shifted into a sitting position, then followed him like a puppy into the kitchen. I was too scared and hungry not to. He chatted amiably about being busy with his 'runnings' and how Tonia would be over soon. I needed to tidy myself up. Get clean. He'd have my favourite dish of rice and peas ready soon. I stared, unable to speak. My mind and body was hollow, wrung out. I was alive, I knew that, but felt dead inside.

On autopilot, I did what I was told and had another brief bath, got dressed in the mini-skirt I'd worn the other night, and meekly sat on the floor, waiting for my food.

Gerald served it on plates he'd brought with him. Chatting away, he talked about a range of subjects from his cousin's new car to his latest theory about police corruption. I nodded along and once we'd finished the meal, he kissed me afterwards.

'We'll go away somewhere soon,' he said, gently. 'Just me and you. Or with Tonia, if you like her?' I nodded.

'Then I'll take her with us. On holiday. Somewhere hot and relaxing or maybe Amsterdam? How about that?' He'd never suggested anything like this before. A tear rolled down my cheek.

'Or we could go to Jerusalem. Like pilgrims of God,' he soothed. The idea of religion, God, Jesus, it was all so abstract right now.

He gently stroked my arm, careful to avoid the cuts. 'Let's have an early night in.'

He held me that night in his arms, as if I was his girl again. I sobbed silently, weirdly grateful he was here. He kept talking about our future, half making me believe one was possible. He was back to being my boyfriend, rather than my pimp again.

For the next week or so, while my wounds healed, Gerald came and went from the flat. He cooked delicious meals and meticulously cleaned up afterwards. I watched, withdrawn and compliant. He brought Tonia over, who winced when she saw my wounds, and helped clean them up. But despite her sunny presence, my sense of numbness didn't lift.

For the first time in months, I had time alone to myself and what happened wasn't pleasant because an unbearably painful bubble of emotion popped. Tears came in floods, like an uncorked bottle of sadness and trauma bursting. I didn't understand what was happening to me, but the headspace allowed all the pain and hurt inside of me to emerge. The past few years had involved attack after attack from boys and men. I still didn't use the word 'rape' but I had been raped multiple times and now I was forced to have sex for a living. This was an endless nightmare with no escape.

But then Gerald seemed to love me. He'd even promised holidays and that things would get better. Maybe he'd change and let me live a normal life? Just as I began to question what was real and what was not, the reality kicked in again. Gerald wanted me back at 'work' the following night.

'You've had enough time off,' he said, his eyes narrowing. I tried not to let him see me cry.

12

There was almost no furniture in Nicola's flat when I arrived but over the weeks, bits and pieces turned up and then disappeared. Sofas, sideboards, tables, and chairs, would be brought in and then vanish. I guessed they were stolen.

One day, while tidying up, I found a birthday card for Gerald in one of the cupboards.

'Happy Birthday Daddy. Lots of love always Jordana,' it read inside.

I couldn't believe what I was reading and vowed to ask Gerald. It took me a week to pluck up the courage.

'Are you a daddy?' I asked, waving the card at him over dinner one night. Gerald cheating always played on my mind when he went missing for days on end. This was evidence for once. Gerald looked surprised and then his face softened.

'Yes, I wanted to tell you,' he said softly. 'I had a baby with Sheree. It was at the same time you were pregnant and had a miscarriage. I didn't want to upset you.'

I stared at him. Sheree was a girl who came and went sometimes in his annexe with his other cousins. He had admitted cheating on me in such a matter of fact way, I didn't know how to react. Who was I to complain anyway? I knew I had no power in this relationship. I swallowed, thinking of what to say.

'I didn't want to hurt you,' he repeated calmly. I knew I couldn't react, otherwise he might get angry and that was the last thing I wanted. I changed the subject and we didn't bring up the matter again, even if it continuously preyed on my mind.

Gerald decided I couldn't return to Stoke, and so said I'd have to go out onto the streets in Dudley with Tonia. I was terrified. What if someone I knew saw me? What if William drove past one night? Or even Mum herself?

I tried to reassure myself they didn't often go out at night, but it wasn't an impossibility. Just the thought of Mum spotting me standing shivering in my mini-skirt under a streetlight made my stomach flip. She'd be so angry, disappointed. I had become everything she said I would.

Gerald and Tiger took us in the car, past the industrial estates, the old steel works and into a run-down derelict area. Our new 'corner' in Dudley was to be a dimly-lit road around the back of Dudley railway station. Gerald nodded to indicate where we were to get out. I shuddered. I was so relieved to be with my Tonia.

Just a few months ago, a prostitute called Janine Downes had been found murdered after walking the streets. She was only 22, a mum of three and her half naked body was dumped in a Shropshire lay-by. Her killer still hadn't been caught. Tonia had told me all about it. She also mentioned another woman called Gail Whitehouse, who was also in her early 20s and had been found strangled like Janine months before. She was also from Dudley but her body had been found in Birmingham. Was there a serial killer on the loose? It clearly scared Tonia, so it scared me witless too.

With my back up against another wall again, my body felt heavy and resigned, but emotions welled up inside like a huge rising bubble. For days, I hadn't been able to control the relentless tide of tears. Yesterday I'd sat on my bed after a cold bath with a towel around me, one Gerald had brought around, unable to stop crying. Gerald came to see what the loud sobbing was about. 'What is it?' he'd asked, impatiently.

'I can't do it. I can't live like this any more,' I'd sobbed. 'I just can't!'

I cried like a baby on the mattress. Gerald kissed his teeth and left me to it. I could hear him join Darryl who was over too, in the living room. Then they began sniggering together.

'Ooh 'I can't cope',' Gerald mocked, in a high-pitched voice. 'I can't do it any more.'

'Noo, I can't either. Make it stop,' Darryl jeered before dissolving into a booming laugh.

Their cruel words made my tears flow faster.

Back on the streets, after waiting just a few minutes, cars began pulling up and another endless revolting night of men and their bodies began. The thought of poor Janine and Gail stayed in the back of my mind all night long.

*

The following night Tonia suggested we moved to the far side of the road, with more suburban as opposed to terrace housing.

'Is it safer here?' I asked her, anxiously. She gave me a cynical smile. 'Yes and no. The only problem is curtain-twitchers calling the cops in surburban areas.'

Tonia pointed to a street running off this one, where housing, a newsagent and a hospital all stood.

'You know that's the last place I saw Janine Downes,' she said quietly, like she was reading my thoughts. So it wasn't safer after all. I stared at the empty pavement, imagining what poor Janine must have gone through. Was her killer prowling the streets around here tonight?

Tonia nudged me while I stared at the headlights flashing past, blurry with tears. 'You're away with the fairies,' she said, squeezing my arm.

'Don't you worry Honey. We'll get through it. You'll see.'

The trouble was, I didn't any more.

By now, I had an unconscious ability to switch into a survival mode very fast. And when my first punter for the night pulled over, that's what I did. I took a short breath, opened the passenger door of a navy-coloured Jaguar and stepped in, barely glancing at who the man was. Unusually, the car smelled fresh, of polish and soap, rather than the more common aromas of BO and fags. I sat down, and put on my seatbelt.

Click.

My head swivelled to the door at the sound of central locking. I had no idea. My heart set off like a drill. I side-eyed the punter, who was staring straight ahead.

'I'm looking for a quiet road,' he said, in a well-spoken voice. 'It's a blow job please.'

There was something familiar about him. The hair. The glasses. I didn't want to stare, but turned my head as he navigated a crossroads. At the moment of realisation my chest lurched in a wild moment of panic. I knew this new punter and I'd realised who he was.

He was my old headmaster from my primary school!

*

Mr Collins was his name and he looked older and greyer. Five years ago, I had been an 11-year-old sitting cross-legged on the floor while he took assembly, talking about values and good behaviour. Now I had to perform a sexual act on him for money.

My breath caught in my chest. I gripped the hem of my skirt as memories of school bubbled to the surface. Mr Collins clapping after a school play, telling my friend off for running in the corridor, walking around at parents' evening to greet mums and dads. Then a memory of my friend Claire telling me that once she saw a teacher on her knees in the Head's office, when she walked in without knocking... Back then, in my innocence, I had no idea what that meant. But I guessed what it meant now. Mr Collins was probably a ladies man. Someone who cheated on his wife. Someone who used prostitutes. I swallowed down bile rising in my throat. My fear was him recognising me, then telling my mum. He kept his eyes on the road.

'Where you from?' he asked, smoothly steering into a side street. He'd clearly picked up girls regularly and had his own parking spot for business.

'Dudley,' I said quietly, hoping he wouldn't recognise my voice.

I wondered if he had access to former pupils' records or former pupils' parents' phone numbers. Mum had kept her old number. Oh my God. She was going to find out and tell everyone.

We pulled over onto an unlit road. I kept my chin tucked down, hair covering my face. Mr Collins pulled his seat back and unbuckled his trousers. Swiftly I took a deep breath and ducked down, not looking at him at all. He was wearing a woollen jumper over a cotton shirt. He didn't lift it up any higher for me, so my cheek grazed against the itchy material. I tried to switch off, but I was so revolted at what I was doing,

I swallowed back the reflex to gag all the way through. Finally he was done. Quickly, I sat back and he drove at breakneck speed back to my beat. His hand passed over £15 and I was back against my wall.

Alone again, my breathing felt ragged. Nausea kept building up, however many times I wiped my lips. I longed to stand under a hot shower and scour my skin. A voice inside condemned me completely. Who had I become? How did that little girl who loved reading The Secret Garden and skipping end up giving her headteacher a blow job for money? Thankfully he hadn't recognised me but what about next time?

For the rest of the night I stood inside the shadow of a wall, the spectacle of giving my own headteacher a blow job playing on a loop in my head. Even if Gerald hit me for not earning more money, I couldn't face another punter tonight.

*

Over the next few nights, Tonia tried her very best to perk me up. A few times, I ended up joining in singing silly songs between punters, or she dared me to do handstands against the wall. Despite myself, I ended up collapsing into giggles on the pavement. I thanked God for my friend. My life had become hellish, but at least she was by my side, making it fun where possible. After a busy weekend, Tonia took me for an STI test at the local clinic. In her usual motherly way, she explained everything about what would happen.

'It's good to look after yourself,' she smiled, brushing a hair from my face while we sat in the waiting room.

I wondered if the staff guessed we worked the streets. The nurse was efficient and barely looked me in the eye before and after the examination. I decided then either way they probably didn't care. Nobody seemed to.

Over the next couple of weeks we were arrested several more times. On one occasion, I was introduced to a senior officer called DC Max Sawyer, a soft, smart-looking copper in his early 40s. A 13-year-old was reported missing from Telford and they believed I could be that girl. I looked young enough. Like before, I gave my friend Becky's name but this time, I was officially questioned. DC Max Sawyer sat across a table in the airless interview room with a huge tape machine whirring next to us. Another officer joined us. This was a formal interview, he said. I was to answer all the questions truthfully.

'I know you're from Telford but I don't believe you're Becky...' he checked his notes, 'Jones.' After my first arrest, Gerald had warned me exactly what to say, or rather what not to say.

'No comment,' he'd said, giving me his hard stare. 'Got that?'

I nodded, not understanding why. These were not words I'd ever use in everyday life but I used them that night.

'No comment,' I said, jutting out my jaw, staring the copper hard in the face. Inside I was scared, but I didn't want to show it. I had to protect myself from Gerald. That was all that mattered. I swung my leg from the chair, eyeballing the copper in a cocky way.

DC Sawyer sighed. 'Who brought you to Dudley, Joanne?'

'No one,' I said. 'No comment, I mean.'

I had slipped up. To hide my mistake I shrugged and sat back.

'I know your boyfriend, who is black, brought you here,' he said. I forced myself to laugh loudly. He was guessing, I guessed.

'I don't know any black men in Telford,' I said, folding my arms tighter. I felt sick now. All sorts of worrying images arose in my mind. Police coming to the flat, Gerald being arrested. Oh God, he was going to kill me.

I masked my fear with a loud giggle as if the idea of someone bringing me from Telford was completely ridiculous. DC Sawyer eyed me furiously. 'For the tape's record, the interviewee is laughing and seems to find this is funny.' He stormed out of the room, leaving the door swinging behind him.

He knows, I thought. *He knows about Gerald, he knows I know.'*

I shifted uncomfortably on the hard plastic chair. The other officer sighed and told me I was free to go. I felt so relieved, like I'd won and beaten the system. Walking back to Gerald's house, the jubilant feeling slowly faded away and my worries about his reaction returned.

I wonder why the police don't just follow me? I thought, looking over my shoulder. It occurred to me how easily police could find out who Gerald was and what he was doing. But they chose not to. I knew if the police followed me and then arrested Gerald I would be free, but where would I go? As awful as this life was, Gerald and Tonia were the only people I had.

I tried to stay in touch with my family whenever I could. Mum was always visibly annoyed, so often I made the visits short and focused on catching up with Anthony when Mum wasn't in. He was 14 by now and growing up fast. He had his own friends and life, but I liked to ask how he was doing. I was glad he still had Buster the dog for company after I'd left.

It had become harder and harder to face my mum, especially because I knew I had lost weight and I didn't want her to find out what I was doing, so I often chose to ring her instead. A few days later, I made my phone call.

'I've had Mrs Jones on the phone to me,' Mum said, without saying hello or asking how I was. Police had contacted her to say Becky had been arrested in Dudley for prostitution but she was sat next to her at the time.

'The only person they know in Dudley is you. What is going on Jo, for God's sake?'

I couldn't bring myself to say anything.

'Is it true?' she demanded. 'Are you working as a prostitute now?'

'I needed money,' I said quietly.

The pause of allowing the words to sink in made tears pour down my face. Shame, humiliation, fear, all my emotions were unbearable.

'Oh my God,' Mum breathed. 'That's absolutely disgusting. How could you? Oh my God Jo.'

'Sorry,' I sobbed. 'Sorry, Mum.'

'How could you do this to me?' she snapped. She was so angry. Like she always was, except this time she had reason to be. I'd let her down, like I always did. She hung up on me. I put the phone down, to feel Gerald standing over my shoulder.

'Your mum doesn't give a shit about you,' he said simply, having overheard the conversation. 'You've only got me now.'

I turned and looked at him. He was right.

A few nights later, the police pulled me in for questioning again. They told me to give them a real address otherwise they couldn't bail me for a court date. So reluctantly I gave them my mum's address. Meanwhile, Tonia had a warrant out for her arrest. She had skipped bail and was on borrowed time.

13

At the end of another long night, I was with Tonia messing around trying to moonwalk across the pavement, when a voice shouted at me.

'Who do ya tink ya are?'

I looked up and a white woman was marching over. She was in her late 30s, had huge eye bags and a hard expression across her lips.

'You tink you're all tha' but you have it comin', let me tell ya,' she spat.

Quickly I put my back against the wall again. I didn't know what she wanted or what she was trying to say.

'Oh God, we're on her corner,' whispered Tonia to explain.

'Why is she speaking like a Jamaican?' I whispered back. The woman, who said her name was Tricia, stood to her full height over me.

'You tink ya man Gerald is jus' ya man, but I know he's not. You're not his number one gal. There tis a lot of 'em,' she spat.

I didn't know what meant. Gerald was cheating on me? I waited until she had finished. She warned us both to leave before disappearing into a punter's car. I breathed out with relief but one thing was on my mind.

'What did she mean about Gerald having more women?' I asked Tonia. Tonia shook her curls and grinned. 'Oh, don't worry. You're definitely his number one girl. Hey, I am not Tiger's number one, because he's married and has kids, but you definitely are. But that's just the way things go.'

I stared at Tonia. How could she be content not to be someone's number one? This was heart-breaking. I tried to relax, thinking that really I was the lucky one. I knew Gerald had cheated on me with that Sheree, but I guessed it was over a long time ago.

'Why does Tricia hate me so much?' I asked Tonia.

Tonia made a throaty noise. 'Because you look like a fresh-faced 12-year-old, Jo. Not like the other girls, who have all been around the block a bit.'

I knew she meant this as a compliment but it didn't feel like it.

*

Over the weeks in Dudley, I got to know many of the working women in the area. One was a character called Kitty, a woman who looked around 60 years old and wore a big blonde wig in the style of Vera Duckworth from Coronation Street. We always spotted her a mile off, trotting down the road in stilettos in a long leopard print fake fur coat grazing her fishnet-clad thighs. She always looked worn out with an open can of Special Brew in her hand.

Quickly, I learned Kitty was the queen bee of the beat. She always said hello and was pleasant enough, but kept away from any dramas or arguing between the other girls. She was above all of that.

Emma was another girl I often chatted to. She was blonde, petite, and had the most beautiful, piercing green eyes I had ever seen. She spoke with an air of confidence I didn't have. Automatically I assumed she was about 19 or 20 so when I discovered she was just 13, I was stunned. This was a child who clearly had no childhood at all. Emma had been in the care system for years, but worked the streets for money after being forced to by her boyfriend. First thing she told me was who her man was. By the way she spoke, I guessed she believed her whole existence revolved around him. Much like I had begun to feel around Gerald. Like her, I had to please him or he'd hurt me. But also it hurt me not to please him. It was so confusing.

One night Emma confided in me that she faced having to go to court.

'It's only a juvenile one 'cos I am underage,' she shrugged. 'That's what happens when you're in the care system – they treat you like a kid.'

I frowned. But you *are* a kid, I thought. Emma also mentioned having a social worker, someone she could talk to, and she had regular payments for housing. It wasn't enough money, she still had to work the streets, but it was something extra. I found myself feeling a rising sense of envy when she told me what life was like in care. Emma had no family who cared, but then neither did I, yet at least she had support of some kind.

By now, I had been arrested so many times, I was dreading being summoned to court. I'd had a few court dates but all of them adjourned. I was never offered any legal representation, but the girls on the streets explained how it worked. They said it was best to plead guilty. If you did that, you got a fine. If you didn't then everything would take longer and if you were then found guilty the punishment would be worse. Yes, it was best to hold your hands up and move on.

I had paid some of the fines but they were growing, fast. My first fine had been just £10, but the latest one was £150. That was the equivalent of sex with four or five men. But I still needed to hand all my cash over to Gerald too.

Then the day arrived. I had to attend Dudley Magistrates' Court at the end of October. It was an adult court and I wondered why. I was still only 17. So when I bumped into Emma the night before the date, I quizzed her about it.

'I am not an adult yet either,' I explained. 'So why do you get to go to a juvenile court but I don't?'

'It's because I am in care,' Emma shrugged, her eyes aglow with the fag end. 'The social services are seen as my guardian.'

She rolled her eyes. 'In the eyes of the law that is,' she added.

I had given my mum's address, so assumed she would be viewed as my guardian. However, this wasn't the case. In one phone call, she even told me she had been warned, in fact, not to house me any more.

'Did you know we could even get arrested for living off immoral earnings if we give you a roof over your head?' she'd snapped in one of our last conversations. I never checked but this made me believe she had been chatting to coppers behind my back.

'My mum has washed her hands of me,' I told Emma. The words said aloud were true but I felt numb saying them. Emma shrugged again. She had such a world-weary look in her eye it was hard to believe she was still a young kid.

*

The idea of standing in court alone was completely terrifying. Aside from what Tonia had told me, I had no idea what to expect.

I turned up outside, shivering in my mini-dress and ballet pumps. I didn't have any other clothes aside from the ones I walked the streets in. When I stepped inside the imposing Victorian building and saw my name written on a board *Joanne Eileen Phillips Vs Her Majesty* made it all too real. Although police had spelled my surname wrong, only with one 'l'.

What if they sent me to prison today? I knew the girls said it was unlikely, but nobody really knew. Filled with shame, I asked a court usher where I should go and was led inside a plush, small courtroom and into the defendant's dock. I sat down on the bench, my head bowed, my heart hammering in my chest. I imagined everyone saw the word 'whore' above my head in lights.

The session began. A judge swept in and presided over it. I was asked to stand and confirm my details, which I did. The minutes felt like hours as I struggled to follow what was going on. Different people spoke and used language I couldn't follow, although the phrase 'common prostitute' was mentioned several times. Then suddenly, ten minutes later, it was all over. I was to pay the fine and be let go.

I walked outside, my head spinning. Had that just really happened? I was now a convicted criminal, I understood that, but I also knew I had no choice but to immediately repeat the crimes. Did the judge know this? How else would I pay the fine?

Although the girls on the street were happy to advise when it came to court cases, few of us spoke about our personal circumstances. Aside from brief information about our families, we never swapped stories about our pimps or who was with what gang. This was the code of silence we'd learned quickly to abide by; we looked out for each other when we could, but that was it.

When it came to injuries girls received, many were also straight to the point. So often girls had bruises or scratches or looked the worse for wear but nobody asked how they'd got injured unless they volunteered the information.

Ginny was an experienced prostitute who shared her stories in a matter-of-fact way. Tonia had known her for years, so she wasn't a threat to us. Tall, with a head of waist-length black hair, Ginny didn't wear makeup unlike many of the others, she didn't seem to feel the need to. One night we got chatting by the wall, and she told me very simply how she'd been raped with a knife.

'An actual knife?' I repeated in horror, instinctively crossing my legs.

'It was a punter,' she shrugged. 'He went mental, took a knife and cut me front to back. I had to have the whole lot down there stitched up.' She showed no emotion whatsoever. Just hearing this story made me wince.

'Did you go to the police?' I asked.

She gave me a look of incredulity.

'Oh, love. You are very new to this game aren't you?'

The following night I spoke to Jenny, another girl who we saw every now and again. She was only 18, but two years previously had been attacked with a knife. She'd held up her hand in self-defence, but the punter sliced right through her palm, cutting the tendons. Now her hand was permanently deformed like a claw. She didn't allow the disability to stop her from working and if she caught anyone staring at it, she casually told them what caused it. Both men who'd caused such devastating injuries were never arrested and nobody was looking for them. In fact, neither Ginny nor Jenny reported their injuries to police.

After hearing this story, when the next punter pulled up, icy fear flooded through me again. The stories from Ginny and Jenny were horrifying. Not only could I be killed or raped, but I also could face serious life-changing injuries and according to both of them, nobody would care. Not even the people paid to protect us.

*

One Friday afternoon, before the first punter of the evening pulled over, Tonia had an idea. 'Let's fuck all this off and go and get fish and chips together,' she beamed.

'But what if Gerald or Tiger catch us?' I shuddered. 'They might be spying on us.' Sometimes I spotted their car cruising by, to check we were busy and not slacking off.

'Oh, we could be with a punter or police,' Tonia giggled. 'Come on, what you waiting for?'

Tonia checked for any signs of Gerald's car and then we jumped into a taxi. Giggling like two schoolgirls bunking off, I was filled with relief at the prospect of a couple of hours off. We arrived at a council estate, picking up fish and chips on the way.

'My mate lives here,' said Tonia. 'Let's go and see them. She's a working girl too.'

She knocked on the door and a tired-looking petite woman opened it. Her face broke into a smile when she saw Tonia and we were invited in. The house was very clean and tidy, ordinary looking but when we walked into the living room, I was taken aback by the scene.

In the living room, a man sat on a chair that looked like a throne, in the middle of the room. His neck was covered in gold chains, like B.A. Baracus from the A Team including thick chains and a heavy cross. Each of his fat fingers had a gold ring on it too. I sat on the sofa, eating chips, feeling like a little mouse.

'You want a drink? Lager or cider?' he asked.

I politely declined and we continued sitting in silence. Meanwhile Tonia and her friend disappeared giggling into the kitchen, while the man eyeballed me. I guessed he was a pimp too.

Several minutes later, we heard raised voices coming from the kitchen. Then abruptly, Tonia returned.

'Well, now we're off again,' she said to me, nodding at the door. 'Bye everyone.' In the cab on the way back, Tonia sighed deeply.

'My mate was angry with me. She said you look like a china doll and you shouldn't be on the streets. Said you're vulnerable and will have your life ruined.'

Then she pulled me into a hug and kissed the top of my head. I didn't know whether that meant she agreed with her friend or not but somehow I sensed she felt guilty.

14

One night, during a cold, drizzly November, where punters seemed few and far between, we were picked up yet again by the vice squad. For some reason, the police realised Tonia's fake name wasn't real so they kept her in. Then she gave them my real name, by accident I assumed. When I was released, Tonia wasn't, so I made my way home alone. I assumed she would come home the next day, but she didn't.

Tonia never returned to the flat in the morning or the afternoon. For the first time I faced walking the streets alone at night, and I was terrified. Without Tonia, I felt so lost and I tried hard to keep my head down when car headlights turned on me. Without her sunny nature and ability to burst into song or make silly jokes, suddenly my situation felt more frightening than ever. But as usual, I began to fear what Gerald would say if I didn't get back out to make money and reluctantly I had sex with a few punters that night, trying to hold back tears each time.

Afterwards, I hoped Tonia would be back at the flat but she wasn't, so I took my bath without her. When Gerald arrived later, I confronted him.

'Where has Tonia gone? I am so worried about her,' I asked him. But he looked completely unfazed and shrugged. Once again, I daren't press him in case he got angry.

After a few more nights alone, I begged Gerald to help me find Tonia. By now I had asked a few of the girls but nobody had seen her. Gerald glared at me.

'Look. You need to just forget about Tonia,' he growled in such a manner that I guessed he knew what had happened to her, but wasn't going to tell me.

*

With Tonia gone, despite having made other loose friendships, the streets felt like an even darker place. By now, I often found myself having attacks of anxiety regularly. Before getting in a punter's car, I'd force my mind to switch off as a defensive mechanism to get through the next half an hour or so. Although the girls warned each other who to watch out for, you always had to stay on high alert at all times. It was exhausting.

One car we knew to watch out for was a lurid yellow car, which looked like the vehicle in Ghostbusters. It was driven around either at high speed or crawled slowly, the driver glaring at girls as he cruised by. I began calling the driver 'Slimer', due to the look of the weird car. He was a pimp and was definitely on the 'avoid' list.

By December 1991, I was sleeping at Nicola's flat and sometimes over at Neil's, depending on where Gerald dropped me off. With Christmas coming he was looking forward to a bonus. 'You'll get tips at Christmas Joanne,' he said. 'It'll be a nice earner for you.' Some of the other girls had told me similar things. 'Punters buy you presents,' one said. By now I had been given cheap rings or jewellery by a few punters. I kept a few rings but Gerald took the rest.

But I had no choice, all my money went straight into Gerald's pocket and I could see he was doing very well out of it too. His wardrobe had grown. He'd recently bought a new car, a BMW, with a big bumper and a spoiler at the back, lowered suspension and blacked-out windows. The first time he pulled up in it, bass pumping from the windows, he looked like a cat who'd got the cream.

'Get in, let's go for a spin,' he grinned. I did as I was told. Part of me was relieved he'd asked me and that he was happy with what he'd bought. Even if I knew it was my body which had paid for it. Gerald also often quoted passages from The Bible to justify his actions. Mary Magdalene had worked as a prostitute, he said, and this was why God didn't condemn this work.

'She is mentioned twelve times in the canonical gospels, more than any other woman,' he declared, between puffs of spliff. 'She was a woman of sin but followed Jesus to his cruci-fixion. God would not have allowed this if he didn't approve. It is a woman's work to provide for their men.'

I stared at him. He often tried to get me to read The Bible but I rarely got past the first page or two. It was so dull. And I couldn't believe a real God would want a life like mine for anyone. Like most things in life, the idea of religion had no meaning for me.

*

While waiting for a punter on the street kerb, a role in the Pied Piper I'd had in a school Christmas play popped into my head. I had played a rat and had to run around with a paper mask, squeaking with other kids in my class. It had been such fun. *Now I run around the streets like a rat, selling myself,* I thought grimly.

I was arrested many more times that December but on Christmas Eve, all was quiet. I found myself standing on the street, dressed in my usual mini-skirt with bare legs and ballet pumps on. I didn't own a coat, just the same hand-knitted cardigan. Shivering, my breath came out in plumes in the cold air. I folded my arms and tried to sway from side to side to keep warm. I looked up to see delicate flakes of snow float from the sky. One landed on the bare skin of my foot, dissolving instantly. But I didn't feel a thing, my skin had turned a tinge of blue and was completely numb.

I imagined most of my punters were playing the role of loving husband and father tonight. They'd be wrapping up their kids' presents tonight and putting them under the trees. Maybe kissing their wive's lips under the mistletoe, pretending to be faithful. I thought of my old friends too. Becky, Sharon, and the Alisons in Telford. They'd likely be doing last-minute Christmas shopping, maybe for boyfriends after scrimping and saving in their part-time jobs. Their A Levels would be soon. Perhaps they'd be treating themselves after sitting their exams.

I shuffled my feet to improve the circulation. I could have been living on the moon considering how different my life was to every person I knew. Nanna and Grandpa would be cosy in front of the TV, faces aglow with lights from her lovely tree. I felt a tear slide down my face. Nanna had sent me a Christmas card with a fiver inside. '*Hope to see you soon Joanne.*' she'd written inside. But how could I see her in this state?

After midnight, I slowly walked back to the flat. My feet were aching and my body was shivering. Gerald was out with his family for a lock-in at a pub somewhere. It hurt me deeply that he never invited me along to any big family events. I knew deep down it was a sign he wasn't committed to me or our relationship. Once again, I simply didn't feel 'good enough', even though he had total control over my life, so I slid into bed and fell into a dreamless sleep.

*

On Christmas morning, I didn't go home to Mum's. I called her from a phone box instead to tell her I wasn't feeling well. She said my dinner would be waiting if I could 'be bothered' but I said I probably wouldn't make it. Gerald didn't turn up. I knew he was out that night, probably taking drugs with his cousins, possibly even seeing another woman. I had no idea. Every time he came near me I flinched too, even if his presence also made me feel less alone.

By the new year of 1992, life continued as it had done for months. Me living in fear of Gerald, going out to work at night, then returning home to hand him cash.

In February, I turned 18. I knew Mum would stress out if I didn't go home for my birthday either, so I called her beforehand.

'Come over on the day and we will take you out for a curry,' she suggested. I was surprised, but couldn't say no. We had never been to a restaurant before, or even out for a coffee.

So I tidied my hair and told Gerald I couldn't work that night. He glared at me but to my relief let me go. He'd not acknowledged my birthday in any way. I didn't expect him to. I was surprised Mum wanted to as well.

I met Mum at her house and she drove us all to the curry house on the high street. Inside, the waiter politely bowed and then took us to a table, handing us menus with a flourish. I scanned the food, struggling to take in the new sights and sounds. Plates clattered, smells of delicious spices hung in the air, Mum and William were laughing and joking about something or other.

I smiled politely and tried to make conversation, but felt empty inside. I had nothing nice to talk about. Even sitting in a restaurant felt overwhelming because I'd never done it before.

Mum was careful not to ask me too many questions, I could tell. In the end I asked William to choose something for me off the menu because I didn't know the difference between a Korma and a Vindaloo. I was hungry, as usual, but tried not to bolt my food when it came.

I watched as my family chatted over their food, breaking poppadoms like they were used to it, making in-jokes. What was obvious was how much of an outsider I'd become. I lived a life far away from nice restaurants and polite banter.

At the end of the meal, William handed me an envelope. I opened it to find a card wishing me happy birthday and a voucher for five horse-riding lessons.

Tears welled in my eyes.

They thought I was crying with happiness but actually it was confusion. This was a lovely gift, but I knew it wasn't horse-riding lessons I needed. I needed help to escape. The stables were about 15 miles away too and there was no way I would be able to travel that far. I couldn't afford the bus fare.

William sensed something was wrong and asked me, so I told him.

'I don't know how I'll get to the stables,' I said. It would cost me time and money and I had neither. William let out a big sigh and said, okay, in that case he would have to drive me every week.

Turning 18 should have been a watershed moment. Instead I felt broken, trapped in a life I didn't want. If I tried to escape, I knew Gerald would track me down and do his worst. I was officially an adult but had nothing to look forward to.

15

One evening in March 1992, I was walking alone on a quiet road near my corner when a man stopped and asked me the time. Immediately I recognised it was 'Slimer' the driver of the yellow Ghostbuster's style car. I didn't have a watch, but on autopilot, glanced at my wrist.

'Sorry I don't,' I replied and sped up, thinking I'd knock off early tonight. I didn't like the look of him.

Seconds later, the hairs on the back of my neck rose, when I heard heavier footsteps behind. Then paw-like hands slid around my shoulders.

'You're coming with me,' Slimer growled.

My feet scrambled like a crab's trying to stay rooted to the pavement.

'Stop! Stop!' I screamed. But he was wrenching me backwards with such speed and force, I lost my balance.

He dragged me to a nearby piece of wasteland on the industrial estate where there was no street lighting and my eyes struggled to focus in the gloom. I opened my mouth and began screaming and yelling like my life depended on it. Which it did.

'Get off, help!' I shrieked. Blows began to land all over my head, face, shoulders and stomach. Any area he could find, he hit me with full force. Then one hand pushed between my legs and I was suddenly up high over his head. With all his might, he threw me onto the gravel floor.

I landed heavily on my side, like a sack of potatoes. In a smooth motion, he crouched down, pulling at the back of my hair and pinching my nose. With his other hand, he took a handful of gravel to funnel into my mouth.

'Grrrughhhhh,' I gasped. Metallic tasting stones clinked against my teeth, causing me to retch and gag. Then he picked me up again and threw me like a rag doll.

'You're working for me now,' he growled. 'Got that? Do you understand that? You're working for me. Nobody else.'

With his face in mine, I couldn't breathe. A feeling of floating began to take over and I imagined the scene from high above. Because that's where I'd rather be. Anywhere but here.

He picked me up again but this time I didn't feel his hand on my groin or the slam of the ground into my body. I was limp and numb. Back on the floor, I twisted my head to the side, to stare into the smashed windows of a disused building nearby. Inside was a basement with bricks and rubble on the floor. Anyone could gain access. Anyone who wanted to bury a body perhaps.

He is going to kill me, I thought calmly. *And then dump my body inside that abandoned basement.* His fists continued to pummel my shoulders and sides.

'You're working,' he yelled, in-between each strike. 'For. Me.'

I stared through the window, at my future grave.

He'll kill me. Then bury my body. I will eventually be reported missing. Probably by the police who haven't seen me on the beat. Nobody will care. Mum and Anthony would go to the funeral.

I coughed, bringing up gravel. I estimated it would take about a week or ten days to find my decomposing body. Very quietly, somewhere deep inside, I accepted this. Suddenly, he stopped and stood over me. I had been beaten so badly, I could hardly move.

'You're going to kill me aren't you?' I said simply, gazing up at him. He looked surprised.

'Look, I don't know what you want to do or what your intentions are. But if you want to kill me, please just do it. If you want me to work for you, that's fine too. Just so you know… I am 14 and grounded. If I am not home by 9pm tonight, the police and social workers will come looking for me,' I said confidently. I was staggered. Where had that lie come from? I didn't even know. Maybe a spark inside of me wanted to save myself. His eyes narrowed until they disappeared.

'Okay,' he said. 'Next time I see you on your corner, you come with me, okay?' He stood up and casually brushed gravel dust from his jeans. 'Lay here and wait for half an hour and then you can leave.'

I watched the back of his jacket disappear into the darkness. I waited for a few minutes then shakily got to my feet and half ran and half hobbled in pain to the main road. I flagged the first taxi down. The driver was a black guy, who I suspected knew Gerald. I was right, he glanced at me then said he was taking me straight to Neil's. On the way, I felt warm liquid running down my face. Only then did I realise I was bleeding.

I knocked at the door, holding my face to stop the blood dripping. Gerald opened the door.

'What the fuck happened to you?' he gasped.

'This black man…' I began. Those first words had obviously been the wrong ones. He was furious.

Whack.

Gerald punched me hard and squarely in the face. I fell backwards, landing on the garden path.

'What have I told you about speaking to any black men? They will bring nothing but grief to my door,' he yelled, standing over me.

He dragged me onto the pavement, reigning blows all over my body. I covered my head with my arms. Then he shoved me into the car.

'I'm taking you back to the flat,' he snarled. 'I can't take you to my cousins in this state.'

He threw me inside Nicola's flat before locking the door. I was left all night crying, dried blood and gravel all over my body.

In the morning, Gerald returned, ignoring all of my injuries. He made me a breakfast of toast and tea. He chatted like nothing had happened, telling me about the latest tune he'd bought and where he planned to take me for a meal out sometime. I nodded, quietly trying to eat the toast so I didn't offend him. I felt a strange sense of dislocation from my body again. A blanket of numbness had thankfully taken over.

'By the way you're working tonight,' he said casually, clearing up the plates. '7pm. Usual spot. Clean up your face.'

That evening, I washed my face again, trying to stop the cuts from bleeding. I couldn't believe Gerald was putting me on the streets in this state. But then I thought of the other women like Ginny and Jenny. They had barely recovered from their devastating injuries before being made to work again. This is what our men did. We were nothing but bodies to them.

*

One evening, when Gerald dropped me off, I moved to the other side of the road. I'd noticed one of the girls had written a list of registration numbers of dodgy punters on the wall. More scared than ever about falling prey to someone like Slimer, I tried to memorise the number plates. I'd seen what pimps and punters on this beat were capable of. The next night, I spotted the yellow car circling on a main road. I ducked behind a shop sign, my palms sweating. How long could I avoid him for? I didn't know. I also didn't know if Gerald would manage to scare him off. All the gangs seemed to be aware of each other but I didn't know how they resolved issues like this.

A few weeks later, I called Mum again. She sounded exasperated with me, but this time she had news.

'I've found you a flat Joanne on Armitage Way, nearby,' she said. 'It's through one of my student friends and will mean I can keep an eye on you.'

I wasn't expecting this. Part of me longed to tell her what was happening but I still couldn't bring myself to. Where would I start? Also I didn't want Gerald to burgle her or worse. I knew she would never believe me and I feared making her even more angry and disappointed in me. No, it was easier to let her believe all this was my fault. That's what I thought deep down anyway. I thanked her for sorting out the flat and arranged to meet her there for a viewing. I didn't doubt Gerald wouldn't make me continue working but having my own place gave me hope I'd have more space.

I arrived in time, keen not to make Mum even madder at me. She sighed when she saw me.

'Whatever have you been up to Jo?' she said, pulling out a foldable hair brush from her handbag. 'Look at the state of you. The side of your face and ear are completely black.'

I had no idea. I never looked in the mirror because I hated what I saw. Mum pulled out the hair bobble from my ponytail so strands of my hair fell over my ears and face. Then I realised she was embarrassed by the bruises on the side of my face and my cauliflower ear.

I stood numbly while she adjusted the hair strands to cover my injuries. Then she hurried me inside. The letting agent quickly showed us around. Mum looked impressed then swiftly took the key.

'This is perfect for my daughter,' she said. 'Now I can keep a close eye on her.' Mum gave him a knowing look as if I was a delinquent.

I moved into the flat in Armitage Way, in April 1992. Gerald wasn't best pleased when I told him but he knew he couldn't stop me. The last thing he wanted was Mum snooping around Nicola's flat. On the day I arrived, Mum fussed around, arranging the basic furniture and bringing me a few plates and cutlery.

'Now this has to be a fresh start Jo,' she warned. 'You need to get yourself a decent job. Ok?'

She didn't stay long. She gave me a curt smile and said she'd be back in a few days to see how I was getting on. I sat alone on the small sofa after she left. I didn't know what to do. I didn't have a TV or any money. I was hungry but there was no food in. I wondered what time Gerald would show up.

It didn't take him long. Almost as soon as Mum disappeared he was on my doorstep, telling me to get back to work.

Over the next couple of nights Gerald was noting the amounts I was earning with a more critical eye. I had to keep him happy but I was on a higher alert than ever, watching out for Slimer. I didn't have to wait long before he was back.

A few days after my move, I was in a punter's car when he pulled up onto another isolated industrial estate on Birmingham Road before driving to the top floor of a nearby empty multi-storey car park for privacy. He began unbuckling his jeans when suddenly my passenger door flew open. I didn't see the face, just a pair of hands, grabbing my legs to drag me out.

'Start the engine and drive,' I screamed, kicking at the hands, which belonged to Slimer. The punter looked horrified, grappling at his belt to do himself up again and trying to twist the ignition key.

I kicked at Slimer's hands with all my might when the engine roared into life.

'Go, go. This isn't my man. Please drive off,' I begged the punter.

In desperation I grabbed the steering wheel to cling on. But now the driver was terrified himself and wanted to get away, so he prised my fingers off one by one and I felt myself be pulled off the seat and onto the gravel. I lay on my side watching the rear lights disappear in a puff of exhaust fumes.

'You bastard,' I thought before I turned to face Slimer who was standing over me.

'You've been avoiding me,' he spat. Then he grabbed a fist of my hair and dragged me onto a piece of grassy wasteland by the railway track. The numbness returned and I cowered with my head down.

'Please don't hurt me,' I said in a small voice. 'I will do whatever you want.'

My insides turned to ice. I couldn't stop looking at the train track. *Perhaps I'll end up under a train or electrocuted on the live rails. Perhaps he'll kill me first and then leave my body to be cut in half by a train.* Whatever was going to happen, it was going to be something terrible.

I didn't have to wait long to find out. Slimer flipped me over onto my back before he ripped off my knickers. Then he roughly covered my mouth with a big hand and raped me. I squeezed my eyes shut. My body had long become a vessel for men to use, harm, hurt and get their own depraved pleasure from. I even felt weirdly grateful this body of mine had little to do with me. When it was over, he made me sit up again.

'I've got a girl called Cherry,' he said, pulling up his trousers. 'You're going to work with her. She's 19 and will look after you. Go home, get your things together and then meet me outside the fish and chip shop at 12 o'clock on Saturday.'

It was Wednesday now. I had just a few days to try and work out what to do. Once again he left and told me to wait half an hour. Then I ran all the way home, my body aching and throbbing all over.

*

Gerald opened the door to Nicola's flat and somehow guessed what had happened.

'What the fuck. Have you seen that black dude again?' he yelled.

I tried to explain but he heard nothing. In fact, the more I spoke the angrier he grew, punching me hard until he became breathless.

I ended up curled on the floor, sobbing. In between sobs I explained who Slimer was and how he wanted me to meet him on Saturday.

'Okay,' Gerald said, suddenly calm again. 'You'll go to meet him. I'll follow you in the car to make sure he doesn't try anything.'

I gasped with confusion. I couldn't believe he was serious. What if he lost the car or got caught in traffic? Or worse, Slimer knew he was being followed by my man? He might rape me again, or worse.

The next day, after another sleepless night, I couldn't face getting out of bed. The thought of what could happen on Saturday made me want to throw up.

I pottered around Nicola's flat for a few hours, pacing up and down the hallway. All I could think of was Slimer's snarling face and his paws on my body. Feeling alone and scared, I went back over to Neil's. Darryl, Neil and a few others were in and out. Gerald was making food. I had nothing at my place and no money, so I was grateful when he offered me some.

Chewing my food, my head hurt so much it felt like my brain had been rattled in my skull. Gerald repeated the plan for Saturday and my part in it. I was to wait for Slimer and then approach his car, and he would catch up with me in his car. Then he left with the others, saying he was busy with more 'runnings'.

I returned to Nicola's flat, half surprised Gerald wasn't locking me in. Maybe he assumed I was so broken I wouldn't run anymore. But he was wrong. Something inside of me had clicked. A flame I didn't think was there had reignited. I wanted out. I wanted to survive this. I had to try and escape. My life depended on it. I waited for a little while before slipping out of the door into the street. Before I had a chance to talk myself out of it, I ran all the way to the nearest police station.

I had been beaten up by other girls, beaten by punters, beaten by pimps and now I was facing regular beating from Gerald for being beaten up!

It was time to ask for help, even if I had to beg for it.

16

I arrived at the counter of Dudley Road police station, breathing heavily and covered in a film of sweat. A sergeant, one I had spoken to before called Nic was on duty. She eyed me carefully when I told her I wanted to report a crime.

'Come this way,' she said, taking me to a side room. There was another officer in the vice squad waiting on the chair next to hers.

Nic sat down neatly in front of me. I could vaguely smell her deodorant and hairspray. Suddenly I felt self-conscious about what I must smell like.

'What is going on Joanne?' she asked, looking serious.

In one swift breath, words streamed out. I told her about Slimer, the first beating, the threats, the rape. I gave her exact times and places, my voice growing thick with emotion. All the while Nic kept her steady gaze on my face,

'Do you want to make a statement?' she asked.

'Yes!' I cried eagerly. 'I mean, isn't that what I am doing now?'

'Do you want to report this as a crime?' she asked.

'Yes! I am telling you what happened to me. I've been raped.'

'I mean…officially report a crime,' she pressed.

I leaned across the table.

'This is what I am doing,' I cried, losing control of my voice. 'Listen to what I am saying.'

Nic let out a sigh.

'Jo, if you do this officially and we sign this off, you'll have to go to court and face your attacker. Do you understand this?'

She stared at me with a steady gaze.

'Yes, I understand,' I said, sitting back down again. I wondered why she wasn't writing this down or recording it. The idea of facing Slimer in court was pretty horrific but if that's what it took, I was willing to do it.

The two officers gave each other a sideways glance. 'Jo,' she said, using a softer voice. 'I don't think you quite understand. You will have to stand up in a dock, in a courthouse, tell a jury what happened and face being described as a common prostitute. You will have to explain to them you've been beaten up and raped by a pimp.'

'Yes that's exactly what happened,' I nodded vigorously. I was frustrated. What part of this didn't they understand?

'But isn't that part of your job if you're a prostitute?' Nic said quietly, studying my face. I sat back incredulously.

'Are you fucking serious?' I frowned. 'Surely it doesn't matter what you are or what you do for a living. If you're being raped you should still be able to get someone arrested.' She shook her head.

'It doesn't quite work like this,' she said softly.

Tears smarted in my eyes, but I shook away the offer of a tissue. All of a sudden the room felt unpleasantly hot and enclosed. I needed to get out.

'So, how does it work?' I whispered. But it was a rhetorical question. They were telling me exactly how it 'worked'. I was a slag, a whore, a prostitute. I didn't have any rights, as far as the punters went and as far as the police went. I wasn't talking to the officers anymore, who sat in their neat uniforms with their neat hair cuts, staring at me. I was talking to myself because I felt like nobody else was listening.

For a split second, I considered telling them about everything. Gerald, Darryl, Tiger, the gang he worked in, the girls, the money I had to make. But I knew it would be no good. If they wouldn't even take this rape seriously, why would they take anything else?

Besides, I knew how stupid telling them everything would be. If somehow Gerald didn't get arrested and charged then I'd be a dead girl walking. And even if he did get put inside, he'd send one of his many 'cousins' to do it.

With no choice but to keep Gerald sweet, I ran back outside into the night air. Breathing in deep gulps I walked back to my beat. I had money to earn.

*

That night, every hair on my body stood on end every time I spotted a yellow car. Each punter who pulled over, I tried to look at more closely before agreeing to anything. I was so scared of being attacked again.

After seeing a few punters, I returned to refresh the registration plates in my mind from the list on the wall. One girl, called Kara, was also reading them aloud.

'Hey, you know I've been beaten up badly by this dude called Slimer,' I said, spotting his reg on the list. Kara turned to me, her face filled with recognition. 'Oh Honey, yes, so have I.'

'Oh God,' I cried. 'You too? Right, well we should both go to the police. They'd have to believe us if there were two of us? I tried to go alone but they weren't interested.'

Kara looked uneasy.

'Please!' I begged her. 'We could go together to the station. Make a statement.'

She shook her head. 'Honey, the police won't do anything. I got my man to sort it out. Please don't think for a second the police will behave like they're on your side.'

My head swam and vision blurred with tears. This was a total nightmare. I was trapped between Slimer and Gerald. There was no way out. I swallowed and looked across to the part of town where the train station was. I'd lost all hope about the idea of jumping on a train and then a ferry to Northern Ireland. Then I imagined turning up at my dad's house or my nanna's, face covered in cuts and bruises. Court orders following me to their address. What shame would I bring to their door? It was unthinkable.

I used the back of my hand to wipe away a tear. Kara gave my arm a quick squeeze before she jumped into the next car. 'Get your man to sort things,' she repeated.

*

The next morning, I avoided the subject of what was going to happen at the weekend. The prospect of facing Slimer was terrifying, so I kept fantasising about other scenarios. Maybe I could run away before then? Sleep on the streets? Hide in another town? But I knew it was just fantasy. I had no money. No friends. I didn't even have many clothes, or at least clothes warm enough to sleep on park benches with. Gerald had a plan anyway. Over rice and beans that evening, before I was driven to work, he explained exactly what was to happen on Saturday.

'I want you to go to the chip shop and stand on the edge of the road,' Gerald said. 'The pavement is wide enough for me to park nearby. I can quickly pull up once you've met him, if there's any hassle. Make sure you stand at the edge of the pavement. Let's see what he does when he arrives.'

Hassle? I thought. *Of course there would be hassle.* I didn't understand what he meant. Slimer was likely to throw me in a car himself and drive off. And then God knows where I'd end up. Like poor Gail or Janine probably. But I didn't dare question Gerald on his plan. His word was always final.

On the Saturday morning, I woke early. My heart was already banging, my chest tight before I opened my eyes. I knew Kara had told me to rely on my man to 'sort things' but the fact was I didn't trust Gerald. I knew he hated being in this position where another pimp was trying to claim me, but I didn't trust he'd protect me properly from him either.

I didn't bother to comb my hair or even attempt to make an effort to look half decent. I just counted down the hours until we had to go.

All the way to the chip shop, I shook with fear. I pushed my hands deep into my cardigan pockets, wishing I could disappear. When I arrived, I could see a queue of people inside behind the glass front. Ordinary people waiting for their chippy lunch. People who had no idea of what was about to happen a few yards away. I breathed a small sigh of relief. Surely in front of all these customers, in broad daylight, I'd be safe?

I stood with my back pressed to the glass. I wasn't going to stand at the road-side edge like Gerald had told me to. I needed the safety of members of the public who could act as witnesses. My eyes flitted from left to right, anxiously looking for the flash of a yellow car. I kept swallowing, wanting to be sick. Then all of a sudden a red car came into view, cruising in a familiar way. Slimer glared at me, signalling with his eyes to get into his new car. I knew if I did, I might never get out again.

I pressed my back further against the glass. I could hear people inside asking for fish and chips twice, the clink of change, the mumble of a mum telling her kids off. For a split second, a memory of Nanna bringing back a chippy tea popped into my mind. The smell of vinegar, handing out the sauce, the comforting warmth through newspaper on my lap. Memories from another lifetime ago.

Slimer's car pulled up and I spotted his eyes glancing up at a flat nearby. I followed his gaze, noticing somehow there were people inside, shadowy figures. Was this his lookout post? Was this where he kept his own girls locked? I could sense he'd guessed something was up, so he pulled away to go around the block again. The next time he pulled up, his eyes stared hard and glittery, telling me I was in deep trouble.

Where are you Gerald? I screamed inside my head.

The reverberation of drum and bass told me Gerald had finally arrived. He was with a few mates, with the tinted windows wound down. I guessed he wanted to look intimidating. His car stopped and they all leaped, shouting and running towards Slimer's car. I turned around to see the mum in the chip shop pull her kids closer to her knees while the red car screeched around the corner. Slimer had gone.

Trembling, I waited for Gerald to return and pick me up. He pushed me into the passenger seat of the car and we sped away.

'You stupid fucking bitch. Why were you standing away from the road? Why didn't you go and speak to him like I said?' he yelled at me.

'I was scared,' I cried.

In-between gear changes he punched the side of my face with a clenched fist. Tears streamed down my face. While the threat of Slimer had gone, now I had to face the fury of my man.

Gerald drove to my flat on Armitage Way, where his rage continued. With an open palm, he went for my face and head, then curled his fist and punched me all over. Next he frogmarched me back to his car to take me to Nicola's flat. He slapped me hard a few more times and then locked me in.

Once again I was alone, with nothing, no food, TV, phone or money. I didn't know what to do. I curled up into a ball and cried.

A few hours later, I got up, hungry. Once again, I didn't know when Gerald would return. When it was getting dark, I wandered into the kitchen to see if any food had been left. Gerald always washed up and cleaned up, leaving the place immaculate after every meal, so there were no left-overs. I looked through every single cupboard and found one half packet of custard creams, so tucked into them. By nightfall the flat was freezing, so I pulled out the old duvet cover and wrapped myself in it, shivering.

After a long sleepless night, I longed to hear the key in the door. But it never came. All morning. All afternoon. By the evening I was starving. I drank cold water from the cold tap to try and fill myself up.

A second, then third night passed. Every hour felt like a day in itself. I began to feel sick with hunger. Several times after pacing around, I'd try the door but it wouldn't budge.

Then, on the fifth morning, the key finally twisted in the lock. I heard the rustle of plastic bags. By now I was so weak and starving hungry. I was desperate for it to be Gerald. He stood over me, holding the bags up.

'Fancy breakfast?' he said. I tried to stand up but felt so faint I saw stars.

I had to wait for him to cook, standing next to him by the stove, I wanted to shove the eggs and bread he was using into my mouth. But he clearly wanted to make me wait, so I daren't. Like always he behaved as if nothing had happened.

He neatly set down the plates and cutlery, spooned the fried eggs on toast on plates and then sat opposite me.

'You're back at work tonight,' he said simply.

17

The next morning, I went for a walk for fresh air, when I bumped into Anthony walking Buster on the street. His face hardened when he saw me.

'Do you know Mum is on medication because of you?' he snapped.

'What are you on about?' I asked.

'Come home and find out,' he said.

Gerald was out that afternoon, so I quickly sneaked around to Mum's house.

Standing in her porch, waiting for her to answer the doorbell made my tummy churn. I could see her neatly arranged antiques through the window in the big dresser. The recently vacuumed carpets. Her pot plants by the front door. Nice things, a world away from my horrible life. I caught sight of my reflection in the window. I had shadowy bruises all over my face. I pulled my hair around my cheeks, hoping she wouldn't notice. Mum opened the door.

'Oh,' she said, looking over my shoulder. 'So you have decided to show up have you?'

She didn't invite me in, so I followed her. Anthony said 'hello' in a furtive way and disappeared upstairs. I felt sad we rarely talked anymore, but I guessed he'd heard nothing but bad things about me now. Mum sat down heavily on the sofa and glared up at me.

'I've had the *Express and Star* on my doorstep,' she snapped. 'They were going to write about you in the newspaper.'

'What?' I had no idea what she was on about.

'I told them I didn't want you in the newspaper because they were going to describe you as a 'Missing Prostitute'. So everybody would know my daughter was a bloody prostitute. Have you any idea how that makes me feel?'

I was mortified.

'Mum, why?'

'You were reported missing Joanne and thought to be abducted,' she said impatiently, her cheeks reddening. 'Don't stand there like you didn't know anything. It was because you reported some dodgy man to police and they noticed you were missing for five days, so all and sundry went looking for you. Have you any idea what trouble you caused?'

My mouth felt dry. I had no idea about of any of this. Mum gave me such a hard look, I felt my insides shrivel. I mumbled something about being sorry but having to go and before she had a chance to stop me, I left.

That evening, I was on the streets again for only an hour or so before a vice car pulled up. They arrested me and brought me into the station. I saw DC Sawyer and Nic behind the desk.

'What the hell is going on, Jo? Nic said. 'We've had every-one up and down the country looking for you. You were put on a missing list. Where have you been?'

DC Sawyer frowned, a look of genuine concern on his face.

'Nowhere,' I said instantly, thinking of Gerald's face if he ever got wind of this.

Nic shook her head slightly in despair, clicked her pen and started filling out another charge sheet. Nothing more was said.

Mum soon got wind of a disturbance reported to police on Armitage Way. The neighbours had obviously heard or seen me being dragged to the car back to Nicola's flat. She was furious when I called her next. 'You need to go and apologise to those poor neighbours. One girl was traumatised by the sound of screaming, so you need to say sorry for all the upset you've caused,' she told me.

Exhausted, I simply agreed. I mumbled an apology to some startled neighbours who clearly wanted to see the back of me. Then I got a bin bag of my things and moved out. I couldn't afford the rent anyway. That night I found myself back at Nicola's flat, with Gerald ready to take me back to work.

*

All of my adjourned cases piled up and I was due to appear at Dudley Magistrates' Court to face multiple charges of 'Loitering for the Purpose of Prostitution.'

I had been back and forth to court a few times since October, but only for a few minutes. Now I had to face another judge with a long list of crimes and was terrified. The charge made things sound so official and filled me with shame. I was a common prostitute in the eyes of the law. But I knew Gerald and his gang were not even on the radar of the police for this and after my conversations with coppers, I didn't expect them to be.

Girls on the street tried to reassure me as the date approached, but I had pleaded guilty to all 22 charges and I wasn't able to afford to pay all the fines. There was no way of knowing if I'd go to jail or not. I recalled what Tonia had told me and cried at the thought of losing my liberty and also at never knowing what happened to her. I didn't feel strong enough to survive a stint in prison.

Beforehand, I had an interview with the probation service who explained they were going to write a social report on me. This time, a well-spoken young man asked the questions, ticking boxes and making notes in another airless room.

'Why are you working as a prostitute?' he asked.

'I need the money,' I said quietly.

The words sounded almost meaningless to me since I'd been asked so many times by police by now.

'Where do you live?' he asked.

'In-between people's flats,' I said, careful not to say too much.

Tick.

'Do you receive housing benefit?' he asked.

'No,' I said.

Tick.

Something took over then. I tried to look at him directly in the eye.

'I need help,' I admitted. 'I want to get out of this. Please can you help me? I have nowhere to live. I have no other way of earning at the moment. I have no savings for a deposit. I need someone to support me, to get me away from this life.'

As soon as the words left my mouth I felt a stab of anxiety. If Gerald ever heard me saying this he would kill me. The man gave a slight nod and ticked another box then turned the paper over and said he was finished.

I wasn't a stranger to feeling scared any more. Different levels of fear peaked during different parts of the day. Depending on which punter's car I got into. What Gerald's mood was. How fast I was running away from the other working girls. Whether I faced arrest again. But the fear I experienced on my day in court was a whole new level.

I had no lawyer. Nobody to go with me. That morning, I got up early and put on the same clothes I wore on the streets, a short mini-skirt and hand-knitted cardigan. Then I walked back to the grey-bricked courthouse, ready to be judged.

*

Due to the number of charges, I wondered whether my case would be reported in the paper. I didn't know and tried to control my breathing as I walked slowly inside the courtroom. My head hung in shame when I told a court usher who I was. She waved me into a seating area for defendants. A judge swept in, wearing a black gown. He looked down upon me and began reading. A probation officer was invited to make a statement first, this all went on for over half an hour, although it felt like 24 hours.

The probation officer who had interviewed me rattled through his findings. Once again, I struggled to understand the proceedings although the description 'common prostitute' was used many times.

The probation guy explained to the judge I had appeared to be soliciting out of choice and therefore I needed to 'take responsibility for my own actions' and so he advocated that I should be sent to prison. He didn't look at me once. To him I was a ticked box.

My stomach lurched, so I put my hand over my mouth to stop myself retching. I hadn't been asked to speak but couldn't stop the words pouring out.

'Oh no,' I cried. 'No, no, no! Please no!'

Fizzing specks formed around the edge of my eyes, while I shakily stood to address the judge. The thought of prison was terrifying and what would happen when I got out? What would Gerald do?

'That's not what I said,' I cried out. 'I said I needed help. I need support to get out of this. I have nowhere to live. God please help me. Don't put me in jail.'

The judge's face didn't move a muscle, but I could see him scribbling notes. Words that would decide what would happen with my life. I held my breath, until he gave his verdict.

'I will advise the probation office to help find suitable accommodation for Miss Phillips, and help her move on with her life,' he announced.

My body wilted with relief. I couldn't believe it. For once, someone had listened. I was ushered back out of the court to wait and then the probation officer told me I had to attend monthly meetings and meanwhile they would help find me a place in a local women's refuge. Then I was free to go.

I wandered back into town. I had nowhere to go but didn't want to return to Nicola's flat. For at least an hour I appreciated a sense of liberty, knowing I wasn't going to prison. It had been a narrow escape. And although I wasn't free of Gerald, I appreciated things could have been even worse.

18

I had monthly visits to my probation officer while they tried to find me a place to live. Meanwhile, I continued being kept at Nicola's flat and was made to work every day and provide Gerald with at least several hundred a week, even if he disappeared for days at a time.

Arrests continued to be made on a regular basis too. I could see the exasperation in the eyes of DC Sawyer every time he handed me a charge sheet and sent me away again but there was nothing either of us could say.

One morning, in May 1992, I glanced out of the window to see Neil and his wife walking up my street, looking flustered and into flat windows. I could tell he was trying to work out which one was Nicola's flat. Neil spotted me looking down and pointed at the door to ask me to open it.

'Gerald has been sent down,' he said simply. 'You can't stay here. Get your things and come with us.'

My mouth dropped open.

'Prison?' I asked. 'What for?'

Neil's wife looked uneasy.

'Four months for robbery,' muttered Neil.

I was horrified. I had no idea what Gerald was involved in but I could tell neither of them wanted to elaborate. They took me to their house where Neil told me I could sleep on their sofa for a few nights. I never asked any questions about what Gerald did, even if my mind was racing.

After a day or so, I began to relax and saw this as much-needed time off. I didn't have to go to the streets because Gerald wasn't around. I spent the days trying to relax, chatting to Neil's wife or walking around town. I still had no money, but even being around normal people doing normal activities gave me hope that one day, perhaps, I could join them. But after three nights Neil told me Gerald had made a plan for me.

'Gerald told me you're to stay with Darryl at Junior's flat,' he said. Junior was another cousin of Gerald's.

'You have to carry on working and give Darryl the money at the end of each night. The money is to be split between Darryl, Gerald and me. Okay?'

I nodded, I knew I had to agree.

Neil drove me to Junior's flat in a tower block. I'd met Junior before briefly and he was a lovely, polite dude who was committed to a college course to improve his lot in life. But I'd guessed they were probably ripping him off in some way, taking advantage of his accommodation while he was away.

Darryl wasn't in when I arrived. I knew he was busy with his own girls and, over the next day or so, I didn't see him at all. So I decided to skip work myself. I watched TV, had long baths and tried to think of anything but the streets.

The next day, with little to do, I dropped around to Neil's when he wasn't in, to see his wife Leanne. When she answered the door, she mouthed: 'Sheree is here.'

She knew that I knew about Gerald having had a baby with her. I swallowed hard and walked in. I didn't want to make a scene and run off. In the lounge was a beautiful toddler girl crawling around. She was a very pretty baby, beautifully dressed. Beside her was a pretty black woman with lots of jewellery on, I assumed to be Sheree. She clearly knew who I was too, but again, not wanting to make a scene, I shyly smiled at her. She stared at my fingers as we made small talk. Then she asked where my rings were from.

'Oh they were just given to me by punters. Oh, and Gerald gave me this one.'

One was a sovereign ring Gerald passed on from prison for me to look after. Sheree eyed me suspiciously. I didn't stay long after this.

With free time on my hands, I decided to give Sam a call. She was my only friend who I was still in touch with.

'Fancy coming over?' I asked her, feeling bold. With Gerald away and Darryl busy, I decided to make the most of it. Sam currently worked in Northern Ireland in an admin job and lived with her mum. She was thrilled to be asked and arranged to get a ferry over the next day.

I met up with her and brought her back to Junior's flat. I was so excited to have a friend to stay, although I hoped I'd get time off because I didn't want her to know the kind of life I was mixed up in.

The next day Darryl came home unexpectedly. I feared he would tell Sam to leave but to my surprise, he didn't. He was polite enough, but avoided her. He didn't even ask me to go to work either. I guessed what was happening. He wanted to keep what we were doing secret too. I could tell other stuff was going on as well, but in my naïvety never understood quite what was happening. One night Darryl was hunched over bin bags, stressing about tissues I had thrown away with the rubbish. I didn't understand why he was so upset and he refused to let me empty the bin or help him. Sam saw what was happening and later suggested he'd lost drugs.

I was shocked, but she laughed at me.

'Drugs are everywhere Jo,' she said. I knew other working girls took hard drugs like heroin and crack, but I'd never seen them do it. Gerald always said he liked the fact I wasn't like other girls who needed to get high. The idea of taking anything scared me, thanks to those '*Just Say No*' adverts from years ago on TV.

Then Sam changed the subject to suggest something more fun.

'Hey, why don't we go to Alton Towers?' she grinned.

I'd never been and had no money but she insisted on treating me and we bought tickets.

I couldn't quite believe it when we made our way to the theme park. This was such an ordinary and carefree thing to do. For the next few hours we screamed with joy on roller-coasters, spun around on rides and ate so much candy floss we were nearly sick. But I loved every minute of it. After the log flume, Sam bought us a photo as a memento. On the way back I couldn't stop looking at it. The girl in the photo was smiling, her wet hair half stuck to her face, looking like she didn't have a care in the world. Could that really have been me?

That night Darryl didn't mention the streets either. He ignored us and went out all hours, leaving us to watch TV. The next morning he casually asked how long Sam would be staying for. Immediately Sam said: 'A week,' so I went along with this. Again, to my surprise, Darryl simply nodded in agreement.

So, for a whole week, we hung around town, ate chips, slept in late, giggled about boys in town and for once I behaved like a girl my age. Not once did I tell her about what was going on or who Darryl was or how Gerald treated me. It never even occurred to me to reveal the truth. Partly because I felt ashamed and partly because I didn't want her involved. Not in my mucky, horrible life.

A week later, I sadly waved Sam off at the station. In a fantasy, I was getting on a train and ferry with her, but I daren't even consider this. Gerald would definitely send someone to come and find me. I had nowhere to stay in Northern Ireland, and also, court cases were racking up. I knew I likely faced prosecution again. What if the police followed me over there too and my whole family discovered the truth about my life? No, I couldn't run away with her. I was trapped.

When I got back, the flat felt empty without her. But I wasn't alone for long. The door soon flew open and Darryl asked where Sam was.

'She's gone,' I said sadly.

'Good. Now she's not here, you're to go back to work. Tonight. You've got a lot of catching up to do. Got it?'

I swallowed hard, trying not to let him see the bubble of tears threatening to rise to the surface.

*

A few weeks later, I was home late, when Darryl pulled out a couple of cans of beer from a plastic bag. He knew I didn't drink so I wondered why he poured it into a glass and offered me some in a way I couldn't refuse. I took a couple of sips. After a few minutes I began to feel dizzy and nauseous.

'I need to go to bed,' I slurred.

The next thing I knew, the room was spinning in a horrible way. I tried to sit up but fell backwards onto the pillow. Then I saw Darryl's bulky frame looming over me. He tugged at my clothes. Next thing, he was on top of me, forcing himself into me.

Oh my God, this isn't happening.

I twisted my head to the side, trying to focus on the window. A fantasy escape route. But of course I know there was none. His heavy weight pinned me to the bed. I knew I couldn't scream or struggle. Instead, I went limp, pretending to be unconscious, to wait for it to be over. He climbed off and left afterwards, saying nothing. I kept my eyes tightly shut, willing sleep to come. The next morning, I woke up wondering if that really happened. I patted the sheets and found a wet patch. Then I started crying. Yes it really had happened.

Gerald's best friend had raped me.

But worse still, what if Gerald didn't believe it was rape? What if he thought I'd slept with Darryl behind his back? I felt like puking up. Gerald always said the best thing about me was how naïve I was. How gullible. How he could trust me. After this, would he become even more controlling now? I'd heard of stories about what happened to girls they didn't trust. At the end of the night when they asked for cash, they strip-searched them. They made them bend over for internal examinations. Tonia had once told me a story of how girls were tortured with electric shocks to make sure they weren't lying or hiding cash somewhere.

The next morning, I left the house to go for a walk. I wanted to avoid Darryl anyway but I needed to work out what to do. Did I come out and tell Gerald or hope he never found out? I decided to confide in Neil. He was his real cousin, a blood relative.

When I sat down and told Neil, my eyes welled up. The idea of Darryl on top of me made me feel physically sick.

'You gotta tell Gerald,' he concluded gently. 'It has to come from you and nobody else.' He placed a hand on mine, in a fatherly way. I knew he treated Leanne badly and had never seen this gentler side to him.

'I have to bring some weed to Gerald in prison anyway,' he added. 'You can come with me then. Help smuggle it in.' I felt my cheeks redden just at the thought of this. But none of this was in my control. I knew I had to do whatever they wanted.

That night I stayed out later than usual, but tried to avoid sleeping with more punters. I always did the minimum of what I had to do before I returned home, trembling at the thought of Darryl being there. Thankfully he wasn't.

*

A few days later, Neil picked me up to visit Gerald in the prison. On the way he handed me a lump of hash in a piece of cling film.

'Stick this inside your clothing and when nobody is looking, give it to Gerald during the visit under the table,' he said, with a sideways glance.

Neil came in with me. I'd never been in a jail before. Prison officers ushered us into the prison in Shrewsbury. A stark, square building that echoed with the sound of clanking doors, keys and shouts of men. I shuddered. Even being here for a few hours was a horrible thought but at the same time, I was glad Gerald was locked up for a while.

Neil and I walked over to a plastic-topped table where Gerald was waiting. He raised an eyebrow when he saw me, like he wasn't expecting me. Shaking, I slid the cannabis under the table. Gerald nodded and took it from me. Neil had a brief chat with him. They spoke in Patois and I didn't understand what they were talking about.

Then Neil turned to me. 'Right, I'm leaving you two alone. Joanne has something to tell you.'

I tried to smile and look relaxed.

'What is it?' snapped Gerald, glaring at me.

'Oh nothing,' I said airily.

Gerald's eyes narrowed. 'What the fuck? What have you got to tell me?'

I opened my mouth to say something but tears smarted in my eyes. What words could I use. *Rape? Forced to have sex? Fear I was drugged?*

I shrugged. 'Honestly it's nothing.'

Gerald slapped open palms onto the table, making me jump.

'You fucking tell me bitch what's been going on?' he spat, jabbing his finger in my face.

A prison officer glanced up, people around us were turning to look. I couldn't stop tears from cascading down my face.

'Okay, okay,' I whispered, desperate not to make a scene. I stared at his hands, spreadeagled on the table.

'Darryl raped me.'

*

Gerald sat back in his chair. I daren't look him in the eye but sensed he was relieved it was this and nothing else.

'Ah. Ok. I had a feeling this would happen,' he said, rubbing his chin. His words felt like a punch to my guts. I hated him. How could he be so casual about this?

'I respect you girl for telling me the truth, the absolute truth,' he said.

Part of me melted with relief. He wasn't angry any more.

He changed the subject and soon the visiting time was up. We said goodbye and he reached across the table to kiss my lips. I walked away feeling a range of emotions. Part of me missed Gerald terribly but also loathed him. And I was terrified of what Darryl would do if he found out I'd told him. It didn't take long to discover. Darryl stormed around to Neil's where I went afterwards, pacing up and down their garden path.

'Where is that little slag?' he screamed. 'Get her out of here.'

Neil and Leanne looked at me in panic.

'You'd better go and get all your stuff out of Junior's flat,' she said.

'But where will I go?' I asked.

They both looked at me with sympathy but neither had an answer. I couldn't go to Nicola's because Darryl would look for me there too.

I waited until Darryl cleared off before dashing from Neil's to the flat. I shoved my few belongings, a few items of clothing, a towel and a Body Shop shower gel into a bin bag and fled.

Once I got outside, I looked up and down the street. *Where do I go now?* I thought. I couldn't go to Mum's. I could only guess what she would say. I couldn't go to Telford. My friends hadn't spoken or seen me for months and I doubted Becky's mum would let me stay anyway. I had no money. No family. No friends and absolutely nowhere to go.

19

This realisation made my limbs feel heavy as I wandered away. It was already 6pm and would be getting dark soon. Clouds gathered in the sky. I'd need to find somewhere sheltered to sleep before it began to rain and night fell.

After walking around the neighbourhood, I wandered into Western Park in Dudley. I walked past the duck pond to see a child's play park, already empty of families who had taken kids home for tea. There was a small playhouse on top of the slide in the centre of the sandpit there.

At least I'll have a roof over my head, I thought grimly, squeezing myself inside. I pushed the black bin bag behind my head to use as a pillow. Staring at the roof, covered in graffiti, I wondered who else visited this hut at night. Shivering, I closed my eyes.

Then I heard the jangle of keys. I glanced up to see a park keeper locking up. If he spotted me he would kick me out but also, what scared me more, was meeting any other night time visitors. If I was attacked, I'd have no escape. In panic, I jumped up, grabbed my bin bag and ran towards the main gate.

After two more hours of wandering around, all my adrenalin had disappeared. I was exhausted and hungry and realised I had no choice. Whatever reaction I faced, I had to go to Mum's house. The second she opened the door, I lowered my gaze.

'Oh, it's you is it!' she barked. 'What do we owe this pleasure for then?'

'Please, Mum,' I mumbled. 'Can I stay here? I really have nowhere else to go.'

She eyed me suspiciously and moved away from the door indicating I could come in. When I walked past, her eyes shot up and down my body with distaste. She disappeared briefly into the kitchen to speak to William and Anthony then returned while I waited in the hallway,

'Alright. You can stay,' she said. 'But first, a few ground rules. You are not to be in this house alone. You have to leave the house by 8am when I go to work. You are not allowed to use the kitchen. I don't want it left in a mess. Or the telephone. Got that?'

I stared at her. I knew Mum cared little about me, but she spoke to me like I was a piece of dirt blown in by the wind. She paused, waiting for me to agree. I nodded and picked up my bag to take upstairs.

'Finally,' she added. 'You're sleeping in the attic.' She handed me a sleeping bag.

'The attic?' I repeated. She gave a brief nod without looking at me.

*

I climbed up to the attic room. The Velux-style window had smashed and been replaced by a bin bag sellotaped to the frame. I could hear rain pattering on the plastic. There was nowhere else to sleep, except underneath it. I managed to doze off, but kept being woken by rain spitting in my face. By 7am, my sleeping bag was soaking wet. Downstairs, Mum was clattering in the kitchen and I could smell toast.

'You awake Jo?' she shouted.

Quickly I got up, dressed and grabbed my bin bag. I was hungry but daren't ask for anything.

Downstairs, William eyed me with the same suspicious look mum gave me. Mum was already dressed and ready for work, in her new job for the local council.

'I'm going now,' I said, to assure them.

'It's raining outside. Where's your coat?' William asked.

I shrugged. I felt embarrassed all I had on was a thread-bare cardigan. He took off his trendy black bomber jacket with a tartan pattern inside. 'Here, you better have this,' he said.

I could sense Mum's disapproval but took it from him. Anthony, all dressed and ready for school, looked at me with pity in his eyes.

'You need something to keep you warm,' William said. I put it on. He was a foot taller than me, so the arms hung over my wrists but I was grateful anyway. Before Mum had a chance to have another go at me, I left. Staying even a second longer in a house where I was so unwelcome made me want to cry and never stop. With nowhere to go again, I walked straight to my probation office to beg for an appointment. They were busy and the receptionist said it was unlikely I could see anyone, so I sat in the waiting room sobbing. After two hours, my eyes were so swollen I could hardly open them, but an officer agreed to talk.

'I need help. Please,' I begged. 'I am homeless. I have no one and no money. I am too scared to sleep on the streets.'

I also had another problem. Gerald had told me via Neil, in no uncertain terms, I was to keep the money rolling in for him. Even if I wasn't living at Darryl's I feared him finding me when he got out. Also, I had such a huge number of fines to pay. I needed to find the money or would face a prison sentence. But I didn't mention any of this.

As if she read most of the worries on my mind, the probation officer said she would see what she could do immediately. Within a few hours, she had found me a bed at a refuge called The Place, in the centre of Dudley.

*

By the afternoon, I had arrived at the refuge door, exhausted and hungry. Based in an old manor-style house, it was set back from the road with big hedges and walls around the perimeter. It would be easy to miss if you were driving past. But despite appearing hidden, I had no doubt Gerald would find me here. He always did.

I walked inside and a volunteer swiftly showed me around. There was a huge kitchen and dining area, where a couple of elderly Pakistani ladies were cooking. One of them welcomed me, and told me she was living in the refuge because her husband abused her and she had nowhere else to go. Her community were ashamed of her, she said. My heart went out to her. 'Everyone helps themselves to food,' explained the volunteer. I noticed how almost all the food was tinned.

I walked towards the corridor of dormitories to find chaos like something from St Trinian's. Women were having loud conversations, one was running up and down the corridor as if she was high on something, while another two were arguing.

I was to sleep in the bottom bunk with an older Asian woman called Maya. She immediately told me her life story and how she too had been rejected from her community for having an affair.

'My husband found out, so I cannot see my kids,' she sobbed.

'I'm sorry,' I said, nervously. Then another woman called Sarah with blonde curly hair approached me.

'Welcome to the nuthouse,' she said. She gave me a brief run-down of who everyone was. There were Romany twin girls called Flo and Violet. Flo was outgoing and winked at me while Violet looked younger and small and stared shyly from under her fringe.

'Like 90 per cent of the girls in here, we all work on the streets,' she grinned. 'We have to give the refuge our Giros so it's the only way we can afford to live.'

Another woman, Julie, was a bit older than us. She was a big girl, with a cynical look in her eye. Immediately she took me under her wing and asked what I wanted for dinner.

I also connected straight away with a lovely girl called Rachel, who had big brown eyes and olive skin and always wore a knee-length skirt, which made her look more respectable than anyone else. She ended up in the refuge because of a troubled time as a teenager. She never spoke much about it, but told me she was in love with a married man and had been in trouble with the police.

Sarah was a character too. With a mischievous grin, she was always cracking jokes and confided in me about her love of shoplifting. I didn't find stealing funny, but the way she told her stories cracked us all up.

There were three support workers who worked shifts and one stayed overnight on the premises. Their jobs were to help find us safe accommodation but aside from this, they left us to our own devices. As long as we weren't away for longer than three nights in a row and were back by 10pm, we could do what we liked. After getting settled on my bed – I only had one small bag of belongings so it took a few seconds – Julie asked me what I wanted to eat. By now I had grown so used to being ravenously hungry, I almost didn't notice it.

'It's mainly tins here,' Julie said. 'But I can knock you up something decent. You're all skin and bone.'

I said I didn't mind. Within half an hour she called me into the cavernous kitchen and dining area, where she presented me with a plate of delicious-smelling sausage casserole.

'There's steam pudding and custard for afters,' she winked.

I was overcome with gratitude, even if I couldn't finish it.

While I ate, I got to know Julie. She told me her alcoholic mum would send her out to shoplift when she was younger. She got so sick of it, she decided one day to get caught because prison was preferable to life at home, so she wandered out of a DIY store with a trolley piled high with electrical goods but the alarms didn't go off and nobody noticed. In panic, she parked the trolley in a bush and headed home. She confessed to her mum who ordered her to go back and pick it up so they could sell it on. 'I ended up homeless after I left Mum's, so they put me here,' said Julie.

That night I lay in bed, staring at the mattress above, listening to all the shouting and hollering in the corridors and wondered how long I could survive it here. But also I was completely touched by the welcome the girls had given me. They gave me a glimmer of hope that people still cared.

*

I put off going back on the streets, but days later, a letter arrived at the refuge for me. I recognised the handwriting immediately. Feeling sick, I opened the envelope, thinking of Gerald's tongue licking the glue.

YOU BETTER HAVE MY MONEY. OR ELSE, it read, underlined in capital letters.

PASS ALL CASH ON TO NEIL.

A tear slid down my face. Nobody was supposed to know we were here and I had no clue how Gerald had found out but it didn't surprise me.

Later that afternoon, I called Mum to tell her where I was. I didn't want her to think I had gone missing again. I heard her sigh.

'Why would a refuge take you in?' she said. 'Life isn't that bad is it?'

I told her I'd call back another time and a few days later, I did. This time William answered the phone.

'You're a little liar, Jo,' he yelled. 'Making your mum worry even more. I called the refuge you claimed to be at and they refused to say you were there.'

'That's because it's all confidential. Women here are under threat of violence so they don't say who is here,' I explained.

'Oh, for goodness sake. Why are you lying like this to us?' he scoffed. I put down the phone. They just didn't get it.

A day or so later, my support worker told me there was a phone call for me. I took the call, expecting that maybe Mum was trying again but it was Gerald, calling from prison.

'Junior has died,' he said. I guessed that's how he managed to persuade them he needed to speak to me. He'd pretended to be a concerned relative with news of a death. I was sad. Junior, from what I knew of him, was a decent sort and had tried to build a better life for himself.

But I knew Gerald hadn't rung just to tell me this. 'You'd better keep the money coming in,' he snapped. 'Don't think the refuge means you're not working.'

I made myself go out to work that night, grateful for the warmth of William's coat. Later I stopped off at Neil's to give him the money. He and Leanne often took a cut for themselves too. Either for travel expenses for going to the prison or they found some other excuse.

That night, after work, I hung up the coat at the end of my bed and fell into a restless sleep on the bunk bed then woke the next day to find my coat had gone. Sarah had disappeared too and I guessed she'd taken it.

By 7pm, when I was on the streets, shivering with cold, I decided to go to the police station. If I reported Sarah, she might give it back. When the officer saw me he raised an eyebrow.

'So what brings you in here voluntarily, eh?' he asked.

I explained the situation. 'I don't want to cause any trouble for Sarah, I just desperately need my coat back. Before I freeze my arse off.' He leaned closer to me over the desk, a look of amusement on his face.

'Come on Jo,' he smirked. 'You work the streets. All you lot are involved with crime. Yet someone takes your £20 or whatever jacket? And that bothers you this much?'

I stared at him. Yes, this did matter to me. But clearly not to the police. They didn't think this crime was worth it. They didn't believe *I* was worth it. And perhaps he was right. The draught from the corridor suddenly made me shiver. I hugged myself, told him to forget it and hurried out.

*

Over the next few weeks, I got to know Flo and Violet, the twin girls. Flo reminded me of Tonia, with her bubbly personality and love of makeup. Whenever she got back from the streets she often told us where she'd been or funny stories about punters. Sometimes she disappeared for a couple of days because she was travelling up and down the country.

Back in her dormitory room, I would often find her covered in fake tan, preparing herself for the night. She was so different to her sister. Violet was child-like and filled with a sadness I couldn't put my finger on.

One afternoon, Violet showed me a picture she had stuck with Blu-Tack on the wall. It was of a tiny baby surrounded by a tangle of tubes in an incubator.

'I had my baby daughter when I was 14,' she whispered. 'She was born premature. They tried to save her, but couldn't.' Her eyes shone with pain like it happened yesterday. Instinctively I put my arm around her. 'I am so sorry,' I said, hugging her tightly. I couldn't imagine how upsetting that must be.

I liked these girls. They were less trouble than some of the others, who were argumentative or clearly on drugs. As naïve as I was, I understood when girls became drug addicts they'd often lied, stole or cheated for money for their next fix.

Rachel was different to the others. She never caused any trouble, except outside of the refuge. One night she asked me to sneak out with her to draw lipstick on the car of her ex. Afterwards we ran off giggling like a pair of schoolgirls. I loved the way Rachel tried to seek revenge. I knew I'd never dare do the same to Gerald but Rachel seemed more courageous than me.

Listening to Rachel's tale and the other girls' stories made me realise we all had similar starts on the spiral downwards. Neglect from our parents lay at the heart of it for many. However, although I could see blame lay at the door of the parents for many girls, I blamed myself completely. Unlike these girls, I was from a 'nice' family. My Mum had gone to university and collected antiques. I had a lovely nanna and dad, who happened to live far away. Mum always told me it was my fault and I believed she was right. I had continued my relationship with Gerald when she told me to stop. I dropped out of school and then college. Mum always said I was good for nothing, like Dad, but actually I was worse. I'd ended up a slag for a living.

Flo, however, didn't seem to mind being on the streets. She told me she'd done it for years after a terrible time in care.

'Hey you should come with me,' she suggested. 'Get some work in a sauna. It's much better than standing on a dark street corner.'

'Is the money any better?' I asked. Gerald was constantly chasing me to increase my earnings.

'Yeah, yeah,' she said. 'Come to Birmingham with me. I'll see you right.'

So the next day I took a train with her, and we went in and out of several massage parlours and saunas asking for work until one place off a high street took us in. Flo quickly explained what was happening after a hard-faced receptionist looked us both up and down then disappeared out the back.

'Each sauna provides a different kind of girl,' she said. 'They'll have a blonde, a brunette, a person of colour, a redhead and someone child-like. I bet you'll be taken for the child-like one. Punters always ask for someone specific to their taste.'

The receptionist returned and offered us both jobs. But all day we ended up sitting around a stuffy massage room because no punters turned up. Quickly, I learned the daytime shift was the worst time to come in. We even had to pay them for our own entrance fee and barely had enough for the train ride back to the refuge.

The next day we found a bigger and more professional-looking massage parlour called Lucy Palmers in Birmingham. This was a five-storey building, open 24 hours a day and the second we stepped inside it had a buzzy air of being busy. We rang a buzzer and a receptionist behind a window let us in through a grilled door. She gave us the once-over and then in a breathless voice took us around the joint.

The first thing that hit me was the smell. It was a heady mix of baby oil, talc and foul body odour. I swallowed back a rising feeling of nausea as we were led around, like the new girls in class.

In the basement were saunas and showers and to the right was a living room. This was where girls had to sit on display on a plush sofa to be chosen by a punter. Behind the living room was a staff room where girls could smoke and chat on their break. Everywhere we looked we could see girls, very young girls, silently eyeing us up and down while we walked past. On each floor was a different style of room. They included a premium suite with a Jacuzzi.

'There are different tiers for business, premium, deluxe and basic,' chirruped the receptionist. She led us back to a room. It looked like an ordinary massage room with a table covered in paper towel, and a basket full of condoms and talc.

'You're expected to clean up after yourselves after every client,' the woman said. 'But girls can't use the showers here because they need to be vacant for clients' use at any time.'

By the end of the tour, the smell of the place clung to my skin. Already I wanted to wash it off. But there was no time, because we were both taken on and our shift was to start immediately.

20

By the afternoon, I had hardly seen any punters. To many men, I was boring, flat-chested and a dull prospect compared to the busty blonde girls who streamed in and out all day. Wanting a break, I decided to make myself look busy by cleaning out the showers and folding towels. I felt disgusting already, my body was covered in a film of oil and my hair felt like a mess. We all had to wear hideous white, tightly-fitted short nurse-style outfits too. All I wanted was to get back to the refuge and stand under a hot shower.

While I loitered in the living room area, tidying up, an attractive woman wearing a Juicy Couture tracksuit came bustling in. She had dyed red hair neatly clasped in a high ponytail, with expensive sunglasses perched above her hairline and an incredible figure. The way she surveyed the room, checking everything was okay, made me guess she was the boss.

When she glanced at me, I was struck at how beautiful her clear blue eyes were and wondered if she had contact lenses in. She seemed to think everything was okay because she soon dashed out of the room, leaving a waft of expensive perfume behind.

'That's Susan,' the receptionist Marie whispered. 'She owns the gaff. She used to work here but became the manager about ten years ago.'

'Oh, right,' I said. Clearly, she was doing very well out of it. She had such an air of confidence and looked so immaculately put together. I wondered what it must feel like to be a person like this.

I knew Lucy Palmers must have been making a killing. Punters paid £20 on the door and then more for services. It was £50 for full sex here and every girl had to give £10 per punter. If a punter didn't pay up, the debt was passed to the girl.

*

I never found out who Lucy Palmers was named after, but the sauna was a meat market. Once my shift started I encouraged my mind to drift, think of something nice and will the minutes away. To break up the day, I visited the staff room for a smoke every hour or so and got to know the receptionists. Marie worked on the day shifts and Beryl worked nights. Marie was a lovely, warm woman in her late 20s, who, for some reason, took me under her wing. In quiet hours she often offered to do my hair or makeup.

'I don't wear any,' I shrugged. She made a surprised face.

'But you're so pretty Jo. A bit of eyeliner, mascara and lip liner and wow. Here, let me help you.' We sat together, smoking and gossiping as she styled my hair.

'You'd look lovely with a bob,' she mused, cocking her head to the side. 'Treat yourself to a haircut soon. Promise me?'

I nodded, although I never had any money to even think about my hair or makeup. I rarely even bothered looking in the mirror. I hated myself and what I'd become so how could changing my looks make anything different?

Beryl, for reasons I didn't understand, took a deep dislike to me. She began making digs about my laziness. Sometimes

I wasn't busy because many of the punters were Asian and they didn't want to have sex with me. I noticed how Asian punters often picked busty girls with blonde hair.

Beryl began making snide comments about me being 'bone idle' and making digs in front of punters. The bullying got to the point even Marie stepped in. 'Jo is always helping tidy up, leave her be,' she said.

Another girl, Catriona, a busty blonde with a filthy laugh, often joined us for a smoke too. We'd sit and talk about our lives, fantasy versions of what we'd like them to be like.

'When I get a flat of my own,' I said, one night. 'I want to decorate it all myself.'

'Ooooh what colours?' Catriona asked.

'Muted, pastels and something classy. Maybe a plush carpet or wallpaper with a William Morris-style pattern.' Catriona did a double-take. 'How the hell do you know about William Morris Nicky?' she laughed. I shrugged.

'My mum,' I mumbled. 'I must have picked it up from her sometime after she got her degree.'

Her jaw hit the floor. 'Oh my God, your mum's *educated*?' She stared at me like I was an alien from outer space.

'Yes, she has a degree,' I whispered. 'And a master's.'

'Sounds like you're from a nice middle class family. So what are you doing here? Girls like you don't belong in this world. How did you end up here, Jo?'

She stared at me, with a mix of pity and incredulity. All of a sudden I felt extremely self-conscious. How *did* I end up here? Was I different to the other girls? I guessed I was. I didn't take drugs. I hated the sex work. I hadn't grown up in care. My mum lived in a lovely house and had been to university. But. But…she didn't care, did she?

Quickly, I wiped at a tear threatening to roll down my cheek. I didn't want anyone's pity. All I could hope was, one day soon, life would change. How, I had no idea.

This wasn't to happen any time soon. Whatever 'class' I was from, I still had Gerald to pay for.

*

By the time I got back to the refuge, I was always exhausted. But sleep and rest wasn't easy back in the dormitories. The chaos seemed to get worse each week. Girls would come back legless from drinking, others would smash the fire alarms so the fire brigade had to come out. They thought this was very funny. Another form of entertainment was to hang out of the windows shouting at passers-by or to run up and down the corridors in a game of 'chase' or have a water fight in the kitchen.

I could tell most of the girls were just letting off steam. I felt for them. They were determined to have some fun in what was basically a stressful and miserable life. Many of us were barely out of our teens and from what I'd heard most hadn't had much of a childhood, if any.

Amid all the chaos, thankfully, I had Rachel to help keep me sane.

Rachel was always a bit calmer, a bit more humorous than the other girls. I found her to be a rock of sanity in what was a rather insane world. Rachel was also into reggae music, just like Gerald liked; white label Jamaican imported stuff. This was the only music I knew about and for once I could briefly pretend to be an ordinary 18-year-old, sharing the love of tunes and gossiping.

During my low moments, when it seemed life became too hard, Rachel always made me a cup of tea or lent me a magazine she was reading. Julie also remained a close friend, perking me up after a bad night or making me a delicious dinner, even if she knew I'd struggle to eat it. In return for the girls' help, I always tried to elevate them when I could see their mood was slipping.

One night I woke to hear a sobbing sound. I looked up to find Rachel holding her fist in her hand.

'What's happened?' I asked, worried.

'I can't even do that right,' Rachel sobbed. 'I can't even kill myself.'

I jumped out of bed to put my arm around her. Julie managed to put her hand through the window in an attempt to slit her wrists a few weeks previously. She was a bigger girl than Rachel. Thankfully she quickly got patched up. This injury looked even more serious though.

I grabbed a towel to help stem the bleeding and another girl called an ambulance. The paramedics came to get Rachel and I promised to join her. With whatever cash I had in my pocket, I got a taxi and made it to the hospital a couple of hours later.

By then, Rachel was sitting up in bed with a middle-aged man and woman by her side. The man, who I guessed was her dad, was gazing at her with sympathy. And the woman, who I guessed was her mum, was holding her hand, desperate to stem the tide of tears coming from her daughter.

I paused in the corridor, watching the touching scene through a door window. Then I stopped myself from joining them because I imagined what her parents would think of me. The words of the judge echoed in my head.

A common prostitute.

I didn't want Rachel's parents to know she called the likes of me her friend. I hung back, checking Rachel was okay.

She looked relieved and wiped her eyes. Then suddenly she spotted me, said something to her parents and hopped off the bed. She came out to the corridor and threw her arms around my shoulders. We held each other tightly.

'You're my everything Joanne,' she murmured into my hair. She tugged at her finger and pulled off a ring with a precious stone. 'Mum and Dad are going to take me home. Hopefully things will be better than they've been in the past. Look, I want you to have this.' She pushed the ring onto my middle finger and kissed my cheek.

Neither of us could speak through our tears.

I thought of Rachel as one of my 'diamonds'. Just like Julie. These women helped keep me going. Their kindness and kinship gave me a reason to carry on. We had one final quick squeeze and she went back to her room. And I left. My heart was broken but also happy for her, even if I knew I would probably never see her again.

*

By the end of the summer, I had been in the refuge for several months and I continued to work at Lucy Palmers on and off. As long as I kept the money rolling in, Gerald didn't care where I worked. Then, in September 1992, he was released from prison. Leanne told me one day when I dropped the money off.

'He's been given his own flat,' Leanne said. 'The probation service has set him up with it.'

I was amazed. I was still waiting for a flat myself, and here was Gerald, who had been done for robbery, all sorted, probably furnishing it with the proceeds from the money I had to give him.

I wasn't wrong. When word came for me to go to his new place, I noticed how lovely it looked. He had a huge leather sofa and the place smelled of beeswax because he'd polished all the wood on a spiral staircase. Portraits of his family had also been carefully hung up on the wall. He had a giant TV and a sideboard for all his records. This flat looked like a man who had a well-paid job, not someone who had just got out of prison.

Gerald was eager to find out how work was going. I shrugged.

'You need to get more busy Jo,' he said. 'I've noticed how takings are going down.'

I looked down at my hands. Nothing I did was ever good enough.

'Listen, girl. I think you should watch the film Malcolm X,' he said. 'It will teach you about real injustices in life.' He pulled out a video and pointed at the sofa. 'I want you to keep watching it until it sinks in.' I didn't know what he meant but did as I was told.

*

I returned that day to the refuge feeling more desperate than ever. Rachel had gone and Julie was also moving out soon as well. I hoped it would be my turn soon. Thankfully I had a bit of good news myself a few weeks later. I had been found a flat on the outskirts of Telford and a volunteer from the refuge took me there to settle me in. They helped sort out the Giro I would need to pay for it and said they'd try and find some furniture too.

It was a small one-bedroomed place in a modern block. The refuge lady looked at me kindly when she showed me around the sparsely-furnished place.

'I have a bag of bedsheets for you,' she said, handing it to me. I nodded, grateful. It was simple but clean and on a reasonably nice estate.

'I hope you'll feel safe here,' she added. I swallowed. I had already clocked the big glass window by the front door. I knew if I didn't let Gerald in when he wanted, he'd easily kick that in. I'd never feel safe, not here, not anywhere. But I nodded and thanked her for the help.

Only a matter of hours later, Gerald was banging on my door. He walked inside like he owned the place.

'Nice gaff,' he grinned. 'Perfect actually.'

Then he told me his new plan. I was to bring the punters back to my new flat for sex. He would install a telephone so he could contact me more easily. 'That way you won't get arrested so much,' he winked.

After he left, I sank down onto the bare floor and sobbed. Whenever something good happened to me, somehow it reminded me there was no escape.

Over the next couple of weeks, I took punters back to mine. I tried to keep things discreet so the neighbours didn't notice but with only bedsheets for curtains it was tricky. When Gerald realised it took an extra hour to drive back and forth to mine, he banned me from doing it.

'It's wasting precious time,' he said. 'Your earnings will suffer. So you're to go back to the streets or the saunas.'

So I found myself back at Lucy Palmers again.

One morning, after a 12-hour shift in a sauna, to my horror, the coming and goings from my flat hadn't gone unnoticed. Walking home by a busy shopping centre, kids circled me in a menacing way on their bikes.

'*Hooker!*'

'*You whore!*'

'*Prossy!*' they jeered. Then one of them spat on me.

I walked faster, head bowed, but they sped up, trapping me in a circle. In the end I had to walk along the side of a wall to break free. Once safely back inside my flat, I cried myself to sleep.

*

Gerald insisted things continued as normal. He dropped me off at my corner, then picked me up at the end of the night. On the first couple of nights I carried on but then police kept picking me up again. However, instead of avoiding them, I let myself be arrested because I had twigged the enormous benefits. The courts finished their sessions around 2.30pm to 3pm. If I intentionally got a warrant for arrest and was taken in, it would be to a warm cell overnight. So I began to work out the shift patterns of certain officers, the ones who I liked, the ones who smoked and would offer me a sneaky fag.

I also worked out if I got arrested by late afternoon, the canteen was still open and I'd be offered leftovers. I had no money for food, Gerald took everything and he only fed me when he chose to or was in a good mood. Often, I had only one packet of biscuits to live off in a week and my weight plummeted to around five stone.

So, in the police station, not only would I get to sit down and relax, I'd get a decent meal of beans on toast or a fry-up. Something hot and tasty. The idea some nights made my mouth water, so I started to actively go looking for the vice cars, then bang on the window and tell them I was soliciting.

'Please arrest me,' I'd beg, eager for a sit down and the warmth of the station.

I began organising my work days around all these factors so instead of being made to have sex with horrible men, I'd find myself sitting in a heated prison cell with a bed, and then a lovely hot meal and a cup of coffee. To me, this was bliss. But to Gerald it was a disaster because my takings took a nosedive. He grew increasingly frustrated about the number of arrests until one day he made an announcement.

'There is only one thing for it,' he said. 'I have to get you working in London. You can go to the saunas there.' He told me he was working on another plan to make this happen.

21

By the end of 1992, Sam got in touch to say she wanted to come and visit me again. I'd had so much fun on her last visit but that was mainly because Darryl allowed it. Now I was back at work, I wouldn't have much time to spend with her. Also, I feared if she found out what I did for a living she wouldn't want to be friends with me any more. After all, who wants to hang out with a whore? But to my amazement Gerald said yes when I quietly asked if she could visit for a few days.

'I'll pick her up from the port,' he said enthusiastically. I smiled gratefully, relieved I'd asked on a day he was in a good mood.

The day Sam came over, I was scheduled for a day shift at Lucy Palmers and my original fears returned. All day I felt physically sick, worse than usual, because I knew my dirty secret would be out. I clung onto the hope Gerald would take Sam straight to my flat and I could pretend I had a different job when I got home.

But on my break, one of the girls told me there was someone in reception for me. I walked in to find Sam waiting. 'Gerald said I should pick up the key for the flat from here,' she smiled.

She glanced around the pink-walled reception, eyeing the pretty girls coming and going. She didn't look fazed at all so I breathed a sigh of relief. Maybe I could pretend I really worked as a masseuse.

As we chatted, a manager stopped by.

'Hey, who's your friend?' the manager smiled warmly.

Reluctantly, I introduced them. Sam smiled, showing the braces on her teeth. I could see the manager assessing her quietly. Sam was petite like me, with straight neat blonde hair. She was pretty. And in this manager's eyes, every woman had their own price.

'Ooh, you looking for work?' asked the manager, casually. My eyes widened. I tried to catch Sam's eye and gently shake my head but her face had already lit up.

'I am always skint if that's what you mean,' Sam grinned. 'I have been working in admin over in Northern Ireland, but could do with extra cash, yeah.'

'I see,' said the manager, her smile fixed to her face. 'Well, we have shifts for lovely girls like you. The work we do involves massages and extras, meeting the clients' needs. Do you understand?'

Sam nodded eagerly. I held back the need to scream. This was the last thing I wanted for my friend, but I didn't want to upset the manager either. Gerald would kill me if I lost this job.

'Fantastic,' said the manager, clapping her hand, like she had done the deal. 'How about starting straight away? C'mon, I'll introduce you.' Sam looked at me in excitement as she got whisked around the joint. Afterwards, she sat with me and Catriona in the staff room.

'This place gets busy doesn't it,' Sam said. She looked relaxed and I didn't know what to say. Was she really up for having sex with strange men?

'Just be super careful,' I warned her. 'This place might not be all it seems. You don't have to do this Sam.'

But she wouldn't listen and I had to get back to work. I told her if she needed me, just to let me know. An hour later, I was due a break so went into the staff area for a smoke. We had intercoms in all of the rooms connected to the staff room and I imagined Sam might be shocked at what she was expected to do and hit the buzzer. I was ready to comfort her and give her my flat keys so she could leave.

About half an hour later, the intercom buzzed so I snatched it up, worried it could be Sam and it was. Her voice sounded hoarse and panicked.

'Can you send up Catriona quick,' she breathed.

'What? Why?' I was confused. Catriona, who was also on her break, shrugged. I was Sam's best mate so why was she asking to see another girl she'd only just met?

'Just ask her!' she cried.

Sam sounded like she was crying, so I told Catriona to go quickly and see what was wrong. Fifteen minutes later, Sam came down, walking like she was in pain.

'Oh my God,' I cried. Sam disappeared to the loo and Catriona told me what happened.

'One of our banned dodgy punters must have sneaked past reception,' she whispered. 'He's the one who always goes for young small blondes and he's anally raped girls in the past. It was a right mess upstairs but poor thing was too embarrassed for you to see it.'

Tears smarted in my eyes and I gulped them down. How could this happen to my friend? I felt so guilty for bringing her into this nightmare world. When Sam returned, I threw my arms around her. She was quivering with shock still, but kept saying she'd be okay.

Not knowing what to do, I went back to the reception to use the phone.

'Gerald, you have to come and get Sam. She's been attacked,' I said.

Gerald sounded genuinely concerned. Within minutes he was outside in his car. I only hoped he would look after her. I had to finish my shift, my thoughts racing with worry. How could I have done this? I should have never invited my friend over. The guilt burnt hot and heavy on my mind.

I couldn't wait to get back to Gerald's that night. I crossed the threshold of his flat, expecting to find Sam crying or worse, but instead peals of laughter rung out from the kitchen. Gerald was frying salt fish while Sam was laughing at something he said. I couldn't believe how relaxed and happy she looked. Gerald left the room briefly to take a call, so I asked Sam how she was doing.

'Gerald took me out for lunch,' she beamed. 'We had a good chat. He made me feel good about myself again. He's so nice, Jo. You're so lucky to be with him.'

I stared at her in disbelief, then quickly smiled when Gerald came back in the room. He could always sense when people were talking about him. I was glad Sam was okay but amazed how fast she'd recovered from something so awful.

I was even more surprised when the next morning she got up early and started putting makeup on.

'Where are you going?' I asked her.

'With you. To work,' she said. She turned her back while she slipped into the white nurse's style mini-dress, the uniform of the sauna, in a way that told me the conversation was closed. Gerald popped his head around the door.

'Ready?' he asked, jangling his car keys.

*

I had no idea what Gerald had said to Sam but knew he could switch on the charm. So much so that Sam said she wanted to stay and work at Lucy Palmers over the next few months. I was horrified, but she wouldn't hear of going back to Northern Ireland. She said her work there was boring and it was more fun here. She'd also fallen out with her mum, whom she'd had a strained relationship with.

'You can't make me go back Jo,' she reasoned.

After that first night, I realised Gerald was also letting her keep half of her money too. To her, the sauna was a way to make a quick buck. He said we could both stay at my flat but he would keep an eye on us.

As sad as I was for drawing Sam into this, I liked having her live with me. Bright and bubbly, she was like a breath of fresh air. Gerald was more upbeat around her and even Darryl seemed to lighten up when he came over.

But when the weeks flew by I noticed she'd begun to change. She started to get more and more giggly, often disappearing with some of the girls outside for a smoke but staying longer than usual. I began to suspect she was taking drugs. But when I asked her, she shrugged. To her, it all seemed like a big game.

Unable to stop her from working, I tried to focus on appreciating the female company again. Like with Tonia, I had a bath with Sam after work and we slept together in the same bed, like sisters.

When she arrived she told me about a strange skin rash she couldn't get rid of.

'It's so itchy Jo,' she complained at night.

I suggested she went to see a GP, which she did and he gave her cream. But nothing seemed to work. The rash kept coming back again. In the end Sam gave up and said it was just eczema. She covered it up with clothes or makeup whenever she could and said she hoped it didn't put off punters. As much as I loved Sam, she wouldn't listen to anyone and soon it didn't go unnoticed. Gerald began to say she was a liability.

'She's going to cause us problems,' he said in bed with me one morning. 'She's not like you Jo. You're completely loyal and keep your mouth shut. And you don't do drugs.'

I nodded compliantly. I couldn't stop wanting to please him, even if he was describing me like I was a pet. He was right, I had no friends, no life, nothing. I might as well have been kept in a cupboard.

*

That Christmas in 1992, I stayed in the West Midlands. Even considering going across to Northern Ireland to spend time with my family wasn't an option. But Sam wanted to go back, so Gerald insisted on us driving her all the way to get the ferry back home. On Christmas Day, when we got home, he then disappeared to spend it with his extended family, leaving me alone.

A few days after Christmas, Sam returned and Gerald presented us with two presents. I was touched to see he had got me a pair of earrings. He'd never got me anything before.

Sam giggled with delight when Gerald handed her a present. She quickly unwrapped the small gift to reveal a box with a silver ring.

'It's from me,' grinned Gerald. I did a double take. Why had he given her that? What was he playing at? I felt myself grow hot with anger.

'Why are you doing this?' I cried to Gerald. I was so hurt, especially as he never bought me a ring. The one he had asked me to look after in prison, he'd taken back. He smirked at me. I could see he was enjoying how riled I had become, while Sam, who seemed oblivious, admired her finger. Within a few days, Gerald took my earrings to a pawn shop, saying he needed the cash because I wasn't earning enough.

The New Year of 1993 continued like the past two years. My days were a blur of men, sex, and handing rolls of cash to Gerald. I certainly didn't make any new year resolutions, except surviving the long evenings and nights and trying to keep Gerald happy. But a few weeks later, he was anything but happy and this time it was because of Sam. She had gone out one night to a gambling house. These were dens full of gang members, often where drug taking took place and similar but not the same as a modern day trap house. It was a dangerous place for a single girl to go. Gerald found her there and brought her home, laughing her head off and high as a kite.

'Your boyfriend slapped me around the face,' she giggled, showing me her reddened cheek. 'But I did deserve it because I told Gerald to fuck off in front of everyone and stuck my fingers up at him.' She laughed hysterically and looked proud of herself. I felt sick. What had become of my friend?

I was at a loss about what to do. Worse still, I'd noticed Darryl had begun flirting with Sam when he came over. Then I found them kissing in the living room. The idea of my friend with a rapist made my blood run cold. But once again, I was powerless to stop anything.

*

A few weeks later, Gerald gave me a copy of What's On

magazine. 'Look at the back for the saunas and massage parlours listed and ring them all. You need to find work down in London,' he said. 'I don't want you getting arrested anymore.'

My heart sank. I tried a few until one agreed to see me. It was called Omega, a sauna in Camden, London. Gerald grinned when I told him. 'Right, let's get in the car,' he said. For the time being, Sam was to stay in the Midlands. I was gutted. This meant no more arrests and peaceful nights in a cell after a hot dinner or hanging out with my friend.

Gerald drove us to another cousin's house in London, with his music blaring from the speakers. I didn't speak to him, already fearing what would happen when we arrived. On arrival, he introduced me to his cousin Leeroy then ordered a Chinese takeaway and to my surprise, I was allowed a big portion. For the first time in ages, I felt like Gerald loved me again and we fell asleep in front of the telly. But in the morning I got woken up by Gerald in a bad mood.

'What the fuck are you sleeping in for?' he snapped. 'Get yourself up and out and fuck off out to work. That's why we're here!' I scrambled up from the floor where I'd been sleeping in a panic.

'Okay, yes, I will,' I said, my eyes filling up. 'But where do I go? I don't have a map. I don't know London at all.'

'Fucking get out the door. Ask someone in the street where the tube is. Stupid bitch,' he barked.

Leeroy appeared in the doorway.

'Why you be so hard on your girl?' he asked in Patois.

Gerald sucked his teeth. ''Cos she knows what she's supposed to be doing,' he snapped. 'And I want you back on the 10pm train to Dudley too.'

Taking pity on me, Leeroy gave me a fiver and vague directions to the tube.

In a panic, I left the house and asked passers-by where the tube was. After an hour or so, I arrived in Camden and eventually found the entrance to the sauna.

Walking inside, I knew straight away this was, thankfully, a very different set-up to most saunas. The place was very clean, smelt fresh and the women were in their 20s and 30s. Many of them were very well dressed. While I waited to be shown around, one girl turned up in a soft-topped sports car parked outside. She came in, smelling of a lovely perfume.

'Sorry I am a bit late. My nanny was late today. Never mind. Kids love her so what can I do?' she said. The receptionist ushered her in. 'No problem. Just come in and get settled.'

I was staggered. How could they afford to live like this? Did the sauna pay this well? Who were their men? These ladies were in a completely different league to the other girls I'd been working alongside. Feeling self-conscious, I ran fingers through my hair, wishing I could afford a bob like Marie had suggested. But I didn't have long to worry, streams of men began coming in and out. That day alone I saw around five punters. All day long, the name of the same madam cropped up from the girls. *Josie Daly*. Apparently Daly ran the most successful of the massage parlours in London. Many girls had worked for her or wished to. I was intrigued. I was under constant pressure from Gerald to earn more money. The look on his face when it wasn't enough always made me wince. I never knew if he was going to lash out, shout in my face or give me the silent treatment.

Towards the end of the day, I was clock watching. I knew I had to be on that train to Dudley by 10pm or else. But the sauna was busy and I daren't ask to leave early. I didn't even know where the mainline station to Dudley was either, but knew Gerald wouldn't see that as a valid excuse. One very attractive girl called Tiffany, who I'd got chatting to, was sympathetic when I told her I had to get the last train back.

'I'll look up the times for you,' she said. 'Your shift finishes at 2am.' I swallowed. I didn't want to walk out early but equally didn't want to miss the train. Tiffany made a few calls and then shook her head. 'Yes, sorry, you'll miss the last train.'

'Oh God,' I cried. 'I'll have to sleep here for the night or something.'

This was common at the Birmingham sauna, with girls nodding off between jobs or curling up on the sofa. Tiffany looked troubled about this idea.

'Oh, well we don't do that here,' she said, concerned.

'I could sleep in a massage room,' I suggested.

She frowned. Her plucked eyebrows were very neat, like a doll's and her glossy mane fell around her shoulders.

'Oh, Honey, I can't let you do that. You'd have to use a massage table as a bed and a towel as a sheet. No, come and sleep at my place instead, eh?'

I was taken aback. This was a complete no-no where I was from. If I returned to her house I might bump into her man who could beat me up or force me to work with him. But then again, from her concerned look, I could tell this offer was made with kindness. She cared enough to make sure I was safe for the night, something nobody had ever done. Tears of gratitude welled up in my eyes.

'Okay if that's alright I will,' I said.

A few hours later, Tiffany walked me to a car park where she pulled out keys to unlock a convertible sports car. My mouth fell open with amazement. Who had bought her this?

She chatted amiably about her son and him being at his dad's tonight so I could sleep in his room. Then she asked about what Birmingham was like. I told her the bare minimum details, not wanting to reveal too much.

We pulled up outside a huge Victorian house with bay windows. Tiffany opened my car door and I followed her into an immaculately furnished hallway and living room. A huge circular fish tank filled with tropical fish loomed from the floor to ceiling. The sofa was plush velvet with plumped-up cushions. Smiling photos of her and her son beamed down from painted walls. I was gobsmacked.

There was no man here. Tiffany looked happy and relaxed, going to her big fridge to get a soft drink. She offered me a cold mineral water and I accepted, my mind reeling.

She is coming and going as she pleases.

There is no man telling her what to do.

She doesn't have to hand her money over to anyone.

Tiffany chatted away about her plans for the weekend. She was going out for a meal, and cinema afterwards. What was I doing, she asked? I stumbled over words, trying to form sentences because inside the realisation had hit home. I was trapped by Gerald and his cousins. I wasn't allowed any money. Or to spend the money on myself. I had a flat with bedsheets for curtains and every single day lived in fear.

'I am not sure what I'm doing,' I babbled.

'It's my boyfriend's birthday on Monday,' she continued. 'I've bought him a food processor.' I stared in amazement.

'You buy each other *presents?*' I began.

She laughed like I was making a joke. 'Yeah, he loves cooking,' she smiled as I stared at her.

The only present I'd ever seen a girl buy her man was a big gold chain like lots of the pimps wore as a status symbol. Tiffany showed me to her son's room, apologising for how small the car-shaped bed was. Like all the other rooms in the house, it was well decorated and cosy. I wished I could have stayed for a week. I thanked her again, before turning the light out while my mind continued racing. This was the first window into how seriously wrong my life was.

I worked in the same 'industry' as this woman, but had nothing to my name and no freedom.

22

The next morning, I woke up to find Tiffany downstairs already immaculately dressed, busy in the kitchen. She had made me a bowl of porridge. I was choked at the thoughtfulness again. I did love porridge although she'd put nutmeg and cinnamon on it, which I didn't like, so I couldn't eat it. She looked a bit hurt and I said sorry profusely because I wanted her to know how much I appreciated her kindness anyway. Before we left, I used her bathroom, an immaculate place with shiny tiles and a big mirror which I avoided looking into as I washed my hands with musky-scented soap.

As I dried my hands on Tiffany's fluffy hand towel, I knew deep down I was to blame for all my failures. I felt like a bad egg who wasn't capable of fitting into normal society. Tiffany dropped me in her car by the nearest tube. All the way, she chatted amiably. I could only stare at her in awe. She was so cool, confident and pretty. Like nobody I had met who worked like me.

'You take care of yourself Honey,' she said with concern. I looked into her lovely brown eyes and thanked her. She had no idea what she'd done for me. In my mind she was another diamond, someone who decided to be kind to me for no reason, except they cared. Little crumbs of kindness like this kept me going.

I managed to find my way to the station and jumped on the first train to Dudley. All the way I held the palm of my hands to my nose to breathe in the musky scent of Tiffany's bathroom soap. A reminder of her kindness and a seemingly happy life. By the time I'd reached the train station where Gerald was picking me up, the scent completely disappeared.

*

I only just got back when Gerald told me of his next plan. His mate had been deported back to Jamaica and the council didn't know, so we were going to squat in the empty flat down in London. And he had regular work lined up in another sauna in Stratford.

'You're coming with Star,' he told me. I had met Star briefly a couple of times, back when Tonia was around. She was a painfully skinny girl, with a gold tooth and a crack cocaine habit. At first I didn't know why she was giggly one minute then depressed looking the next and smelled strongly of smoke. It was Gerald who explained she was a crack addict. I liked Star. She always made an effort to chat to me, and was friendly, unlike so many others in this circle.

'I want to get Star off drugs,' Gerald continued. He didn't need to elaborate. I knew he liked girls to be clean, because it meant more money for him and he could trust them.

I didn't ask anything. What was there to say? I knew I had no choice. Sam, meanwhile, was happily working at Lucy Palmers and when I saw her, told me she'd catch up later.

Days later, we arrived at the council flat in Leytonstone. It was in a run-down council estate and was in a terrible mess. Gerald began cleaning and bleaching everything straight away. I tried to help but he shooed me away like a cat.

'What are you still here for?' he barked. 'Fuck off out to work bitch.' He threw an address on a slip of paper for my next work venue, another high street sauna.

*

The sauna in Stratford was run by three brothers of German descent. Tim, an obese chain-smoking man who reminded me of Jabba the Hutt, his younger brother Jonny, who loved playing cards for bets with the girls and Marc, a property owner who ran the business in his name. This place was nowhere near as nice as the other one, but was busier, which was why Gerald was happy for me to work there. It meant I'd make money for him faster. The set-up in the sauna included a flat where girls could stay at night if they needed to. On breaks, I got to know many of the girls. Listening to their stories, I realised how many walks of life women came from.

There was a loud Greek lady called Soraya, who was in her 40s, and was determined to provide a better childhood for her kids. She worked in the sauna to pay for a private education for them. Every day she could be heard yelling down the phone at her latest nanny who couldn't speak English.

Robyn was a girl from New Zealand. She was travelling around the world, and planned to go to Harlem in America after Stratford. She was here to make extra cash. I didn't ask how she'd fallen into this business but clearly it must have been hard times. I also met two girls who had a flat-share nearby. Paula and Sandra were a giggly pair of twenty-somethings. They invited me over to theirs for the night once and Gerald happened to be away, so I said yes. Their place was a big studio flat, upstairs in a small terrace, nicely decorated with pictures on the walls and throws on the sofa. They were both relaxed and made me feel welcome, but I didn't know where to put myself. I felt nervous and shy, like I had been at Tiffany's.

'Are you hungry?' asked Paula. 'Go and help yourself to whatever you want in the fridge. Make yourself at home.'

I opened the fridge. There was so much food; fresh salads, yogurts, cheese, bacon, eggs, milk, ready meals, I couldn't believe it. In all the flats I stayed, the fridges were always empty. A yogurt fell onto the floor at my feet. Shaking, I picked it up. I didn't want to seem greedy, I didn't know what to do or what to choose to eat.

'What's wrong?' asked Sandra. 'Don't stress out. Have what you like. Shall I make an omelette or something?'

I hated being so shy, but by now it didn't take much for my nerves to show. Sandra took eggs from me and whipped up a meal. While we ate she spoke about their plans.

'We want to join a strip club,' she said proudly. 'Get out of this sauna game.'

'Yeah,' Paula chimed. 'High-class escorting and stripping is where the money is.'

They grinned at each other. I couldn't understand why stripping was viewed as a nicer job, the idea made me shudder.

'Have you worked for Josie Daly?' I asked.

They exchanged glances. Then Sandra smiled. 'Not me, but I know plenty who have done. She pretty much runs London's massage parlours. A legend on the scene. I am sure I can get a number if you want.'

I thanked them. Maybe if I found even more work Gerald would get off my back a bit more. That night I watched a film with the girls. They laughed and joked, teasing each other playfully like they didn't have a care in the world sitting on their comfy sofa. Once again, I couldn't believe how different their lives were to mine.

*

A few days later, I arrived back at the flat in Leytonstone to find Gerald in a bad mood. I had no idea what had happened and he wasn't going to tell me. But he was going to take it out on me. He slapped me across the face a few times, before raining blows all over my body. I curled into a ball, begging him to stop.

'What have I done?' I begged him. But he didn't even answer. It appeared he just needed someone to vent out his anger on to. Then he ordered me to strip naked. I looked at him in horror. I'd already brought back a few hundred quid. Why was he punishing me? The look on his face told me not to argue, so I did as I was told and slowly undressed. Shivering, he told me to lay on the front doormat.

'What?' I cried. 'Why? What's going on?'

'Just do it,' he spat through clenched teeth.

Humiliated and sobbing, I sat on the doormat, trying to cover my modesty. It was made from coir and felt rough and uncomfortable. I daren't move until he told me I could. It was already late, around midnight. Then he told me he was going to bed and I was to sleep on the doormat.

'Why?' I cried. 'Why are you treating me like this? I am doing the best for you. I made all that money for you haven't I?'

Crying, I curled into a ball and sobbed. Unable to sleep, but shift uncomfortably all night, I finally got up at 6am when Gerald said I was allowed to. He never explained why he had treated me this way or even acknowledged what he'd done.

The next day, a kind Indian neighbour in the flat above ours approached me as I left the flat. 'If you ever need a chat or anything please knock on my door,' she said, looking worried. I thanked her but never did because I knew there was nothing she could do.

*

One piece of autonomy I was granted was the right to look for more work. So when one of the girls passed on a phone number for Josie Daley's 'people', I decided to ring it. Immediately they offered me an interview at her Roman Road sauna in central London. When I told Gerald I was going, he looked at me with something like pride.

'Oooh, I like to see you making an effort,' he smirked. 'Do not be slothful in zeal, be fervent in spirit, serve the Lord,' he quoted from The Bible. I didn't know what he meant or how to reply to that.

When I rang Josie's 'people', I was told to turn up with my birth certificate. Luckily, through all the ups and downs of the last couple of years, it was the only piece of identification I'd kept safe.

On the day, I wore my usual mini-skirt and cardigan. I even combed my hair and borrowed some of Star's mascara. Everyone always told me how young I looked and this was my attempt to look older. I pushed away the conversations I'd recently had with the other girls about Josie from my mind. When I mentioned I had an interview, Soraya, the Greek girl, told me Josie was a monster. 'The girls have to work 24 hours a day, sleep on the floor and are not even allowed a shower,' she'd warned me.

Josie's sauna was in a discreet, old converted building. I was ushered inside by what looked like a bodyguard down a corridor and into a windowless side room. It was almost completely dark inside, except for one spotlight on a desk. Behind the desk sat an older woman with unruly frizzy red hair shooting out in all directions. She had a slightly humped back and a huge, hooked nose and reminded me of an elderly Bette Midler, like the witch she played in Hocus Pocus. I was shocked at how frail Josie looked. How could this eccentric old woman have such a formidable reputation? Although, from her clothing and jewellery, I could tell she had lots of money.

Next to her was a bench with a few girls, who all looked very young, sitting neatly with their hands folded on their laps. They were all very well groomed, dressed in nurse outfits which looked like lab coats and had strange blank looks on their faces. One was clasping her hands so tightly her knuckles were white. All of them looked like they were on display and sat to attention. I could see none of them looked comfortable or happy. I wondered what were they waiting for? Then, from the shadows stepped out a man, a huge, tall, intimidating black man who stared straight ahead, like a soldier on sentry duty or a copper.

I breathed through my mouth trying to stop the rising tension building inside of me.

'I'm Josie,' said Josie, in a gravelly voice. 'And you are?'

I told her my real name.

'Right. Where's your birth certificate?'

I pushed the piece of paper across her desk. She stared through me, before picking it up. Squinting, she glanced at it.

'And this is your birth certificate?' she said, squinting at me.

I knew what was coming. I was 19 now but still looked at least five years younger. I sat up straight.

'Yes,' I said, in what I hoped was a confident voice.

'Where were you born?' she asked.

'Belfast,' I replied.

She pushed the paper back and shook her head. 'Come back when you're older,' she said. Then she turned her head slightly to indicate the interview was over. I held the birth certificate to my chest and thanked her before turning to the door.

Later, I told Soraya in the sauna what had happened. I couldn't stop thinking about what I had seen. Clearly Josie was a very wealthy woman. Everyone knew who she was and what she was doing, but nobody was stopping her. It played on my mind.

'I don't get how someone as old and frail as that can work in this industry for so long. She must make so much money from all these girls, who all have pimps and it's all going on under the noses of coppers,' I said.

Soraya shrugged. 'I've heard her minders are even ex-policemen. They must be all in it together.' I thought of her bodyguard. He had the air of a former policeman. Maybe she was right.

*

For the next couple of months, I worked mainly in London, but regularly came back to the Midlands, often working at Lucy Palmers and occasionally back on the streets too. One punter from the streets was a regular with many of the girls. He was a softly-spoken chap called Sean and when he picked me up, he chatted proudly about working as a councillor on the Parish Council. Like many of the punters, he was middle-aged and married.

'If there is anything you ever need council-related,' he winked, as he pulled up his trousers. 'Just ask.' I openly laughed. The idea of me needing an insider at the council was ridiculous.

Sean became one of my regulars too. He was always in the area because his wife worked near the red light district. He dropped her off first before coming to pick one of us up. One night he asked me if he could take me back to his house. I agreed. It made a change from the usual set-up – inside a car on a piece of wasteland.

He drove me to a detached house. When he opened the door, he led me into the living room with leather sofas.

I looked around the room, marvelling at how plush and clean it all was. It had been a long time since I'd set foot in a room like this.

I perched on the edge of the sofa, politely waiting for what he wanted. He got a drink from the kitchen before deciding he wanted to have sex in his marital bed. This became part of his routine once a week. I was always struck by Sean's confidence. He never seemed to fear being caught at home by his wife.

One time, while I sat waiting on a stool next to his kitchen island for him to decide when we were going upstairs, Sean's answerphone clicked on.

'Hello Councillor,' the voice began. 'I need to ask you a question…' It was a complaint from a member of the public about an issue with local traffic. Sean rolled his eyes at the answerphone.

'I've already told them,' he sighed. 'That area is not in my constituency.'

Once again it occurred to me how I lived on the fringes of ordinary life. The person calling the local councillor would never have guessed in a million years their moan about traffic would be listened into by a young prostitute. Sean was never jumpy like other punters when he picked me up either. He never put his foot down in case his number plate was spotted or sped up away from the kerb. He always drove off calmly, like he was a father picking up his daughter from the cinema for a ride home. He was so confident, I even wondered if he knew the police and they turned a blind eye for him.

Before and after the sex, we often chatted about our lives. I told him about moving over from Northern Ireland and not fitting in at school. I told him everything, except the parts about Gerald. Often he listened impatiently before switching the conversation back to himself. He loved talking about his importance on the council, even insisting I went away with his up-to-date business card.

One day, when Sean invited me into his house, I found a couple waiting in the living room. The woman was aged around 50 and wore a denim mini-skirt. Her legs were covered in varicose veins and her large glasses reminded me of Deirdre Barlow, the Coronation Street character. She sat in a wing-backed armchair while a man in his 40s stood behind her. Sean looked pleased with himself when he introduced me.

'Meet Nicky,' he said. 'I thought I'd introduce her.'

The woman's eyes flicked up and down my body behind her owl glasses, while the man, who I guessed was her husband, gave a small smile.

A feeling of nausea crept over me. I wasn't up for a four-some. I didn't care how much they paid me, the thought of it made my skin crawl more than usual. Sean kept talking.

'Now, when can we arrange an overnighter?' Sean asked.

I gave a watery smile. I didn't know what to say.

That night, Gerald quizzed me on who I had been with. I'd not earned as much as usual, so eager to please him, I mentioned Sean's overnight request. A smile spread over Gerald's face.

'If he wants you overnight, tell him it's a grand,' he said.

This was a bit of a jump from the usual £30 and I doubted Sean could stretch to that. The following week Sean picked me up like always and I named my price for my participation in the foursome. He shook his head. Instead he went for a hand job, said cheerio and I never saw him again.

*

By now, my relationship with Mum had reached a new low, but I continued very occasionally dropping in on her. I knew she worried about me, even if she was always inexplicably angry with me. One afternoon, she invited me in, and blurted out her latest news.

'I have three things to tell you Jo,' she said. 'Number one, I am getting married. Number two, I am pregnant and number three, the dog has died.'

She spoke in such a terse, matter-of-fact way, I wasn't sure how to respond. I was really sad to hear about Buster. Although I never saw much of him these days, I'd loved that dog and knew Anthony was very fond of him.

'Congratulations,' I said to Mum. She gave a small, quick smile and changed the subject.

'What I am most upset about Joanne is how Anthony was left with Buster at the vet's. Quite frankly, I am disgusted with you for not being there for him. Did you know he had to make a decision to put down the dog himself?'

I didn't even know Buster had been ill or died until this very moment. How could she hold me responsible for what happened at the vet's too? I opened my mouth to respond but didn't bother arguing. Mum would always find a way to blame me for everything.

Mum got married a few months later in the spring of 1993, in a low key ceremony at a register office. None of the family came. I was invited to the after-party with Anthony held at William's large house.

He owned a huge country pile in Wem and they'd put up a marquee in the grounds. It was so fancy it took my breath away, but I hung back from the crowds, nursing a Cola all night. I didn't want anyone to ask any questions about my life.

From afar, I watched Mum look radiantly happy, pregnant, with her successful new husband on her arm, living in their fancy house and felt like I had no place in this. And neither, it turned out, did Anthony. Mum had left him to live alone in the Victorian house in Dudley. She told everyone it was so he could finish his exams but I felt sorry for my poor brother. When I tried to talk about it he shrugged the conversation away.

*

Back in London, Gerald took me over to Brixton to visit Nicola, the girl whose flat we briefly stayed in. Star was very good friends with her and came with us. Nicola's place was absolutely disgusting. The carpets and walls were filthy, the kitchen looked as if it hadn't been touched in years. The smell was horrendous.

To my shock, Star pulled out a pipe and began preparing drugs.

'It's crack,' Gerald whispered. It was as if he wanted me to see this. Nicola joined in and they sat together on a grimy sofa, puffing away, giggling. I didn't know where to look.

I lit a cig myself. I had started smoking when I was 18 and although I rarely had any money, I often managed to cadge a cig off the other girls. I mouthed to Gerald, asking him where an ashtray was. He rolled his eyes and smirked. 'Just use the floor,' he whispered. 'They're crackheads. They don't care.'

It was true the carpet was covered in cig burns and dirt but it still didn't feel right to disrespect someone's home like this. I looked at Gerald, slightly panicked. Star and Nicola were high and clearly couldn't have cared less and neither did he. But something inside of me still did. I waited until the pile of ash on my cig end was so long it fell off anyway. Then I quickly rubbed it with my foot and hoped nobody would notice.

Weeks after arriving in London, I felt under more pressure than ever. Star earned a lot more money for Gerald than I did. I began to realise he hadn't brought her down here to get her off drugs, it was because she had the gift of the gab, flaunted herself around punters and picked up loads of work. Gerald began comparing me to her.

'You should be more like Star,' he shouted. 'She puts it out there. She gets the money in. I like her. She's *worth* something.'

I began crying. I was shy and unforthcoming. I never offered myself. I only went with punters when they picked me. I couldn't bring myself to behave in any other way. But at the same time, Gerald made me feel even worse about myself.

23

By spring 1993, I was shuttled between London and the Midlands by Gerald virtually every week. Sam was still very much part of our household when I returned home, I still appreciated her being there. She broke up the monotony of the long days and nights and on our rare nights off, was always up for a laugh. She'd had a fling with Darryl but then he ditched her and started sleeping with Ginny, the prostitute who had sustained terrible injuries. I could only hope for her sake he'd never attack her too. Tiger had disappeared, since Tonia had gone, but he was the only one who had a 'regular' family and indeed even a job, I had heard. The gang life had been his double life, much like Neil who always seemed to maintain an air of respectability by claiming to be a family man too.

One night, the streets of Dudley had been unusually quiet and we hadn't made any money. This was never good news to return with but once we got into the car, I sensed things were about to get a whole lot worse.

Gerald was driving. Darryl was in the passenger seat but I could tell by the way Gerald shifted in his seat and gazed from the window something was up. Darryl was also quiet in a menacing way I had come to recognise. Sam hadn't witnessed their terrible tempers as much. Gerald only ever beat me up when nobody was around and I had become used to hiding my injuries. So she was oblivious to the thick atmosphere in the car.

'Boy, it was a quiet night tonight,' she giggled. 'Can't wait to warm up though. Need a bath I do. What's for dinner?'

'Have you got any money?' Darryl asked curtly.

'Nah, sorry,' said Sam

Gerald turned to me. 'Did you make anything Jo?' he asked in an unusually gentle voice. I shook my head apologetically.

'Okay, okay,' he said kindly before turning back in silence.

I hardly dared breathe with the anticipation of what would happen next. Sam, still none the wiser, continued chatting normally. Then Gerald revved the engine and took off at some lights, making us slide on the seats. Sam gave me a funny look, finally twigging something was up.

Gerald turned off the main road, down a deserted lane and then again onto a dirt track. There was no street lighting here. Nobody was around.

'Stop,' ordered Darryl.

Gerald turned the engine off with what I sensed was a reluctant air. My guts lurched. Darryl, despite his bulk, twisted his torso to face Sam over the seat. In a slow, menacing tone, he spoke.

'So that itchy skin rash you got Sam,' he said very slowly. 'Turns out it's not eczema…' He paused, allowing the words to sink in. Instantly Sam's grin vanished, she shrank back, closer to me.

'It's ringworm,' he spat.

Darryl leaned further over the seat, his sour breath hot in our faces.

'And my girlfriend Ginny now has ringworm,' he said, narrowing his eyes. 'And my woman has ringworm. And even my kids have ringworm…'

Whack!

The first fist flew into Sam's face so fast she had no time to react. Her head flew backwards, hitting the head rest. Instinctively I tried the door but it was locked. In panic Sam tried to move closer to me, but she couldn't escape as Darryl's fists flew into all areas of her body. Her stomach, her sides, her head, her neck, her legs.

Bam, bam, bam.

She clutched her head, shrieking. Blood blossomed across her face and hands. I looked desperately at Gerald. He winced but he told me with his eyes not to intervene.

Say a word and Darryl will lose it even more.

Darryl pushed his bulk between the seats to gain more access to Sam, punching and hitting in between shouts.

'You're a dirty little slag,' he screamed.

The sounds of his big knuckles pummelling her head made me want to vomit. Tears streamed down my face while I covered my ears. Listening to my poor friend being hurt like this was unbearable. I would have preferred to take the beating myself.

Darryl took hold of the back of Sam's hair and whacked her face hard onto the middle of the gearbox. More blood bloomed from her nose and mouth.

'What are you?' he snarled like a dog. 'A dirty little slag. Say it! *'I am a dirty little slag.'* Through a broken nose, Sam repeated his words. He made her repeat them many times.

'*I am a dirty little slag,*' she mumbled, spitting blood. '*I am a dirty little slag.*'

By now I was beside myself. Helplessly watching my best friend beaten to a pulp in a tiny car was one of the most horrifying things I had ever witnessed.

Satisfied at the damage he'd caused, Darryl moved back behind his seat, breathless, then slipped out of the car. Gerald looked visibly relieved. Sam made a low, howling sound so I pulled her onto my lap, to stroke her hair.

'It's going to be okay,' I whispered.

'Please go,' I urged Gerald. 'Just drive!'

Gerald quickly started the engine and began driving away, leaving Darryl to walk off.

Gerald dropped us off at my flat and I offered Sam my arm to help her walk. The crook of her arm was trembling just like mine, while I struggled with the key. After we got inside, I sat her down on the sofa but she was agitated and jumped up.

'What the fuck was that!' she slurred through a thick lip. 'What's happened to me! I need to go,' she cried. 'Get home. How could they treat us like this?'

Her face had swollen up like a football. Her nose had spread to the side of her face. Blood dripped off her chin. The horror of it all made me weep. All I could repeat was 'fuck' over and over again. I wanted to cuddle Sam, soothe her wounds, but knew she was too angry. She seemed to recover her senses faster than me. 'Come on Joanne. You need to pack your stuff.'

But I didn't move.

'Come on quick,' she yelled. 'I've got some cash. This is your chance to escape.'

I shook my head slowly.

'We both can't leave,' I said, my voice hoarse with emotion. 'I'll have to stay to cover for you. If they get wind both of us have gone to get a train they'll come for us. Let me stay and reassure them you've just gone to hospital to get things checked out. They have to be reassured you're not going to the police.'

'But we should report them to the police,' Sam cried.

'It's no good,' I sobbed. 'They won't do anything.'

Sam stared at me, wiping blood off her face. I prayed she wouldn't look in the mirror. It would frighten her.

'This is crazy. You can't live with these people...' she whispered. I gently reached out and touched her face.

'Please get away before Darryl comes back,' I whispered. 'Just go when you can.'

We clung to each other for a few seconds, before Sam gave me one last long look. 'I will call you when I get home,' she said, and she dashed out of the house and disappeared down the street to flag down a cab to the station.

After Sam left, I shivered, staring at her blood, smeared and sticky on my hands. I was desperately worried about her getting away. But when Gerald returned, and asked where she was, I tentatively told him she had left.

'She's gone to get treatment,' I said, vaguely. He looked relieved.

'It's best she's gone,' he sighed. 'She was always going to cause us problems.'

Noticing he was not bothered about it, I knew Sam was going to get away with escaping. They were letting her go. Fearing I had ringworm too, Gerald forced me to cover myself head to toe in a special lotion. Only after that would he relax, he said.

Two days later, Gerald asked me for Sam's mum's number. I froze. But he gently said he just wanted to check she was okay. From the beating she took, there was a chance Darryl had caused real damage. Sam's mother answered and was furious he had even called and put the phone down.

For weeks afterwards, every time I closed my eyes I still saw Darryl's twisted face and heard Sam's anguished cries. It was a sound to haunt me for years to come.

A few days later, I sneaked out of the sauna, pretending I needed some painkillers after a punter paid me. Thankful to have some money at last, I wandered into town to get myself a few toiletries and extra food. In the pharmacy I picked up a pot of aspirin. Staring at the label, I realised there were 100 tablets inside. Enough to kill a person.

My hand grew sweaty when I tightened my grip on it. I was going to buy these. I needed the option of a way out of this. I knew nobody could help me escape this awful life. Not friends, not family and not even the police.

Watching what they did to Sam was a reminder of how dangerous they were. Although Gerald never laid a finger on other girls, I had borne the brunt of his rage so many times. It wouldn't take much to take things too far and kill me. I had to have an option to be able to do it myself.

*

It was as if I'd had a crystal ball predicting danger. Later that week, I was in the hallway of my flat when Gerald came through the door with a piece of rolled-up carpet. He unrolled it on the floor, and then pointed a gleaming grey shotgun in my direction.

Instinctively I shrank back, the blood draining from my face.

Instantly, I was back in fight or flight mode, my heart hammering in my chest, my eyes darting to look at the door for a quick exit.

Was he going to kill me? Threaten me? If he wanted to scare me it had worked. But he laughed.

'Nah girl, this is a gun I need to keep somewhere safe, so it's staying at yours. I need to get it sawn down you see? There's a job I need to do. You get me?'

He went on to explain in detail how someone can saw down a shotgun to make it more deadly and easier to shoot someone.

I sat on the sofa and hugged my knees, my eyes fixed on the weapon. I'd never seen a gun before. Like it was a precious gift, he polished it with a piece of lint and then rolled it up in the carpet again. Then he propped it up in a side cupboard.

That night I could hardly sleep a wink, thinking of the gun in my house. I opened the cupboard after work the next night and noticed it had fallen onto its side. But I didn't want to touch it. I didn't want my own fingerprints on an illegal weapon. The next day, I overheard Gerald tell someone how he had the gun. He talked about a post office. And something about 'gear'. I didn't understand everything but there was clearly another gang of men who were intimidating him and his cousins. I tried to keep my head down. I continued working, handing over the money and, when I could, tried to keep in touch with Julie from the refuge. By now she had moved into a YMCA hostel and often asked me over to hers at the weekends. When Gerald wasn't around, I went to visit her.

Although I considered Julie a friend, she had no idea about what my life was really like. Julie even met Gerald a number of times and, like always, he was a charmer to the ladies. She had spotted the odd bruise on my face and even tried to talk to me about domestic abuse in a relationship, but I brushed it off. I never told Julie the truth about our relationship and how he'd forced me into the game. She viewed Gerald simply as a controlling boyfriend.

Occasionally I saw the odd woman coming or leaving the various flats we stayed at, but while Gerald chatted to them, I wasn't encouraged to, although sometimes I'd snatch a few details like their names or where they worked. One of them was a lady in her 30s called Tracey, who wore jeans and drove a car. There was something well put together and mature about her and I couldn't understand why she was so wealthy, but assumed she had better paying clients and not all her money was taken off her. Gerald often flirted with her, but I turned a blind eye. There was nothing I could do about it anyway.

My Auntie Barbara was even sucked in by Gerald when she came over to visit me in my flat. She was the only relative from Northern Ireland I had regular contact with, and the only person to offer to come. She arrived with her new boyfriend, who she was marrying. I was so pleased to see her, even if I knew I couldn't tell her anything about what was going on. As if on cue, Gerald made sure he was in my flat when she arrived.

Like always, he shook hands, called her 'ma'am' and showed real interest in her and her life. Barbara seemed happy to chat to him while I made the tea. Towards the end of the visit Gerald left, and it was then Barbara looked at me with concern.

'Are you *sure* everything is okay Jo?' she asked. 'You have lost a lot of weight.' I could see her looking around my bare flat, and eyeing up the lack of decoration or contents.

'Yes, all's fine,' I said and changed the subject. 'Money's a bit tight, that's all.' Then I asked after Nanna and Grandpa, who Barbara sometimes saw around. At the end of the visit, Barbara asked again if I was okay and I put on my best fake smile.

*

But to other people, the abuse was becoming more obvious. Although Gerald was always very careful not to hit me in front of people we knew, sometimes he slipped up.

One afternoon, Gerald dropped me off at the Stratford sauna. Just before I left the car, he punched me hard on the side of the face for something or other. My head bounced off the window. I arrived at work, rubbing the sore spot, and then ruffled my hair over any impending bruise.

I assumed nobody had seen it but the sauna had mirrored windows, so people could see out but not inside. Soraya had been in the reception area and clocked Gerald's punch.

'Did your bloke hit you in the car?' she asked, shocked. She stared at me with such concern, I almost cracked then recovered my senses. Swiftly I shook my head.

'Nah, I am fine,' I smiled. But I could tell she was not convinced.

All day, I dreaded going home. Especially if Gerald suspected anyone had seen him hit me or that I had been telling anyone. My paranoia about how this situation could worsen kept growing.

Shortly afterwards, I went back to my flat to find one of Gerald's 'cousins' waiting for me outside.

'Gerald is back inside, this time on remand' he said gruffly. 'But this makes no difference to you. Got that?'

I was staggered. What had Gerald done? Once again he had never mentioned to me being arrested, charged or going to court. I knew he led a double life at times and God knows what he was doing with that gun. That's when I remembered. The gun. It was still in my flat.

A few days later, Julie asked me over for dinner.

I'd only just arrived when she waved a local paper in my face.

'Arrests made for Gang Rape,' the headline read. In the paper was Gerald's name.

My mouth gaped open. Julie shook her head. 'You keep your nasty boyfriend away from me, thanks,' she said. Then it was her turn to look surprised.

'Joanne, didn't you know what he was up to?' she asked.

Tears smarted in my eyes. I tried to read the words but they swam everywhere. A violent gang had raped a girl in retribution for a drugs deal gone wrong by the girl's cousin.

'This is awful,' I said. 'Poor girl.'

Julie nodded grimly. 'I hope he's been put away for a long time.'

Days later, a letter arrived in the post from Gerald demanding I went to visit him. I didn't realise I didn't need a visiting order because he was on remand. I applied for one, as usual, but then he wrote a second, angrier letter,

'Why aren't you fucking coming to see me?' his words spat.

I decided I'd visit in a few weeks' time. In the meantime, with Gerald safely behind bars, for now at least, I could taste freedom.

The next day, I hopped on a bus to Telford, wanting a break and to consider what I was going to do next. I felt lonely, isolated and the need to make friends, or look up old ones, but I didn't have any luck with old school friends. I thought of everyone I knew and, for some reason, the lad Kevin popped into my mind. He had raped me, along with the other boys, but had also shown me kindness with cups of tea and allowing me to watch Australian soap operas. Crumbs of kindness really, but enough to make a lasting impression. Without anywhere else to go and barely thinking of the consequences, I decided to knock on his door.

Waiting for him to answer, I realised how crazy this decision was. I had no idea if he even lived here anymore.

24

The door opened. Kevin had filled out and looked older than his 20-odd years but he recognised me straight away.

'Hey, what you doing here?' he said, in a surprised but not unkind manner.

'Do you want to go for a drink?' I blurted out. A smile spread over his face and he grabbed his coat.

We went for a walk. I told him nothing about Gerald but gave a vague account of working in London and coming home for a bit and wanting to look up old faces. Kevin explained he was working in a biscuit factory. He'd just had a baby boy called Leon but said he'd split with the mum and the baby lived with her.

After reconnecting, Kevin took me back to his house. Like years earlier, he made me a cup of tea and put on the telly. Then one thing led to another and we had sex.

Voluntarily having sex was a novel thing, although I tried to block out the flashbacks of when Kevin and his friends used to attack me. Afterwards, we lay together, reminiscing. I pretended the memories were fun for me, even though they were not. Kevin didn't acknowledge anything he or his friends had done, so I guessed we were both in denial. Then it was time for him to do his late shift and I had to go. He kissed me goodbye and said he hoped to see me soon. Afterwards, when I walked past his dad's bedroom, I noticed a baby's cot in the room.

For the next week or so, I saw Kevin a handful of times, often starting in a pub and ending up back in bed at his house. On one occasion, a woman came towards us with a buggy, and Kevin jumped up and led me away by the elbow quickly. I half feared it was his baby and that was his girlfriend but he didn't say anything. But then he stopped taking my calls. On the last arrangement to meet, he didn't turn up. But being dumped wasn't the only shock. A month later, I realised I was pregnant.

Instantly I knew it was Kevin's baby. I hadn't been made to work the streets for a couple of weeks or slept with anyone else. I was especially shocked because after my last miscarriage, I had been told by a doctor I wouldn't be able to have children. Getting pregnant was the last thing on my mind. After the news sunk in, I began to look forward to it and decided to go and tell Kevin. But each time I tried to meet up, he either didn't call me back or seemed to be avoiding me.

The other positive to keeping the baby was the situation with Gerald. Being pregnant would provide me with protection because he could no longer make money out of me. Punters wouldn't want a pregnant prostitute and he'd also not want me if I was expecting another man's baby. Could this really be the best way to escape? I began to think it was.

Unable to put off Gerald any longer, I went to visit him on remand in prison to try and keep the peace. When I arrived, I had to give my name to the visitor reception.

'I am the girlfriend of Gerald McAllister,' I said. 'Here to visit him.'

The officer warden cocked her eyebrow in a way that told me she knew something. Immediately I guessed it meant I wasn't the only girlfriend visiting Gerald.

'I'll go and see if it's okay for you,' she said, looking anxious.

When she came back and said she wasn't sure if he was allowed extra visitors, but I could wait until the end of the visiting period. I said no thanks. Even if it had taken three hours to get there, I didn't want to see Gerald if he was being visited by another woman.

I stormed out, my cheeks burning with humiliation. Despite everything, I couldn't believe Gerald was cheating on me. Although I was terrified of him, I was devastated too. I wondered who it was, it could be any number of girls. By the time I got back to the flat, I felt more rational. As much as him cheating on me hurt, the fact was, I had cheated too. I was even pregnant. This was my big chance to finally break free and I had to try and think positively about the future.

I grabbed a paper and pen. Then I started writing a Dear John letter, outlining how I think we should end our relationship. After I popped the envelope into the post box, I let out a big sigh of relief. I couldn't believe perhaps this nightmare might finally be over. Would it really be as simple as this?

The next day, I decided to start seriously thinking about my future. Although I still struggled with sleeping, eating properly and having flashbacks, I really wanted to improve my lot before the baby arrived. Considering all options, I decided to go for a secretarial training course. I needed to learn how to type properly. So many life skills had passed me by. This seemed like a sensible option.

The next time I dropped into Mum's house, I shared my plans. I hoped she'd be proud of me, finally. I wasn't ready to tell her I was pregnant but I explained I wanted to return to education.

'I want to learn how to do shorthand,' I said. 'So I can get a proper job and earn a decent income.' If I expected her to smile or give me a hug, I was wrong. Her face fell.

'Why bother with that?' she said. 'Courses are for academic learning. You could learn all that basic typing stuff on the job, no?' I stared down at the hoover marks on her carpet. Whatever I did was never good enough. Why hadn't I learned that by now?

But days later the bubble of fantasy around doing a course and getting a job popped. Gerald sent another letter and the words leapt off the page like he had his hands around my throat. '*Get your fucking arse in this fucking prison tomorrow,*' it read.

I turned up on the dot when visiting hours began. Gerald glared at me when I sat down, launching into a tirade about me not earning him any money. Then he told me a story of another prisoner who had sex in a waiting room with a girl with a long skirt. His eyes bore into me when he spoke. I guessed he was actually speaking about himself.

I listened, nodded along and then left. I felt humiliated and also angry. How long had he been cheating on me? I would never find out. Not knowing what to do, I decided to return to my flat and wait to see what happened. Gerald faced a huge trial for the gang rape of a woman whose cousin was involved in a drug deal that went wrong and a date had been set.

However, weeks later, during the beginning of the trial, the gang threatened the girl's family and she quickly dropped the charges and the case collapsed. Once again, Gerald got away with it.

*

Gerald came over to my flat soon after he was released. It was clear he believed he was above the law. And he was right. Having spent most of his life in crime, Gerald and his lot knew how to play the system. No physical evidence was left at the scene of crime, he said proudly. But I could also tell he had something else to say. Sitting shiftily on the sofa, he made a confession.

'Sheree is pregnant again and the baby is mine,' he said softly.

I didn't react. I tried to process what I was feeling. The familiar twist of jealousy emerged, but then also a wave of relief flooded through me. I placed my hand gently on my stomach. I had been looking at baby clothes recently, even started thinking of names. I was looking forward to this more than anything. I loved this baby already. It meant a fresh start. It meant escape.

'I've something to tell you too,' I said, trying my best to look him steadily in the eye. 'I'm pregnant as well. And it's not your baby.'

Gerald's mouth fell open. He stared at me in silence. I could tell he clearly never thought I had it in me. Then he gathered himself.

'Well,' he said eventually. 'Congratulations.'

I watched him brush invisible dust off his trousers, stand up and leave. When the door closed I sat quietly absorbing all of this. He couldn't be angry because he'd also been unfaithful but he also wouldn't want me anymore. I couldn't earn him any money, so I was worth nothing to him now.

*

Over the next few days, I set about sorting out my life. I tried to save some money from the Giro, eat as much fresh food as possible and look for work. But it was hard. I was struggling with adapting to normal life again. I still had disturbed sleep and found myself jumping at every knock on the door. I was only 19 but struggled to relate to carefree young people my age. I didn't know how to pay bills or cook, Gerald had had control over everything. I'd become institutionalised. Used to being on the streets and being controlled. I also felt burdened with a deep sense of shame about what I'd done.

In the eyes of the law I was a 'common prostitute' with convictions to my name and unpaid fines hanging over my head. I worried about any potential employer finding out and it wasn't easy finding regular casual work where I lived.

I knew I should do all the normal things a pregnant woman does like have a scan, but I didn't. Anyone in authority scared me. I even feared perhaps social services might get involved. And if I fell onto their radar, they could take the baby away.

Above all, I was lonely too. Deep, darkly lonely. Without the girls on the streets, I had few peers. I saw as much of Julie as I could, but I was wary about bringing my own problems to other people's lives. She had enough burdens of her own. I was essentially estranged from my family too. Mum barely saw me. Aside, from the one visit from my Auntie Barbara, I never saw anyone from Northern Ireland. I'd not even heard from Dad or Nanna and Grandad in ages, and even Sam had lost touch with me.

Cut adrift, I tried to focus on myself for my new baby. I dreamed this baby would be someone to love and care for and set my life back on track.

*

A couple of months later, there was a knock on the door I recognised. It was Gerald.

'I was just passing by so stopped by to see how you are,' he asked kindly. 'Is everything okay with the baby's dad?'

I was puzzled by this sudden appearance but was honest and told him I'd not told Kevin yet, but planned to. I wanted to tell him face to face to give him a chance to be involved in the baby's life if he wished. 'Actually, I am due to go to Telford and meet him tomorrow,' I confessed.

Gerald looked deep in thought. Despite myself, it was nice to talk to someone, even if it was him. I often went for days on end without speaking to anyone.

'Let me give you a lift there?' he suggested.

I did a double take. I didn't want to spend any time with Gerald but at the same time money was so tight. I'd still not found regular work and was surviving on benefits. It would save me a train fare.

Gerald cocked his head, waiting for my reply.

'Okay, thanks,' I said.

He drove me in his car, the bass of the drum reverberating the windows as usual. He even tapped along on the steering wheel, amiably. He seemed in a good mood. I felt a weird pang of jealousy he was with Sheree now, but relief too.

An hour later, Kevin never showed up to our meeting spot and my heart sunk. Walking away, I got the train back alone, promising the baby I would do this all alone. A few weeks later, Gerald turned up at my doorstep again.

'I am going to the launderette,' he said. 'Do you need help?'

He knew I didn't have a washing machine and I was surprised, but also touched that he was thinking of me. Although Gerald behaving generously was unusual, I thought of the lift he'd given me previously and how nothing untoward had happened. Perhaps he had moved on with different girls. Perhaps it was possible he was just being kind again.

'Thanks,' I smiled. I had plenty of washing to do, I was trying to live a more organised life. Practising for when the baby arrived. I was three months pregnant now, or so I thought according to my calculations, although I'd still not seen a doctor.

'You don't want to be hauling big laundry bags in your condition' Gerald chuckled. 'Let me drive you.'

I was grateful. I still had no friends around and the launderette was miles away. I got my washing and then stepped into Gerald's car. He said he was dropping into his house to pick up his own washing en route.

'Won't be long,' he said, dashing into his flat.

Half an hour passed with me waiting in the car and still no sign of him. I began to need to pee. So I knocked on the door to ask to use his loo. Inside, Gerald was gathering washing. What had he been doing for the past half an hour? Something was up. Quickly I went to the loo, thinking I just needed to get out of his flat. I had made a big mistake taking up his offer and coming here.

A familiar rising sense of panic gripped me as I quickly washed my hands. What had I been thinking? How stupid had I been trusting him. He was never going to change, when would I learn?

When I unlocked the bathroom door, I realised it was too late. Gerald was waiting for me behind the door and pushed something cold and hard into my tummy.

I looked down. It was a medieval looking metal contraption, I didn't know what it was at first and then cold realisation washed over me.

It was a crossbow. And Gerald was pushing the tip of the arrow into my baby bump.

My knees turned to water. Silently, I said a quiet goodbye to my baby, because every instinct told me he or she wouldn't survive this.

25

'If I release this trigger you will die. But I am not doing life in prison for the likes of you. Instead, you're going to get that fucking baby out of your stomach,' Gerald spat, his voice full of hatred.

My eyes daren't move from his finger poised to shoot.

Before I had a chance to react, he suddenly tossed the crossbow onto the carpet then grabbed my arm, dragging me into his bedroom and threw me onto the bed. I curled into a ball sobbing, bracing myself for what was to come. I didn't have to wait long.

Whack!

I felt the pain of a long broom handle come down on the side of my body.

Whack!

Again and again, he held it high over his head before bringing it down on my thighs, the sides of my arms, my back, any area he could. I shielded my tummy the best I could, silently telling the baby how sorry I was. Gerald only stopped when he grew breathless.

Next I heard a key in the door. I was locked in again. I lay, clutching my growing tummy, saying aloud: 'I am so sorry. I am sorry.' Over and again. Because I knew I couldn't have this baby now. Bringing an innocent life into this sordid, dangerous world was the last thing I could do.

Aching all over, I sat up and waited on the floor. Tears fell down my face thinking about losing the baby or if I didn't, I'd need an abortion. I steeled myself to being left in the flat for days again, but Gerald reappeared the next morning with his friend called Jay. I had overheard rumours from the other cousins over the years about Jay, because he had a reputation for being involved in organised crime, and was someone many people were fearful of. My heart thudded as I listened to them chatting amiably downstairs, like I wasn't here.

I didn't know what to do, but a voice from deep within told me to get out if I had the chance. Shaking, I walked downstairs, past the room where they laughed together and straight out the door. I expected someone to stop me, but nobody did. I ran as fast as possible all the way back to my flat and locked the door and closed the curtains. I knew I daren't leave it.

Very unexpectedly, the next few days were quiet. I didn't go out in fear of bumping into Gerald and lived off whatever food I had in. I didn't look into having an abortion either because deep down I desperately wanted this baby. I hoped for a miracle and maybe Gerald would leave me alone now because I couldn't earn him any money. I fantasised about buying baby clothes and moving away. Maybe I could even have a fresh start in Northern Ireland. Yes, I had a few more fines hanging over my head, but maybe it was possible?

Exhausted, I spent the next few days eating and sleeping. On day three, I was sitting down to eat beans on toast when the door banged. Instantly my heart reached my throat: it was Gerald.

'You're still fucking pregnant aren't you?' he screamed at me.

He picked up the plate and threw the beans over my head. I reached to wipe my eyes as he grabbed my shoulders and threw me against the radiator. Then he gripped a handful of my hair and repeatedly began banging my head against it. I managed to let out such a loud scream, he let go. Then I raced into the kitchen to take a knife from the drawer.

'Leave me alone. Get out! I can't take any more,' I yelled, brandishing the knife.

The voice that emerged didn't belong to me. It belonged to a mother who wanted to keep this baby. A protector. A woman who had had enough. I was shocked by it.

Gerald moved like lightning, knocking the knife from my hand and picked up a glass on the counter and smashed it hard over my head. He dragged me onto the floor, on top of the shards of glass, wrestling me to the ground.

'Who the fuck do you think you're talking to?' he snarled, his spittle landing on my cheeks. Glass stuck into my hair as I tried to get up again.

I struggled slowly to my feet, not knowing what to do next. I didn't want to leave him in my house alone, but I had to get away from him. I shut the bathroom door and sat quietly on the toilet. This was no good. This was no life for a baby. What was I even thinking, trying to bring an innocent baby into this world? I couldn't have normal things like normal people. Like a loving family, or a normal job or motherhood. A terrible bubble of grief emerged and made me fumble in the medicine cabinet. I couldn't go on. I just couldn't take any more of this.

I popped the lid off the bottle of the 100-tub of aspirin, and gulped down two handfuls. I needed water, so took some from the bathroom tap. By now Gerald was banging on the door. He could hear me crying and shoved it open.

'What are you doing you stupid bitch?' he cried. 'Do you really want to die?' He grabbed the tablets from me.

'Okay then,' he shouted. He pulled my head back by the hair, forcing my mouth open with one hand, then he poured the bottle of pills down my throat, pinching my nose closed. Gagging and retching, I began foaming at the mouth.

'See!' he yelled. 'If you wanna die, then die!'

He then opened a bottle of Ribena he had brought and began pouring that down my throat too. Gagging, I had no choice but to swallow with my head clamped between his hands. Part of me didn't care, but the other part still thought about the baby.

Feeling dizzy, I tried to stand up. I was retching and gagging but nothing but foam was coming up. All I could think of was getting outside for help. I staggered into the street with Gerald watching me. Through blurred vision I spotted a red phone box, so I made my way over and dialled 999.

'Ambulance please,' I slurred.

By the time they arrived I was struggling to stand or keep my eyes open. I could feel someone laying me on a stretcher and another voice repeating: 'Don't sleep. Don't sleep.'

With blue lights flashing, I was rushed into the Royal hospital. Straight away my blood was tested and then my stomach was pumped with saline solution. I felt someone take my hand.

'I am here for you,' said a female voice. 'I've seen the toxicology reports and you might not make it, so I am staying to see you through this.' The sound of her soft and compassionate voice made a tear roll down the side of my face before I drifted into unconsciousness.

Hours later, I woke in my own room with an alarm going off. A saline drip into my arm needed changing. Blinking in the artificial lights, I didn't know what time or day it was. A gentle sounding nurse told me I had been very lucky.

'You were just one or two tablets away from dying,' she explained.

Then I closed my eyes and fell back asleep.

For the next 48 hours, I woke to the sound of the alarm before falling asleep again. On the third day, I woke and stayed awake for ten minutes when a nurse asked me who my next of kin was. I couldn't bring myself to say Mum, so gave her Gerald's number.

Finally, I managed to stay awake for longer and was transferred to another hospital. I was taken to a ward, where I lay and cried. I had no idea what damage I'd caused the baby, so asked a doctor. He said nobody would be able to tell until I had the 20 weeks scan.

A week passed in hospital. A nurse asked about my mum, and I reluctantly gave her the number. Hours later, I opened my eyes to see Mum's flushed face over mine.

'As soon as they called I knew it was you and I guessed you'd done this,' she sighed. 'Look at the state of you.'

I hadn't even noticed, but my hair was still crispy and had baked beans and glass stuck in it. With the catheter and wires in my arm, I'd not been able to have a shower.

'Give me the keys to your flat and I'll go and get things you need,' she said. I was too exhausted to argue but I knew what would happen. Sure enough, she returned hours later looking more annoyed.

'Jo, I couldn't find anything! Where is your makeup? Your toiletries? You don't even have any clothes. The flat is bare.'

'I know,' I shrugged.

'Then why are you doing this? Why would you choose to sell yourself on the streets if you're not making any money from it?'

She stared at me agog and I felt so embarrassed.

'Is it really worth it?' she continued.

'Mum, I am pregnant,' I sobbed. I couldn't stop the well of tears falling now. She gave a deep sigh.

'I guess that's something else that needs sorting out.'

We had nothing left to say, so sat in silence for several minutes, then Mum stood up and said she was leaving. I didn't say goodbye.

*

The next day Julie arrived at my bedside, her eyes glistening with tears. She was furious. Mum had pushed a letter underneath the door of her YMCA hostel. She knew Julie and I were friends and where she lived. The note read: *'Please go and visit Jo for me. She is on the upper ward, seriously ill in hospital.'*

Julie wrapped her arms around me and stroked my hair.

'Your mum is a piece of shit for leaving you alone like this,' she soothed. 'But I will help you in whatever way you can.' Just by being there, she had already had.

'You're one of my diamonds,' I sobbed.

Julie stayed with me while I slept. She bought me food and helped me to drink from a straw when I was too tired to sit up properly. She returned over the next few days watching me grow stronger then turned the conversation to Gerald. Thinking he had been let off the terrible gang rape, she didn't consider he was so bad after all.

'Are you going back to him?' she asked, concerned. I hadn't told her it wasn't his baby or that he had forced me to eat the aspirin. I was so wary of burdening her with my problems.

'I don't know,' I sobbed.

Later, I saw a psychiatrist. They questioned me briefly and then concluded I had tried to take my own life because I was pregnant with someone else's baby and my boyfriend had found out. Like always, it felt impossible to tell them what really happened. I was simply too scared and they didn't seem to care. A few days later, after more treatment I was finally discharged. Because I had given Gerald's number to the nurse as my next of kin, he was called to collect me. I walked slowly to the car, him guiding me by the elbow.

'Don't worry I will have an abortion,' I promised him.

*

Gerald dropped me off at my flat and drove off. Once again I was left alone. I spent that night in tears, saying goodbye to my baby. How could I ever contemplate bringing a baby into a life of fear and violence, even if I already loved it?

The next day, I knocked on Mum's door. She let me in, wordlessly as usual. She didn't hesitate to ring the GP to try and organise an abortion. Her face a neutral expression, she wasn't surprised I'd made another mess of my life.

William and Mum drove me to the doctor's the next day. I had an appointment for doctors to sign paperwork to say I could have the termination. However, I needed two signatures and it was a struggle to find another GP to help. So I waited in the car while Mum sorted it out. Sitting silently with William in the car, I could tell he was fuming with me. Once again I felt like the bad apple who had brought nothing but trouble to their perfect middle class lives.

Eventually Mum came out with two signatures. 'I had to insist someone helped,' she said triumphantly to William.

'I told them tax payers like me pay their wages and I wasn't leaving until I got the signature.'

Before we left, Mum nipped to a nearby Sainsbury's to get chocolates to thank the receptionist. Back in the car, William pointed out the receptionist was only doing her job, so they ate the chocolates themselves.

*

The surgery was arranged for the following day. Nobody knew how far along I was but doctors guessed it was around the cut-off date for an abortion, so I needed the op as soon as possible. The next day, Mum dropped me off at the hospital at 8am. I wanted her to come with me, or have someone there. I had no idea what to expect. But she didn't offer and I didn't want to ask.

I walked into a seating area alone. On one side were people waiting. On the other were curtains covering beds. There were several young girls there, some only school age. They were all on their own, only the older women had partners or husbands holding their hands. Nobody spoke or looked at each other.

One by one we were called over. I had to remove my clothes, put on a gown that gaped at the back, have an internal examination and then was handed a pessary.

'You'll just feel a bit of pain,' a nurse said impatiently.

Walking back to the waiting area, I felt so exposed in my gown and could see other teenage girls did too. Suddenly one young girl fell to the floor, clutching her tummy and screaming in agony. She was clearly in labour. Quickly nurses took her away. Nobody said anything and the room fell silent again. Then it was my turn. I had to get onto the bed and be wheeled away for an injection. I felt the cold spread across my arm and soon everything went black.

I woke up, feeling exhausted and like I had period pain. But I was also relieved it was over. I was wheeled into a recovery room where I got chatting to another young girl, who was friendly and helped me feel better.

'Hey, let's go and have a ciggie,' she suggested. 'We can pretend we were going to the loo or something.' I was a bit nervous doing anything we weren't supposed to do, but she lightened the mood, so we wandered off. We lit a cig in the corridor and blew smoke out of the windows, giggling. The nicotine made me dizzy, and I found myself passing out. I came around with an angry nurse telling me Mum was going to pick me up in an hour.

Mum and William drove me back in silence to Wem, where they lived as newly-weds. Neither needed to say how disappointed they were with me, I could sense it. When I arrived, Mum and William sat me down in the large plush living room filled with books and leather sofas. They had clearly spoken together and wanted to make a speech of some kind.

'We have decided you can stay here,' Mum announced. 'To rebuild your life. All this nonsense has to stop. Do you understand Jo?' I nodded.

'You can stay here, find yourself a job and then sort yourself out,' William repeated. 'I would suggest the job centre would be a good place to begin.'

The following day was a Saturday. When I woke in the unfamiliar surroundings of William's spare room, what I had done sunk in. There was no baby to look forward to anymore. I closed my eyes and sobbed.

I went downstairs to find Mum and William had gone shopping. So, left to my own devices, I watched TV before quickly nodding off. I woke up later on and burst into tears. I couldn't seem to stop sleeping or crying and had no idea what was wrong with me. On the Sunday, I stayed in my room and, on the Monday, made myself go into town to the job centre.

Being out and about made my head go dizzy. Everywhere I looked I thought I saw Gerald or one of the gang. I didn't

'Well, it's not exactly clothes fit for an office,' sighed Mum. 'But better than that awful mini-skirt.'

She left me that afternoon alone again, saying she had chores to do. Later that day over dinner, William and Mum asked me what jobs I'd applied for. When I said none, Mum lost her temper.

'What's wrong with you?' sighed Mum. 'You're being given the chance to stay here, rent-free, and time to find work and yet doing nothing all day!'

'You need to sort a CV out,' William chimed in. 'Do one tomorrow and we can check over it.' I stared at him. I didn't have a clue how to write a CV, let alone know what to put on it. I found myself in tears again. 'No point in crying,' said Mum. 'Time to stop feeling sorry for yourself.'

That night I lay in bed worrying about Gerald. I half expected him to break in and try and kidnap me. But then the other half was worrying he wouldn't know where I was. He'd have tried my flat by now and realised I wasn't there. The next morning when Mum was out, I quickly rang Gerald. I kept the conversation short and reassured him I was staying at William's after I'd had the abortion. He said that was good and I should come back soon and hung up.

After over three years together, I was both frightened of him but also felt bizarrely co-dependent.

*

After a week at Mum and William's house, I still hadn't found a job and was struggling with intense feelings of anxiety. At the same time, I was left alone all day, had nothing to do and was very bored, so began jotting down my thoughts and feelings. I picked up a pad and pen in front of the TV and allowed a stream of consciousness to emerge. All my weird thoughts and feelings poured from the pencil onto the pad.

'Dear Gerald. I am so sorry I wasn't good enough. I am so sorry I didn't work hard enough. I am so sorry I didn't make enough money for you…'

I re-read the words. I was sorry, it was true, that I'd ever got involved with Gerald. And I hated how he made me feel not good enough all the time. The words were half in sarcasm, but also cathartic.

'Maybe I will be better next time,' I continued. I put the pencil down. It felt good to get some of the crap out of my system, I had no other way of processing all the intrusive thoughts. If I had my time again, I would do everything differently.

If only I *could* re-live my life. Make different decisions. I knew it was hopeless thinking like this but I couldn't see any way out. I simply didn't know how to begin to live a normal life like Mum wanted. Where did I start? Feeling overwhelmed, I turned back to the TV, before dropping off again. It had become a habit recently. Wherever I sat, I slept. I knew Mum and William saw it as proof of my laziness, but I couldn't help it. Not wanting them to come home and find me asleep, I went back upstairs, leaving the notebook and pencil behind.

*

The moment I woke to hear William shouting my name, I guessed what had happened. I ran downstairs to find him waving my notebook in his hand, his face pale and deadly serious.

'You wrote this?' he breathed, shaking the pad in my face. 'Is this a letter you were about to send to your boyfriend?'

'No!' I began protesting. But I didn't know how to explain it was just ramblings to release the pressure inside me.

'Then what is it?' he demanded. But then he tailed off, and went into the kitchen to ring Mum. I knew whatever I said he wouldn't believe me. I returned to my room upstairs, all I could think was: *fuck!*

Mum came home shortly afterwards and I could hear William stomping around, with raised voices. Then she came into my room, looking shaken.

'Joanne, I am sorry but you're going to have to leave this house right away. William read the letter you were going to send to Gerald,' she said.

I stared at her. For a split second I thought I should explain, but the look on her face told me not to even try.

'But where am I meant to go?' I asked her instead. Rising panic filled my throat again. My flat was over 30 miles away. I had no money. No car. It was 6pm and already dark.

Mum shook her head and told me to pack immediately. Quickly, I shoved a few things I possessed into a bag and walked downstairs, my head spinning. I couldn't believe this was happening but the way Mum followed me in silence, confirmed it was.

I turned and she looked at me with something like sympathy. She leaned in and for the first time since I was a very small child, held me tenderly in her arms like she acknowledged this was a terrible moment for me. I was about to walk back out there. Into the void. Or back to what I faced, something I knew she didn't comprehend, and I could never explain.

I could tell she pitied me, but at the same time, was going to do nothing to help. My mother had given up on me, so without looking back I walked out the door back into the darkness.

*

247

I turned into the empty street. Once again, I had absolutely nowhere to go. I wandered down into the main high street of Wem. It was already getting dark and the cold wind was blowing. There was an Indian restaurant called The Shabab which had a side entrance and door open for the hot air of the kitchen to blow out of. I decided I might be able to keep warm there, so huddled in the doorway opposite. It was only one brick deep, but was enough to squat down on. Then I put my head on my arms and sobbed.

After an hour, I could hear chefs clattering about, starting their shift and feared being moved on. But where would I go? The job centre was closed. I didn't know anyone in the village. I could try and reverse charges on a phone call and ring an old school friend, but that would mean explaining what had happened.

I brushed away my tears. No, I had no choice but to make the one call I didn't want to make. I found a phone box, reversed the charges and called Gerald's mobile. His voice perked up when he realised it was me.

'I am coming straight away Jo,' he reassured me. Within half an hour he'd bombed it down the M54 and was parked up in the road.

'Let's get you home,' he said, gently, ushering me into the car. 'I'll make you some good food.'

I sat in silence in the car, barely able to process what was happening. I had thought I'd escaped. But here I was, back here again already.

*

And so, within days, I found myself standing on the same spot of pavement where I first started. First for a night or two in

Dudley and then Gerald took me back down to Stratford in London.

A new girl called Nicky had started in the Stratford sauna just before I'd left. I had to change my name because there couldn't be two Nickys. But I didn't mind. She was such a warm, kind-hearted girl who liked a laugh and shared cigs between breaks. When I arrived back, she was so pleased to see me she swept me into a hug.

'Everyone has been asking where you disappeared to,' she said. 'I tried to track you down. We were so worried, Jo.' I gave her massive hug, grateful for her concern. She was the only person to have shown any. 'It's okay, I am back now,' I said, not wanting to give any details.

On our break Nicky quietly quizzed me on what happened. 'You don't have to tell me,' she said. 'But I am here for you. What happened?'

I stared deep into her concerned eyes. I knew she cared. Without thinking, I began to talk. I blurted out about Gerald tricking me into his flat, the crossbow. The fear I had. The abortion. Nicky was horrified.

'That's horrendous. You can't live like this Jo,' she said. 'This isn't right. He can't get away with it.'

Minutes later, one of the managers, Tim, was standing at the door, his face twisted with concern. I had forgotten there was CCTV in the staff room and he must have heard every word.

'Why the fuck didn't you tell me what was going on?' he demanded, protectively. 'Do you think the other girls live like this? Your boyfriend has to go.' Nicky nodded with agreement. 'I know people who can get rid of Gerald,' she added.

'The police won't do eff all,' said Tim, warming to the theme. 'But we can help.'

I looked at them while they bounced ideas of how to get Gerald out of my life. It had been three years now since this began, and this was the first time someone had offered to help. As touched as I was, I was also already deeply regretting ever opening my mouth.

'It's okay,' said Nicky, noticing my face. 'We're going to sort this out for you.' I burst into tears. I knew they thought I was relieved but it was the exact opposite. I was terrified.

I left the sauna and never went back. Over the next few days, I locked myself in my own flat. Gerald banged on the door but then left me to it for a few days. I guess he saw my spirit was broken and I wasn't going anywhere. He was right. I stopped getting dressed and washed. I sat like a zombie on the sofa, crying. I'd reached a point of reflection that was so painful, even breathing was an effort now. This was because I realised nobody could help and get me out of this.

When I was a schoolgirl, I'd been raped by kids walking home from school and none of the teachers noticed anything. I'd reported a rape by Slimer to the police but they refused to handle the case. I'd stood in front of a judge and been quizzed by probation and nobody asked if I was being coerced or tried to get to the truth. I'd been in hospital, seen doctors and a psychiatrist and nobody, not once, realised the situation I was trapped in. And my own mum had once again washed her hands of me. Instead they all said it was my own fault. So there was only one thing to believe; it must be true.

I am never going to escape, I thought. *This is my life. Probably forever now.*

I didn't even cry. There was no point. Nobody was going to comfort me. It was as if all the tears had dried up.

*

A few days later, Gerald was banging on my door, demanding I got dressed 'or else'. He had plenty of work for me and wasn't going to wait any longer, he said.

For many weeks I was shuttled between several saunas, based in Bromley in Kent and Chingford in Essex and occasionally Leicester. Gerald would drop me off and I'd stay there until he picked me up, sometimes three or four days later. By now I felt hollow and totally resigned to my fate.

Often I'd end up spending the night on the sofa in a sauna reception or dozed uncomfortably on a massage table. I was exhausted, but also now existed on complete autopilot, like a husk of a human being. My body was used all day by horrible men before another man took all my money and I completely accepted this like the slave I was.

The days and punters quickly merged into one. My only memorable conversation at the time was with a woman in the Bromley salon. She told me she used to be one of Hugh Hefner's Playboy bunnies. I had seen photos of the girls in magazines before and they all seemed so happy and beautiful.

'It was fun,' the girl, called Tara, beamed. She was a very pretty blonde, with huge boobs. 'I loved America. I lived in the mansion with Hugh for several months.' I didn't ask whether she slept with Hugh, I assumed she had and never asked how she'd ended up from there to here, in a sauna in Bromley. But really, once again, it proved to me the industry was all the same, even if from the outside it looked more glamorous.

That Christmas in 1993, I was at rock bottom. I had no money for presents for anyone and hadn't seen Mum since I'd left. I feared seeing Mum too. Gerald kept disappearing for days but to keep me in check, he'd begun using new threats against my family.

One morning, he came back in a bad mood and told me I'd not earned enough for my keep.

'You do know I know where your mum lives don't you?' he snapped. 'I know she's pregnant and home alone most of the day.'

My blood ran cold. Another time, he told me he knew Anthony now lived alone.

'Your mum doesn't give two shits about either of you,' he sneered. 'You know it and I know it. That's why you have to rely on me. You've nobody else.'

I didn't even cry any more. I just agreed to whatever he wanted and tried my best to squeeze more punters in the next shift to please him with more money.

On Christmas Day, William came to pick me up to take me home for Christmas dinner, which I ate in near silence. Nobody asked me where I was working or what I was doing. It was like they'd given up on me. Which was fine because by now, I had given up on myself too. Mum's main emotion she showed me was anger.

'We never see you anymore,' she said. 'Why don't you even bother to visit?'

I wanted to tell her it was for her own protection. What if Gerald followed me? What if he harmed Mum or the unborn baby? I knew what he was capable of. But I stared miserably at my plate of turkey, saying nothing. What horrors could I have bought to their nice, stable lives?

At the end of the meal, William offered me a lift home and drove me back in silence. He didn't have to say anything. I knew I was nothing but an inconvenience.

*

I had no money for electricity, and no money for gas, so it was cold and dark in my flat when I opened the door. William flicked the light switch but nothing came on. Saying nothing, he turned and left. I sat in the flat in darkness and then a few minutes later decided to go to Julie's room at a hostel. She was on her own for Christmas too and had clearly been crying when I turned up. When she saw it was me, a smile shone from her face.

'Thank God for friends, eh,' she said. She turned on her CD player, blasting Abba out of the speakers. Dancing around in the shared kitchen, she pulled me to my feet from the dining room chair.

'Come on, I am not dancing like an idiot alone,' she said.

I joined in and within a few seconds found myself giggling and laughing again. Once again, one of my diamonds had temporarily pulled me out of the hole I had fallen into and made everything okay again.

Afterwards we collapsed, knackered, onto her sofa and she offered me a chocolate from a box of Roses. 'Seeing you is better than Father Christmas,' she smiled, unwrapping a chocolate.

I giggled but knew this feeling wasn't to last long. By Boxing Day, after he'd spent his Christmas with his extended family like always, Gerald picked me up from my flat to take me back to London. In Christmas week I was back in the saunas, forced to have sex.

*

In the New Year of 1994, my mum gave birth to a baby girl named Matilda, but Tilly for short. But I didn't find out until several weeks later when I visited because Gerald had disappeared for a few days and I felt safe to do so.

When I stepped into the living room and saw my baby sister, I completely fell in love. I couldn't get over how perfect she was. Mum let me hold her and I marvelled at her tiny fingers and shell-like ears. I could smell her lovely new-born smell and wanted to hold her forever.

But Mum looked at me angrily while Tilly curled her hand around my index finger. 'Tilly was unwell when she was born. She had jaundice and you weren't there.'

'But Mum,' I spluttered. 'I didn't even know she had been born! Nobody told me.'

Mum tutted and took Tilly back. Her face softening when she looked at her. Then hardened again when she looked back at me.

'There's always an excuse with you, isn't there?' she said. 'We hardly ever see you these days. You can't be bothered can you?'

I wanted to cry and tell her the truth. I was terrified of Gerald following me to William's house and then him finding out where they lived and putting everyone at risk. Then another thought occurred to me. Baby Tilly. She was so fragile and tiny but I wouldn't put it past any of the gang not to hurt her. The thought made me feel physically sick with panic.

I stayed for a brief cup of tea and then returned to my flat, looking over my shoulder. The worry of something happening to my baby sister was so extreme, that night I could hardly sleep.

The next day, I found myself back on the streets, exhausted but desperate to make extra money for Gerald to keep him away from people I loved. To stop the endless threats.

*

Months later, after working around the clock, Gerald had a new venue for me.

'It's Tracey's flat on Edgware Road in London,' he told me. 'Nobody else can cover her shift so you can do it. This isn't a sauna, it's a brothel in a flat.'

I did a double take. Tracey's name often cropped up. I'd caught him on the phone to her a few times. I suspected something was going on. Sheree had had a little boy, but Gerald told me the relationship was finished.

Gerald had more instructions. 'I am known as 'Chris' there and say I am just a friend of yours. Don't tell anyone you've worked on the streets and don't say where you're from. This is high-class stuff. Got it?'

I didn't say anything. I had no time to even pack a bag, and he drove me to the address in central London. Edgware Road was a busy, straight road for ten miles linking Marble Arch with Edgware. The flat was part of a Victorian mansion block above a restaurant, at the end closer to Hyde Park. The three-bedroomed flat inside was set up like a sauna, with a little receptionist desk inside the door. The receptionist managed the phones, looked out for the girls, took the money and then handed it over when one of the men arrived.

The girl behind the desk that day was a bubbly Aussie called Maddie, who found herself here to make extra cash on her travels. Instantly I liked her and we got chatting when Gerald left and she showed me around. There was a living room, and one bedroom was set up for girls to sleep in and another two for the business. Next to the bed was lube, condoms, and small bottles.

'What are they?' I asked, picking one up, opening it and sniffing it.

'Poppers,' Maddie laughed. 'Haven't you heard of them before?'

I hadn't and put it back, not wanting to show my ignorance.

Over a cup of tea, I listened to Maddie's stories from her travels, giving accounts of what life was like in Paris, Rome and other places she'd been to. Listening to her was like a form of escapism. It ignited a longing to travel myself. I loved hearing about other cultures and later found myself dreaming of other places far away while I was waiting for the men to finish.

*

The flat was busy with punters coming and going, day and night. I didn't know how long I was to stay and had arrived at the flat with the same clothes Mum had given me, leggings and a roll-neck. Without any other outfits, I had to wash them in the sink, in between clients.

After a few days, I decided to quiz Maddie about Gerald. By now, he often went for weeks barely seeing me. I had deep suspicions about Tracey, but could never prove anything. The last time I'd spoken to him on his mobile however, Tracey had answered. She'd passed me over to Gerald, but I could hear her giggling in the background. Maddie knew Gerald as 'Chris,' so I casually asked about him, pretending he was a friend.

'Do you know Chris well?' I queried in between clients.

'Oh you know I've seen him a few times. He's often in and out with Tracey,' she shrugged.

I took my chance and asked outright if they were in a relationship.

'I guess so,' she shrugged. 'After all, I walked in on them once in the back bedroom. There was a lot of cocaine around.

They've gone away this weekend to Blackpool, just the two of them. Tracey was telling me all about it.'

I tried to control my face but inside a rage was building.

'So I am, like, covering Tracey's shift while she's on holiday?' I enquired.

'Yeah,' agreed Maddie.

First Sheree and now Tracey…

I made an excuse and went to use the bathroom to cover my emotions. It felt like a match had been lit in my head. I felt so full of rage I could hardly breathe. My thoughts were like a boiling cauldron.

Gerald is cheating on me.

He was probably with Tracey when I was being treated in hospital.

Now they're on holiday together paid for with money I've earned.

27

I wanted to scream but I managed to say goodbye calmly to Maddie. I waited for her to leave before I allowed the fury to spill over, and then I began raking through the flat. Who was this Tracey? I didn't know what I was looking for, but I turned over every drawer, every cupboard, pulling out expensive designer clothes, shoes, makeup, photographs, bits of bank statements. Then suddenly I stopped. Inside one cupboard, I found a handgun.

Stunned, I stepped backwards. This was the second gun they had. One here and at my flat. How many more were there? What were they going to be used for? To scare someone, or worse? I wanted to be sick. I closed the cupboard again, my heart banging so loudly I thought it would pop from my chest. What was I going to do now?

Gerald didn't come back that night, so I eventually fell into an uneasy sleep on the couch, only to be woken by Maddie returning for her next shift.

I was exhausted, my mind had raced all night. For so many years, despite everything, I had assumed Gerald was my boyfriend, but now I knew he wasn't anything more but a pimp. The past few years had been nothing but a nightmare and nothing had appeared what it seemed, even my so-called relationship. The violence had also escalated to the extent I was petrified about what would happen next. He had threatened me with a crossbow. Would it be a gun to my head next? My mind turned over about what I should do next. Feeling groggy, I got up and the anger quickly returned when Maddie breezily asked how I'd slept and if I needed a coffee, but I couldn't think of breakfast.

'You know Chris, who I was asking about, is really called Gerald,' I blurted out. 'And he's my fucking boyfriend of three years.'

Instantly Maddie recalled our conversation from yesterday and went pale.

'Oh shit,' she said quietly. 'I had no idea.' Instantly I regretted telling her this, for all I knew she was a best friend of Tracey's. I forced myself to smile.

'Still, better get on with the work today,' I said in a fake sing-song voice. 'I'll deal with all this later.'

*

By the time I had finished for the day, my emotions of fear and anger returned. And in the end, the anger won. I called Gerald. I wanted to scream at him, say I knew all about Tracey. But when I heard his voice, I didn't dare. Dealing with an angry Gerald was so scary, so instead I ended up showing my irritation.

'You have to come and get me. I am not working here any more,' I said frostily. 'I mean it. Come and get me now!'

My words instantly triggered his rage. 'Shut your fucking mouth bitch,' he spat darkly. 'Do your fucking job or I'll come and smash your fucking teeth in.'

I quietly put down the phone again. Who did I think I was? I was never going to get away. He was going to kill me.

I closed my eyes and imagined that gun being pointed to my forehead.

By switching off as usual, I managed to get through another long working day, with punters in and out. Although we were in a wealthy area of London, the men were all the same. Aside from a few lads on stags dos, the odd teenager wanting to lose his virginity, the majority remained middle-aged, professional, grey-haired, desperate for sex. How I hated them all. And every time they touched my body I thought of Gerald touching Tracey in a hotel on a holiday I'd paid for.

Gerald clearly knew I was in a state because he called me back that evening time. 'You're to stay where you are Jo. I will come and get you, but it will be late tonight.'

'I can't stay here,' I sobbed, thinking of Tracey and him together. 'Please.'

'You fucking well wait for me,' he snapped.

Maddie quickly cashed up that night. I had been busy with customers and Gerald clearly hadn't been down for a while, so there were bundles of notes from weeks of work. She carefully put it all into a grey hessian bag and handed it to me.

'You need to give Chris, I mean Gerald, this,' she said, her eyes full of sympathy. 'Are you okay?'

'I'll be fine,' I told her breezily. She gave me a brief smile and said goodbye. Suddenly I was alone again.

I breathed, trying to control my rising anxiety. I dreaded hearing Gerald at the door. At the very least he was going to batter me for being rude to him. If I didn't get out of here, I was going to end up leaving in a body bag.

I sat and stared at the hessian bag in my hand. I pulled out a roll of the notes, watching one fall onto the floor. There must have been a few grand in this bag. Slowly it dawned on me. For the first time ever, I had been left alone with a huge stash of money and a gun.

This had been a huge mistake, but if I ever had a chance to escape, it was now.

*

I breathed deeply to gather my thoughts. I was broken inside, but closed my eyes to channel this anger into courage. Without allowing myself to waste any more time, I grabbed the bag, ran out of the flat, down the stairwell and into the street. It was really late, after midnight, traffic was thinning out on Edgware Road and only a few people were staggering home from a night out. I had no time to waste. Gerald was on his way and I needed to get out of London asap.

In London, you are not supposed to flag down a mini-cab but I had no time to call and pre-book, so I banged on the window of the first cab I saw. He unlocked the door so I could jump in.

'Please take me to Telford,' I said breathlessly.

He moved around his seat to take a good look at me. 'No way I can take you there. It's too far…' he began. 'I also can't pick up in the street. I'll have to go back to the cab office to pre-book.'

'Look, I need to get away,' I said, struggling to sound calm. 'I have the cash on me. Please get the cab moving. We can discuss on the way.' I slumped in the seat to hide from the window. The cabbie switched on the ignition, clearly sensing I was in big trouble.

We quickly arrived at the cabbie office, where a receptionist seemed to take forever to fill out the details for the journey. It was going to cost £150.

'Fine,' I said quickly. 'I can pay up front.'

I handed bankrolls of notes over and then finally got back into the taxi. This time I sunk right down, trying to hide myself. It was around 1am and the streets were very quiet. The cabbie had to turn back onto Edgware Road to reach the flyover out of London. Then, to my horror, we stopped at traffic lights directly outside Tracey's flat. It was then I peered over the window and froze.

Gerald's car was parked almost right next to ours.

I could see him on the front seat, cuddling a girl with blonde hair. Tracey. With the internal light on in his car, I could see they were kissing.

My sense of panic rose to a point, I thought I might faint with fear. All Gerald had to do was turn his head slightly to the right and he would see the cab I was in. I tried to reassure myself his internal car light would obscure his vision as I willed the red light to change. Every second felt like an hour. Finally it turned to amber, then green, and we lurched forward.

'Please go,' I urged the cabbie. He put his foot down, and away we sped.

*

On the whole way to Telford the cabbie didn't say a word to me, which was fine because my own head was busy with thoughts. I could only return to my flat. It wouldn't take long for Gerald to discover I had vanished along with the cash and my flat would be the first place he looked for me. But where else could I go? I didn't want to waste the money on hotels. I needed it to rebuild my life.

Three hours later, we finally arrived. It was getting light now, so I jumped out of the cab, desperate to get indoors. I closed and locked my door, breathing heavily like I had run all the way from London.

I switched on a light in the gloom. My flat was just as I had left it. Practically empty, with little food or anything else. Then it suddenly occurred to me, if Gerald saw the lights on, indeed, if I used any electricity at all and he checked the meter outside, he would know I was here. Quickly I snapped the light off again.

I tiptoed into the kitchen and living room, half expecting Gerald to be waiting for me, even though I knew this was impossible. Swiftly, I closed all the curtains and then sat on the sofa. Waiting. For God knows what.

All morning nothing happened, so I dozed off, then woke to look for some food. All I had in were a couple of packets of custard creams and tea, but I daren't boil the kettle. The afternoon dragged on. I couldn't watch TV and had no books, I had to sit and stare at the walls, willing the time to pass. The next day, nothing happened again. By the Monday, I began to wonder where I could go next. Perhaps I could go and stay at Mum's and explain vaguely I was in trouble. But I squashed that idea. She had no sympathy left for me and was busy with my baby sister. Besides, I didn't want to put Tilly or Mum in danger. What if Gerald followed me there?

Before I had time to think of anything else, there was a bang at the door. I slid from the sofa to crouch behind it. I hardly dare breathe.

'Joanne, I know you're in there,' Gerald yelled. 'Come out. Now!'

He banged and banged. My head felt giddy with fear. What if he kicked the door in? What if he smashed a window? What would he do to me if he got inside?

Then I thought of the gun, sitting like Kryptonite under my stairs. And the penny dropped. Gerald couldn't kick the door in, because if neighbours called the cops they would find his illegal weapon. Incredibly, the gun which scared the life out of me, was actually protecting me now. I held my breath until I heard his footsteps disappear and the sound of his car engine roar away.

That night I barely slept a wink. Then, sure enough, Gerald returned the following morning to shout through the letter-box again. Luckily, I was by the couch, so dropped to the floor and sat still. I didn't even leave a shadow for him to spot if he tried to see through the bedsheet curtains. Again, I waited until he left.

Later, the answerphone clicked which Gerald had installed for me so I could make him more money. The sound of his voice filled my living room and I sucked in a breath as if he was in the room with me.

'Hi Joanne,' he said in a soft, gentle voice. 'Are you okay? I'm really worried about you Jo. I need to know you're safe. Please call me.' Then he replaced the receiver.

I exhaled.

*

After two more days of waiting, like a sitting duck for Gerald, I decided to take action. I didn't have a purse big enough to carry all the money, so I hid the rest in a washbag and left it in the flat. Then I peered through my curtains, making sure the coast was clear and then quickly ran from my flat and flagged down a taxi to Mum and William's house in Wem.

Only when I arrived did I realise how dreadful I looked. I was completely dishevelled, having not even dared have a proper bath for days. I was still wearing the same clothes I'd left their house with. But I didn't have time to worry too much.

They looked surprised to see me, but invited me in. William had two large Chesterfield sofas opposite each other in the lounge. They sat together on one side and invited me to sit on the other one, as if I was being interviewed for a job. I had no plan of what to say, but it was clear I wasn't going to be welcome here. In that case, I thought, the only other place I can go is to Dad's.

'I think I need to go and live with my dad,' I blurted out, wondering how Mum would react.

Mum nodded straight away. 'Yes, that sounds like a good idea,' she agreed hastily. I could sense she knew I was in trouble, really big trouble. But she wasn't going to ask why and I guessed she didn't really want to know.

William and Mum turned to each other, as if they had already discussed this idea.

'Jo will have help there to set up her own place,' Mum said.

'Yes, I'm sure the family will provide second-hand items like a cooker or fridge,' William agreed, even though he'd never met Dad or his family. They nodded and chatted like I wasn't even in the room. Then they both turned to me.

'I hope things work out Jo,' said Mum politely. She stood up, indicating I was to leave.

Shaking, I quickly left, taking another taxi back, looking over my shoulder, expecting to see Gerald's car. Back inside my flat, I washed my clothes quickly in the sink, hoping they'd dry by the morning. Then I sat shivering in a towel, hoping Gerald wouldn't return tonight. I planned on leaving for Northern Ireland tomorrow and never come back.

28

I barely slept all night and, by 5am, peeked from behind the curtains to check the coast was clear before slipping out of the flat into a taxi to the station. Even inside the cab, my heart was in my mouth as if I expected to see Gerald's car appear in the rear view mirror any second.

I made it to the train station and jumped on the next train to Liverpool. Every few minutes on the journey, I found myself glancing up and down the train carriage, expecting to see Gerald's angry face. On arrival, I got a taxi to the ferry port and then jumped on a ferry to Belfast. Next I ordered a taxi to go to my dad's council estate in Londonderry.

Thankfully Dad wasn't at work, and opened the door. His eyebrows shot up to his eyeline when he saw me, tired, dishevelled and carrying one small bag.

'Can I stay on your sofa for a bit?' I asked him.

'Yeah, of course Jo,' he said, opening the door wide. I stepped inside and felt my shoulders relax for the first time in months. Dad's council estate was one of the roughest in the area. Even if Gerald tracked me down he'd think twice about trying to kidnap me from here, I thought.

My stepmum, Jude, appeared from the kitchen, a quizzical look on her face.

'Everything alright Jo?' she asked.

I shrugged, I didn't know what to say. From Dad's worried expression he knew something had happened, but what was I supposed to say...

'Hey Dad, I've been working as a prostitute for the past few years and now I want to start my life again. Oh, and my ex-boyfriend, who was also my pimp has a gun, probably wants to hunt me down and kill me.'

'You can stay but only for a few weeks, yeah?' said Jude anxiously.

They made me a dinner of oven chips and burgers, watching me wolf down the plate as they exchanged worried glances. Dad then made up a second bed in my stepsister Victoria's room.

'I'll have an early night,' I said.

That night, I waited until Victoria was asleep before I cried myself to sleep. I might have escaped physically, but mentally I was still tormented.

*

Dad's way of dealing with this was different to Mum's. He didn't press me for information or tell me to get a job. He just gently asked how I was every day and left me to my own devices. I knew he guessed something had happened but he respected I wasn't ready to say.

Terrified Gerald would come and look for me, I quickly decided to try and put his mind at rest, so I rang from a call box. When he picked up, he sounded pleased to hear from me.

'I am just having a rest and staying with my dad for a few days,' I explained.

'Are you okay?' he asked.

'All fine,' I said, putting on a cheerful voice. 'Don't worry about me Gerald. Honestly, I am okay and will be back soon.'

'How is your nanna?' he asked.

I swallowed. I didn't want him to bring my nanna into this. I hadn't seen her yet. But I assured myself he didn't know where Dad lived or Nanna. He had no contacts I knew about over here either.

'I am seeing her soon,' I said cheerily.

We chatted for about five minutes. The conversation felt like a cat and mouse game. I wanted to reassure him so he wouldn't come looking for me while he asked more and more questions, angling to find out what was going on. He must have known I'd stolen the money but he hadn't said anything. When I ended the call, I told him I hoped he was okay too.

'No I am not okay because my girlfriend has left me and I am heartbroken,' he said in an exaggerated, sad voice.

I made myself give a small laugh.

'Don't worry, I will see you soon Gerald,' I said. I put the phone down, knowing he'd probably try and trace the call.

*

Over the next couple of weeks I fell asleep whenever I sat down for more than a few minutes, even upright in a chair. Dad always left me to doze, only waking me for meals or bedtime.

I had no idea at the time, but sleeping all the time was the result of living through years of trauma. My body had lived off adrenalin and been sleep deprived for so long, it had now collapsed.

Two weeks after I arrived, Dad asked how long I'd be staying for.

'I am not going back,' I said quickly. 'I can't.'

'But I thought you had your own place,' he began.

'Please let me stay here' I begged, tears forming in my

eyes. He gave me a hug and told me not to worry. I could stay as long as I needed to get myself sorted.

*

I arranged for a van to pick up the rest of my things, driven by one of my stepmother's relatives who was a bit of a hard nut. I knew if Gerald saw him, he wouldn't mess with him. I didn't have much left to bring back, just a few clothes, a sofa and a TV Gerald had left. Dad said he would inform the council I wouldn't be continuing with the tenancy. He supported me giving up my flat, even if he didn't understand why.

Then I remembered the gun. I knew I had to get rid of it but couldn't do it myself. Near the local park, I spotted a phone box and imagined ringing the police and telling them everything. Surely possession of a firearm would be enough alone for Gerald to be arrested?

But then I realised the gun was in my house, so I might be charged. But then what if he got off the charge? What if he was released and came to hunt me down? He might go after Dad, Victoria or maybe Mum, Anthony or Tilly. I knew it was too risky. Instead I rang Gerald again to try and reassure him.

'I am staying here for a while longer,' I said. 'But you need to get rid of the gun. There is a spare key hidden in the electric meter by the front door.'

'Okay,' he said simply and then unexpectedly put the phone down. I breathed out, hoping perhaps he was accepting things were over now.

After about six weeks, my energy levels improved and I promised Dad I'd get a job. I also contacted Sam to reconnect with her. She was living back in Belfast and was so pleased to hear from me and that I had escaped from the gang.

'You know Darryl fractured my skull,' she told me. 'I could have died Jo.'

I wanted to weep for my friend. I was so relieved she was safe. She told me she was working as a waitress and was often busy. Aside from this, we never mentioned the past when we spoke, it was all too painful. We both longed to put it behind us.

I found a job myself, working in a café nearby but I found reintegrating into normal life very hard. I had constant flashbacks, I thought I saw Gerald or Darryl everywhere. I had nothing in common with the other young people who were more carefree and into things like music and clubbing. I didn't know what the latest dance moves were or who was cool and who wasn't. It was the mid-1990s by now and I was 20 but felt like a child learning about the brave new world while pretending there was nothing wrong with me.

I had to work out how to shop for food. Eat properly. Budget. Every day after work, I was itching to ask for the payment straight away like we did in the saunas. I was used to getting paid immediately after sex, so why wasn't other work the same? It felt so bizarre having to wait until the end of the month for money.

Every day I woke up and went into work trying to put on a brave face but felt like I was painted with black tar. My shame followed me every hour of every day as if customers and co-workers could see inside my body. Nobody knew what I had done or gone through but what I had lived through made me who I was, like someone had etched *Slag* indelibly onto my forehead.

I stuck to my job, and began to reconnect with Dad's family too. It took several weeks to pluck up the courage to see Nanna and Grandpa, however much I missed them. Like always, Nanna welcomed me inside her cosy house with a big smile on her painted lips.

'Ooh Joanne your arms are like sparrow's kneecaps. Come in and sit down and let me get you something decent to eat.'

I could have sobbed with gratitude when she brought out one of her delicious stews from the oven. Nanna watched me closely as I tucked in.

'You are okay aren't you love?' she said. I nodded, but was unable to finish my plate.

'I am fine Nanna, I am sorry it's been so long.'

There were so many things I wanted to say, but I couldn't tell her anything. Instead I joked about having a smaller stomach and then asked for Arctic Roll. I knew she would have it in for me and she did.

Afterwards I went and sat near Grandpa's chair while we all watched Countdown, like time had stood still over the past six years.

Only Sam understood what I had been through, but whenever I arranged to meet up she was always working in her restaurant. Then a few weeks after I'd collected my stuff, she called.

'Why the fuck have you told Gerald where we are now?' she asked.

'Sorry?' I said, my heart immediately leapt to my throat.

'I've had a girl come into my place of work asking for work herself. Says she's from Dudley and her boyfriend is called Gerald,' Sam explained. 'That's too much of a coincidence no?'

I was absolutely horrified.

Instantly I decided to call him from the phone box again, I had to find out. I knew he didn't have my dad's address but he could have followed me from work one day. It was best to know.

Gerald answered his mobile straight away when I rang.

'Where are you?' I asked.

'Home of course,' he snapped. 'Why?'

'Well you have a chatty girlfriend,' I said. I knew I sounded cocky, but I had to be. I didn't want him to know I was scared.

'Ooo-ooh, says who?' he jeered.

'So you have someone over here looking for us?' I asked.

'No,' he said. 'But we have girls over there now. Belfast is good for business…'

I put the phone down and held my head in my hands.

Later, I arranged to meet Sam to reassure her I didn't believe Gerald was around after all. She asked me to wait at the corner of the road rather than at her place of work, which I thought was strange. Then I realised one of the saunas was at the far end of the street. Afterwards, we went back to her flat and I was shocked at how untidy it was. Her clothing was strewn everywhere, including thigh-length boots and mini-skirts. It was then it clicked. She was still working in saunas and didn't want me to know.

I didn't say anything but my heart went out to her. I wholly understood the decision. Reintegrating yourself into a 'normal' life was bloody hard. Working for a normal wage, living with the flashbacks and a feeling of disconnection was a nightmare of another kind.

*

If Gerald's phone call had worried me, things were set to get even worse when an envelope with my name on landed on Dad's doormat. The courts in Dudley had tracked me down to Dad's address.

I managed to open the envelope without Dad around, but knew keeping my past secret might be impossible now. The court appearance was for Belfast courthouse for unpaid fines and I knew reporters could attend the case. My name was likely to end up in a local newspaper.

In desperation, I called my mum in tears from a phone box to ask her what I should do. She let out another big sigh.

'Joanne, you have to go regardless,' she said. 'Get this over with. Offer to pay the fines weekly or something.'

This time I turned up in court wearing jeans and a baggy jumper to face the judge and braced myself to hear the words 'common prostitute' again. To my relief, however, they didn't mention the actual charges, only the unpaid fines. And thanks to the money I had stolen, I could pay them all off at once. I walked out, head held higher than usual. I had no intention of ever being arrested again, so I hoped this would put my past to rest.

*

At work, I met a new boyfriend called Paul. He was a local lad, heavily into music and going to live gigs. I didn't know who anyone was in the charts and he found it very funny. I'd never heard of the Manchester band Oasis, who were all the rage.

Having a boyfriend who didn't want me to sell my body was a relief but I felt clingy and paranoid about our relationship. I wanted to spend all my spare time with him and followed him everywhere like a sick puppy. During sex I still disassociated my mind and body and I became like a Stepford Wife, completely agreeable to anything he wanted to do.

One day, I was at Paul's house, watching a movie where the characters used sawn-off shotguns.

'Oh, you know how they do that?' I said before going on to explain how a sawn-off shotgun was made and operated.

Paul burst out laughing. 'What would a young girl like you know about the sort of guns gangsters use?' he jeered. 'Pull the other one Jo.'

I'd never told anyone about what had happened and didn't expect this reaction.

'I did know a lot of criminals,' I said indignantly.

Paul's face fell.

'Stop talking shit,' he snapped. 'I didn't know you liked making up silly fibs.'

I closed my mouth and vowed never to mention it again.

Around six months later we went to a music festival. I was so excited to attend my first big music festival where Paul and I shared a tent. But on the second morning, we woke to find our tent had been robbed. In the night thieves had unzipped the tent and taken money from our coat pockets. While Paul reacted with anger, I had a complete meltdown. In total panic, I began sobbing.

'I could have been stabbed or raped, anything could have happened,' I cried. Paul thought my reaction was over the top.

'Why are you behaving like this?' he demanded, quickly turning to anger.

I didn't know what was wrong with me either, but I was very triggered. Such was my panic, I refused to come out of the tent to watch Oasis play. Soon afterwards, we split up. Paul said he had no idea what was wrong with me, and neither did I.

29

About a year after arriving in Northern Ireland, I put my name on a waiting list for a council flat, but was refused. The council said I'd made myself intentionally homeless by giving up accommodation in Telford, so I told them I was a victim of domestic violence and that I feared for my life. After this, they gave me a dilapidated flat, riddled with fleas, which I wasn't allowed to refuse. I cleaned it up, had it fumigated and then moved in, paying my way by working in the hospitality industry.

In 1996, I met a short, stocky lad called Callum in a nightclub who was immediately smitten with me. At this point, I had no idea what love was.

A friend at work told me she believed love was something that grew, and I decided I should give him a chance. Callum had grown up in care and had been through bad childhood experiences, so I felt connected to him, even though I never dared tell him exactly about the abuse I'd experienced, not after how Paul reacted. I fell pregnant within weeks of meeting Callum and was in no doubt, I wanted to keep the baby. Callum proposed at the same time and all of a sudden I had a wedding to plan.

I was young and naïve for my age and had little clue about how to plan a whole wedding. I booked a register office in Belfast, bought a second-hand dress and hoped the rest fell into place. In the end, my Auntie Barbara paid for a sit-down meal on the day, and a friend of Callum's bought flowers last minute. Dad couldn't make it because he had to work, otherwise he'd lose his Christmas bonus, and Mum stood with my stepdad, observing and judging the rather shambolic event.

But by the end of November 1996 I was a married woman, and we settled into a three-bedroom house in Belfast. I might not have been madly in love, but for once I felt very safe.

For me, this was truly a fresh start.

In January 1997, I gave birth to a baby girl called Jennifer. Holding her in my arms, made me realise what true love was. Emotionally, I was hit by a truck too, because a protective mothering instinct went into overdrive. I was so determined she would never endure a life like I had. Quickly, I settled into a new routine, working part-time and juggling looking after our new family. We struggled managing our finances and a household but muddled along.

In 1999, I had another baby who I fell equally in love with, but with tight finances and unresolved childhood issues between us, Callum and I quickly grew apart. We split up in 2000.

Thankfully, my mum's brother Dermot, who owned several properties, stepped in and gave us somewhere to rent. Knowing I was going to be the sole provider on my own with two babies, I suddenly felt more determined than ever to improve my lot in life, so applied to do a degree at Ulster University.

I contacted the university directly and fortunately a professor was impressed with my application, even if I didn't have the required qualifications. He said if I passed two sample modules, I could join his course – and I did. For the first time in years, I was going to return to full-time education. Finally, it seemed, I could make up for lost time and focus solely on a better future. But like always, life often had other plans.

*

Subconsciously, over the years, I developed a technique to help me feel 'safe'. It involved immediately scanning a room to see who was there. I did this everywhere, including shops and pubs when I was with Paul and later Callum. Wherever I was, I noted exits and who was coming and going.

Now I was at university, with students coming and going from every direction, I found myself struggling to use my technique. Between lectures, when everyone stood up to move to the next class, I began to feel a rising sense of panic. People walking behind me made me jump.

One day I was walking to a lecture when my arms and legs slowed down as if I was walking in sticky tar, until I couldn't walk at all.

This happened so regularly I began to believe I had something seriously wrong with my muscles, perhaps something serious like multiple sclerosis. Upset, I told my nanna over tea one weekend when I went for a visit. 'Maybe you should go to see a doctor,' she said. So I made an appointment, but my GP could find nothing wrong with me.

This went on for around nine months and at the same time I developed insomnia. I began to fear going to bed.

When the kids were tucked up and asleep, my flat was so deadly quiet I got flashbacks about being locked in Nicola's flat. The only way I could get through the day was by drinking coffee and Red Bull.

Jittery and anxious, I spent hours studying and then after school took the kids to activities they loved like ballet, sports and kayaking. I wanted them to have a childhood I never had while I worked towards my goal of gaining a degree.

Aside from putting my energy into the kids, I copied music online to help make extra money. Unable to sleep, I spent hours and hours learning my way around a computer until I was good enough to fix them for people, earning more cash. Focusing on something else gave my brain a rest from thinking about the trauma and whiled away the lonely hours.

Meanwhile, I met a wonderful woman called Carla, a mum of two who was also a single parent. We hung out together, and I felt inspired by this passionate and determined woman. Not only did she live for her kids, she knew how to fight the system when it came to benefits and exes. Like me she had no family support, so we began to support each other.

*

In 2003, we went to a concert together with our kids. Having a ball, it was there I met Ade. He took a shine and after asking for my number, came over from Liverpool to visit. At first we became friends and then a year later, we got together as a couple. Ade seemed like the perfect gent, hard-working and someone who cared about me.

But the moment I fell pregnant, our relationship changed.

Ade accused me of cheating on him, while I suffered postnatal depression. Later, I took time off my degree to focus on my family but the relationship soon fell apart. I'd begun to suffer night terrors, imagining I was being beaten up by men in my bedroom at night. Unable to explain to Ade about what had happened in my past, I felt like I was going mad and he reinforced this by telling me he thought I was too.

Once we'd split up, I found myself homeless and also fighting to stay on my degree course. I'd taken a year out and was told to graduate without an honours, but I refused. I wanted to get a proper degree, it was my dream and something by now I'd spent years working towards.

One female tutor told me I didn't deserve my place because I wasn't like other students who had worked hard and completed their A Levels.

Determined not to fail, I found myself temporary accommodation in a block of flats for homeless people just outside Belfast and threw myself into catching up on the course. I took the kids with me into university, breastfed in lectures and let the kids play in the crèche while I feverishly studied over books in the library. Unable to write essays particularly well due to missing so much school, I even took on extra tuition with a Masters student to get better grades.

Then, six months later, I moved into private rent in Londonderry, around the corner from Dad's and continued my course to see if I could complete it.

I found I had developed OCD when it came to certain topics. Like teaching myself about computers, I took up various sports obsessively, doing them at every spare opportunity. In my mind, filling my days being busy with kids and improving myself helped keep the wild anxiety at bay.

It took ten long years, but I finally managed to graduate with a second class honours degree.

The female professor who tried to throw me out came up to me and apologised. 'You deserve this after all your hard work,' she said.

To my amazement, my mum and dad also came to my graduation. After the ceremony, Mum threw her arms around me and told me how proud of me she was.

'To gain a degree while looking after kids as a single parent is a real achievement,' she said. I basked in the glow of her pride. It was such a strange feeling, like I was floating on air. I had done it!

The whole point of gaining a good degree was to improve my job prospects to provide for my family, so quickly I set about applying for positions. Yet my employment options were limited as I was continually asked to provide a DBS check which meant that I couldn't apply for many jobs.

I decided to join a local business network, to see if I could find work another way. But every time someone asked me to help their business or apply for funding grants, I had to say no. Once again DBS checks were needed.

I had heard on the grapevine news of Muslim gangs grooming young girls, but I didn't stop to consider what that meant or relate it to my own experiences because the gangs then had been of Jamaican or black origin and we were being sold to mostly white men. I desperately, desperately wanted to forget about it and ignored it all.

With a busy life as a single mum, working full-time, I had little time to dwell anyway. I worked hard at my job but remained vigilant. I never drank at work events just in case I ended up saying something I regretted about my past and when the chance of promotion came up, I always turned it down.

After all, I would need a DBS check if I climbed up the ladder. Then, one day, I thought about applying for a job regardless of whether they'd see my DBS.

So what if they read my criminal record? I thought in despair. *Maybe I should hold my head high anyway?*

But then I considered what the reality would mean. I'd be invited in for a job interview and would be 'known' as a prostitute before even meeting my potential employers, and who wouldn't judge that?

*

Then one day, I made a snap decision. Gerald had become such a bogeyman in my head I had to see if the reality matched up to this. I also had a fantasy about showing him I'd made a success of my life. I had escaped, I had got a degree, a good job and a family. The need for him to see I was worth more was overwhelming, even if the idea of confronting him was madness.

One day I decided to jump on a ferry and go and confront him. My heart beat so fast as I approached his flat, I thought I'd throw up, but I forced one foot in front of the other, telling myself he might not even live there any more.

The front of his flat didn't look the same. The windows were filthy, grime covered the paintwork and the door was grubby. *Maybe he's moved out,* I thought with relief.

By now, my curiosity was so strong I couldn't walk away. Taking a deep breath, I knocked on the door.

To my horror, Gerald opened it right away.

30

'Woaaaah, hi Jo,' he beamed, stepping outside. 'How are you doing?' He threw his arms around me like I was a long-lost friend, before I had a chance to react. I was rooted to the pavement in shock. Gerald looked very unwell. His arms and legs were rake thin, like they could snap easily. His eyes looked tired and he'd aged badly. I could smell alcohol on his breath.

He invited me in, but I stood on the doorstep, not daring to go further. I could see over his shoulder what a mess his flat was in. Walls were covered in mould, the sofa was ripped and rubbish strewn everywhere. This shambolic man was a far cry from the proud peacock who had once owned my life.

'I was passing by,' I said confidently, looking him straight in the eye. 'I wanted you to know I have a university degree and a family. I have done okay.' I tapered off. Why did I feel the need to tell him this? None of it mattered. Gerald looked absolutely delighted for me.

'Oh, you made it then girl,' he grinned with a genuine smile. Then his face dropped as he realised I had seen the state of his flat.

'I am getting this place cleaned up, and rented out,' he began. I stared at him with pity. He was no longer the kingpin but a sad, middle-aged man whose life had spun out of control. All my old fears around him had evaporated within seconds.

I couldn't believe this was the Gerald who had dominated my life for so long.

He grabbed his coat and closed his front door.

'Can we go to the shop?' he asked. I was walking that way anyway, so reluctantly I let him follow me. We stopped at a corner shop and he asked me for money. I paused momentarily. How had I found myself in this position with Gerald asking me for money again? But of course it was nothing like years earlier. Here was a pitiful man, needing a drink.

Without hesitation, I quickly bought him a can of cider for £2. I wanted to go now, I had seen and heard enough.

Outside the shop, I began to say goodbye when another black man came over. Another 'cousin' of Gerald's.

'Hey, you see this girl,' Gerald said in Patois. 'You wanna respect her innit. She from the ghetto and once had a shottie.' He meant a shotgun so I stared at him with incredulity. He knew very well this wasn't true. If anything I was now the type of educated, middle class white person he used to loathe.

He asked for my phone number and I gave it to him in the spur of the moment. Then I walked away, wondering why I had felt the need to do any of this. The last thing I wanted was harassing phone calls.

Gerald rang me a few weeks later when he was in trouble with the police. He clearly saw me as someone educated who could help him. I listened politely but couldn't wait to get him off the phone. After this, I never heard from him again. I had the closure I needed. I could finally put the past behind me. But once again, it was never going to be that straightforward.

*

Over the next couple of years, I was very busy with single parenthood, still working full-time, and keeping everything together. I often hid my feelings when ever-present anxieties from the past arose and so I decided not to focus on romantic relationships. Instead, for the time being, I focused on my lovely kids.

About a year later, in March 2018, I went around to my daughter Jennifer's house for a coffee one Sunday morning. She was reading a newspaper and couldn't wait to tell me about the big story of the day.

'Mum, I've read about horrible Muslim gangs in Telford. They're abusing young girls!' she said.

I shook my head.

'Honestly, you don't need to worry. It's not girls like you the gangs are after,' I assured her.

I still avoided all news and never read up about these gangs, I preferred to think ignorance was bliss.

'Read this Mum, there's a huge number of girls involved,' she said. She pushed a copy of the *Sunday Mirror* in front of me.

I always avoided newspaper headlines but, 'Worst Ever Child Abuse Scandal Exposed' screamed out.

'That's terrible,' I tutted. 'However, you don't need to be scared.'

'But Mum,' Jennifer persisted. 'What's weird is the report says teenage girls worked as prostitutes, but it's impossible for a girl under 18 to be a prostitute isn't it?' I stared at my innocent daughter who was full of indignation and disbelief.

'Well,' I spluttered, unable to swallow my coffee. 'I dunno. Sometimes, you know, life can be terrible for young people. Especially if they don't have a family looking out for them. Young girls can find themselves on the streets, yes.'

I had never told any of my children what had happened to me, or any of my family. It had never occurred I'd end up having a conversation like this with my daughter either.

Jennifer looked confused and scanned the paper again. This time, I read the article, by the journalist Geraldine McKelvie, properly. It was absolutely damning.

Hundreds of young girls have been raped, beaten, sold for sex and some even killed over 40 years as authorities failed to act. Up to 1000 children could have suffered in Britain's worst known abuse scandal. Sex gangs targeted girls as young as 11. Five deaths linked to abuse in Telford…

A girl was interviewed and told how she had been groomed and abused by a gang of men. The report went on to describe how a mum and four girls had died in tragedies linked to the abuse. One girl, Lucy Lowe, 16, was killed alongside her mother and sister after her abuser set her house on fire. Lucy was just 14 when she gave birth to her abuser's baby.

I felt sick and closed the paper.

Poor girl, I thought. In the back of my mind, I wondered if Gerald had been in one of these gangs, especially if it went back over 40 years, but dismissed this.

Back home, I waited until the kids were in bed before googling: 'Child Sexual Exploitation'. Going down a rabbit hole, I read article after article about various abuse rings. It appeared in Telford that Asian gangs had taken over from the other gangs after I'd escaped. In 2013, a gang of seven men were convicted for child exploitation offences, but that was it. In the towns of Rotherham and Rochdale there had also been child sex rings exposed and enquiries, but no further action seemed to have been taken.

Then I came across an official definition stating it was illegal for a child to work as a prostitute under 18 and it usually only happened when men groomed the child. Grooming, I read, was when an older person coerced, tricked or prepared a child into sexual exploitation or sexual offences.

I sat like a deer in headlights.

Bloody hell, I thought. *That's what happened to me. I was a child forced into prostitution and groomed by Gerald.*

My understanding of my past suddenly felt crystal clear. Horribly so. I had always blamed myself for getting mixed up with an older, dodgy boyfriend and then trapped in a life I didn't want. But had, in fact, I been the victim here?

I became obsessed. Every night, once the kids were settled, I flicked on my laptop to research more.

I read every single media report I could find and discovered what modern slavery was and how large scale it was, but virtually none of the gang members are ever caught or face justice. I sighed deeply, images of my past flashing through my head like a ticker tape. I wanted to forget all about this, but something had stirred up inside and I couldn't shut it down.

The next night, during another four-hour stint of reading the internet, I discovered there was a National Referral Mechanism, a process which had been set up to identify the victims of trafficking. It urged people to come forward to the police and report the crimes. For the first time, I wondered if I should report what had happened to me.

*

Over the next few days, I struggled to process all the information I had read. But instead of avoiding the subject, I sought more information out. Then Holly Archer, the girl who had spoken out to the press about being abused by a gang in Telford, appeared on Good Morning Britain. Sitting with her back to the camera, Holly was interviewed by Piers Morgan about her experiences and eloquently spoke about being groomed by a gang from the age of 11.

The journalist Geraldine McKelvie also spoke on camera. She told how more and more Telford victims came forward after reading her investigation in the paper.

Devastatingly, she also revealed how Telford residents even went to the police numerous times, as far back as 1996, but were told there was not enough evidence to prosecute. Once again I swallowed down bile rising in my throat. It was only because of this brave reporter's digging and subsequent article that any of this came to light.

Holly had also written a book, called 'I Never Gave Consent: A Schoolgirl's Life Inside The Telford Sex Ring' so I bought and read it in one sitting.

Although the gang members were Asian, there were many, many parallels with my story. Like Holly, I was a vulnerable girl, whose early sexual encounters were filled with shame and humiliation. Like me, Holly ended up in a gang who raped her and threatened her family. I could identify so much with her story, especially how she felt unable to tell anyone what was happening.

After devouring her book, and reading other books by survivors of trafficking gangs, I knew I needed to speak to someone so managed to get in contact with Holly.

'You need to get in touch with the police,' she replied,

after I told her I'd been abused too. Holly offered to come with me but I declined. I was determined to sort this myself.

I rang the local police station who gave me a phone number for the Child Sexual Exploitation specialist department of the police. Then I made an appointment to speak to them and went to Telford police station to tell them my story. I didn't mention Gerald by name, but wrote all the events down and they said they'd be in touch. Next I was passed onto another officer, who was not part of the CSE team.

It turned out West Mercia didn't have a modern slavery team, so instead passed me onto another officer, who treated me like I'd experienced a random rape attack on the street. So I ended up referring myself to the National Referral Mechanism via the Modern Slavery Helpline. I told them my story over the phone briefly and they agreed – I'd been trafficked.

Then Victim Support contacted me but they told me outright they couldn't offer any help because my case was too 'complex'. Through the NRM I was expected to get financial and legal support to help my case but that didn't happen either. I was supposed to get help but then they turned me down for various reasons. Then in a major blow, a week after I joined the NRM, the police contacted me to say they were closing my case. When I asked if they were doing this because I'd joined the NRM, the officer simply said: 'What's the NRM?' It was then I realised what a shambles the whole system was.

Eventually I was given a support worker from the NRM but they didn't show up for our first meeting. Then finally I was assigned another support worker called Steph who was really proactive and tried to get me legal help. All of this happened over the course of a year or so and each twist and turn was exhausting and demoralising. The support system put in place for girls who'd survived sexual exploitation clearly wasn't fit for purpose.

*

Meanwhile, my obsession with researching everything to do with CSE continued. One night, deep into the research, I came across the Edwards Report. This was an 80-page document entitled 'Prostitution, Whose Problem?' funded by a Safer Cities Project and written by Dr Susan Edwards, now a professor, from the University of Buckingham. The reason for the report was to make the streets safer for women.

In this detailed report, Professor Edwards focused on prostitution in the West Midlands, highlighting how it was 'increasingly controlled by male pimps… where women were physically forced or more subtly coerced into committing other crimes… where kidnapping, imprisonment and sexual torture is not uncommon.'

She examined the legal system, pointing out women were known as 'common prostitutes' and shamed while the punters were not called 'kerb crawlers' or anything derogatory. Men did not suffer the same stigmatization as women.

You can say that again, I thought grimly.

Professor Edwards examined the cycle women became trapped in, how they had to return to the streets to pay for their fines; how they asked to be arrested sometimes and how if they reported sexual violence it wasn't taken seriously. She interviewed the women and local people on the impact on their lives and the environment. What she had discovered basically mirrored my own experience.

I was shocked, but then came the worst part. The report

had been written way, way back in 1991. This was the exact year my ordeal began. So, when I was living through the nightmare as a vulnerable 17-year-old girl, all the authorities knew about it and had even written a report about it. The words in front of me went fuzzy as my stomach sank. I had to get up from my desk and focus on breathing.

In. Out. In. Out.

The realisation that the authorities knew was like a hammer-blow. Everyone knew. And yet nobody did anything.

It was staggeringly upsetting. Once again, in my mind's eye, I thought of myself aged 17, being forced to stand shivering on a dark street, waiting for the next car to stop. Could someone have swept in and stopped this? Stopped years of mental torture and physical abuse?

Somehow I managed to track down Professor Edwards' email and I told her who I was and how devastating it was to read that the authorities understood exactly what was happening but did nothing.

'What you wrote was word for word what happened to me back then and nobody did anything,' I told her. She called me straight away.

'I am so sorry Jo,' she said. 'Changes did come about as a result of the report but they didn't come into effect until later. I am sorry it didn't benefit you.'

I appreciated her words but my need to know more continued so I tracked down DC Sawyer, who was now retired.

'I don't know if you remember me,' I wrote. 'But I am investigating what happened back in the 1990s…'

DC Sawyer emailed me back. 'Of course I remember you,' he said. 'You were one of my girls. I remember you being a thin, very vulnerable girl who I wanted to protect and the only way we could do this was by arresting you. I had lost Janine Downes and Gail Whitehouse, I didn't want to lose another of my girls.'

My eyes pricked with tears as we spoke because this ex-copper clearly had in fact cared. Max Sawyer said he had hoped my case would be taken up with a social worker after my convictions. It seemed like every authority hoped another authority would step in. Except nobody stepped in. This was a systemic failure to protect girls at every level.

It wasn't my fault boys attacked me after school in the woods or in my own bedroom. I also realised those boys from school and in my bedroom hadn't been 'boyfriends' – they had actually raped me.

I wasn't to blame for being groomed by Gerald, nor for being repeatedly raped and regarded as a 'common prostitute.' The eye-opening revelation none of this was my fault was incredible. Suddenly I viewed the terrible experiences through a prism of compassion not self-hatred and blame.

I also understood more about the gangs and the scale of the number of girls who had been abused. I was far from alone. In fact, I was actually part of a huge, undefined number. It was if a 20-year black cloud of shame hanging over my head had been lifted.

Next I got in touch with Holly once she was in the process of setting up The Holly Project, a special service to help advise survivors of Child Sex Abuse. More tears emerged when I heard about this venture. This was something I had needed for years, but the idea other girls could now have somewhere to turn to was overwhelming.

Holly asked me to keep in touch if I wanted to help other survivors and I promised I would.

*

In May 2018, Holly invited me to join her on a silent protest outside Telford council. The councillors were meeting to discuss whether to hold a full inquiry and vote at the end of it.

Nicola Lowrie, a local councillor, read out a letter written by a few of the abuse survivors. It was a no-holds-barred letter, describing in explicit detail what these young teenage girls lived through. One even described how it felt to be forced to give a strange man a blow job. Recognising these sordid details made me sob in the meeting room. It was surreal hearing a world so secretive and filled with shame be described in a respectable council meeting room.

What Holly had achieved was incredible. Although we hadn't known each other for long, I felt like her biggest fan. She was standing up for justice and speaking the truth when all of us, for so long, had been told we were to blame or made to feel like criminals. One councillor who saw me in tears, mouthed: *I am so sorry.* At the end of the meeting, the council voted unanimously to hold a full inquiry into all the failings of the authorities. Everyone also stood up and gave Holly a standing ovation too. Holly shrunk in her seat, terrified at having her identity revealed and I felt for her. But also I had never been so proud of anyone in my life.

At the end of the session, I had so many emotions from all directions, I couldn't stop crying. All the councillors apologised to all of us and were clearly moved by what they had heard. Thanks to Holly, the abuse had been brought out into the open in a way nobody could ignore. I knew I had nothing to be ashamed of and everything to be angry about instead. That evening left me feeling recognised, validated, determined but also devastated. I'd spent the past 20 years blaming myself, and feeling like I had a dirty secret to hide. Now I was left with a criminal record after surviving years of being trafficked and this was something I had the strength to confront now.

*

Later on, I was asked to help Holly with the Holly Project, a group set up to help other Childhood Sexual Exploitation survivors come forward and receive the help they needed. Incredibly, although we could only help over-18s, we had girls from aged 13 to women of pension age come forward for help. Like we had discovered, it's very hard for kids who have grown up being abused to receive help to recover. Many experience mental health issues, and battle their way through life. After so many years of not being believed, it's very hard to trust anyone.

Meanwhile I continued with my own fight for justice. One big question I had for my support worker was this: If I had been recognised as a victim of sex trafficking why did I still have a criminal record?

I was referred to a lawyer to help take my case higher. I was also referred to the Centre For Women's Justice who had begun a campaign called HOPE (History Of Prostitution Expunged). Their mission statement said they wanted all criminal convictions of women in street prostitution wiped from the record, so they can live freely without stigma.

Other girls had tried similarly to take their cases to court, but one was told by the defence that police have a 'right to know' of a criminal past, even though she won the right to have her convictions 'hidden' on the DBS. I don't think we should accept our offences being 'hidden'. I believe they should be removed completely. After all, we are not criminals but victims and survivors of a heinous crime.

Unbelievably when I began to take legal action, I was warned I was stuck by limitation. They told me I should have appealed my court case within 18 months of my convictions. This was just ridiculous considering I was still a victim of trafficking then and a child without any legal knowledge! If I have my convictions expunged, I will be able to move on with my life. As it stands, it will always hold me back in my career and how I am viewed by society.

For so many years I tried to put my story behind me. Through fear of not being believed to simply wanting it all to go away. But today I use it to highlight the systemic failures within legislation and how those failures can potentially effect a child's life even after they have managed to escape the abuse.

Epilogue

In 2019, after months of co-operation with the NRM, the National Crime Agency, and the Home Office, it was confirmed that yes, I had conclusive grounds for being recognised as a child sex trafficking survivor.

It's incredible for me to think that just a few years ago, I still blamed myself for what happened. But that's how manipulative gangs operate. The gang leaders recognise and target vulnerable youngsters and use their isolation and vulnerability to their advantage.

People often ask: But why didn't you tell someone? Well, I hope this book explains why. The fear was deep-rooted. I had also been groomed, although I loathed that word. 'Groomed' implied I had been given gifts when actually I had been forced under the threat of violence and manipulation.

I was isolated from family and friends, and even imprisoned at times. My spirit was often broken and my trust in adults was non-existent. Nobody stepped in when they could have done so. Not the school, not the truant officer, not the support worker in the refuge, not the probation officer, the GP, the psychiatrist and over many years, definitely not the police.

Other revelations over the years have been soul-destroying for me, as a survivor, to read about too. For example, Josie

Daly, the infamous madam, finally faced courts for her prostitution racket in 2000 and terrible allegations emerged. Not only did she earn around £7.5 million over the course of two years from running three saunas, where 1500 men visited per day, she even advertised their services in police magazines. I recalled the bodyguard who reminded me of a cop, who had stood to attention next to her — the chances are he used to be one!

Daly escaped a jail sentence due to ill health and old age. But she went on to live for another decade and when she eventually died in 2011, mourners packed out the crematorium in Golders Green, many driving BMWs and Mercedes-Benzes.

Known as 'Madame Stiletto', Daly was nostalgically remembered as a successful, no-nonsense businesswoman. Her fortune from illegally running brothels, which was supposed to be seized by police, was said to be split between her children.

Also I discovered what happened to Susan, the pretty blue-eyed woman in the Juicy Couture trackie, who ran the Lucy Palmers sauna in Birmingham. She spoke openly about her work to the press in 2006, obviously not feeling the need to cover up what she did. She stated she used to work there as a girl, but moved up the ladder to become a manager. She admitted helping run it between 1981 and 2003, and talked about the high turnover of girls and how popular it was. But police never investigated or took action against her. She spoke about becoming a Christian since then, as if that made up for her crimes.

I also reported Sean, the councillor to police. He's still working in public life, despite using me, an exploited child, quite confidently. But I was told he might not have known I was underage. Currently he is still working for the council, with nobody knowing about his background. I also reported my old headteacher, concerned he might be still working with children. But he's dead now and no action was taken. Criminals are getting away with it and justice is not being done.

*

Over the years, I have often wondered what happened to Tonia. Incredibly, she appeared to be working as a support worker for women in court. I wondered if she was using her life experience to help others. I assumed so. I don't bear any grudge against her or any ill-feelings. She was just as much a victim herself.

Earlier in one of the saunas, I also ran into the girl who had held a knife to my throat. By then she had had a baby and was clearly a drug addict. I recognised her, but she didn't recognise me. It made me realise how desperate some of the girls had been to use violence and threaten others. I was so grateful again not to have been placed in this position where I was forced to hurt other people.

And what happened to the other gang members? Neil, I discovered, died of cancer. It appeared he managed to keep his double life of gang member and family member successfully separate.

I never knew what happened to Tiger. He disappeared at the same time Tonia did. But he was married and had kids, and I wondered if they ever discovered the truth either. I looked up Darryl too. He is now running his own company. I doubt very much it's legitimate, but he hasn't been investigated and there is no sign of it happening either.

Sadly, I lost touch with my friend Sam in Northern Ireland. I last saw her when I bumped into her whilst shopping in Belfast, and she had a long-term partner and looked healthy and happy, I was so pleased to see.

I managed to get in touch with Sharon, the classmate who once impressed me so much with her painted nails and older boyfriends. Turned out the lads she was seeing were also abusive, cajoling her into underage sex and grooming her too. She never ended up on the streets but she was vulnerable and for the rest of her life she struggled to deal with the trauma.

*

When it comes to my extended family, there is no happy ending for mine. Although I still see Dad, my Auntie Barbara and my grandad, my mum's family fell out when my nanna sadly died.

Around this time, Mum said to me: 'Although you think I haven't been a good mother, you haven't exactly been a good daughter. Think of what I have been through, having to keep your dirty little secret all these years.'

I was lost for words and after this knew it was impossible for me to have a mother-daughter relationship with her. We are now estranged. However, I recognise I have her to thank for the education I did receive. Without that, I am sure, I would not be where I am today.

I am determined my own children will have a very different childhood. Every day, I am grateful for my own children. I am so proud of them all and they are what keep me going and fighting to make this world a better place.

*

Since working at the Holly Project, I was approached by an NGO and the next thing I knew I found myself sitting in a big glass office in London, being listened to by other experts in the field.

I went on to help with many kinds of work including developing a module to help identify victims of trafficking. I have even found myself sharing my experiences with students at universities. Standing in front of a lectern, openly describing my past to students was a moment I never imagined happening in a million years.

I went on to become the first recognised British trafficking survivor to sit on the Victim Support ministerial board, have spoken internationally and been asked to speak to the United Nations. I currently work as a modern slavery and human trafficking consultant and actively promote survivor inclusion into policy making. We can only change the system from within, and that's what I am helping to do.

Currently, in the eyes of society and the law, I am still viewed as the criminal, but the men who made money from me are not. I am still waiting for the courts to decide if I can remove my 52 convictions for prostitution. It's taking years and years but I won't give up. A similar case is currently with the Supreme Court. Although I can never change what happened to me in my past, I can hopefully help change what will happen in the future to girls like me, who society said was worth so little. I am proof that being sexually and criminally exploited could happen to any child, it doesn't matter what race you are, what class, where you live, or what your dreams are. Exploitation is inclusive of everyone.

In the 2020 United Nations Global Report on Trafficking in Persons it states that in higher-income countries, children that are trafficked are mostly sexually exploited, and that traffickers may use the child's vulnerable curcumstances as a means to exploit and that in many cases they will feign romantic interest and not always resort to violence. It also states that once the child is criminalised they are less likely to report the crime, which reduces victim co-operation and means that many traffickers are never brought to justice.

In the same year, the Home Office noted that more than 6,700 victims were identified as being exploited in the UK and almost 60 per cent of these victims were under 18. In contrast to the UN report, 26 per cent were female. This is due to increased awareness of 'county lines' and criminal exploitation. That said, many victims of CSE are also criminally exploited, as I was – much of which has been omitted from this book – yet the criminal exploitation of girls is often further hidden from sight and ignored by authorities. The Prison Reform Trust reported that in 2017, almost 80 per cent of women that were sent to prison were actually victims of sexual or domestic abuse.

I was sold alongside girls from every race and every country. I was even sold alongside girls that were trafficked internationally and had had their passports withheld by their traffickers. Likewise, the traffickers are also from every race and we were sold to anyone with money. The punters, although mostly white, also included every race and nationality. So far Rotherham, Rochdale and Telford have been exposed, inquiries have taken place but we've yet to stop this from happening.

At the end of the day, the most vulnerable in our society deserve our protection. Gangs still operate all over the country today and every young person is at risk. The fight for justice is ongoing, and I am proud to be part of this.

Acknowledgements

This book would not have been possible if it wasn't for the direct support that I have received from some incredible people. Whilst I can't include everyone, I would like to say a huge thank you to Professor Susan Edwards for highlighting the injustice and bringing about change; Max Sawyer for your kindness, blankets and also for the bucketloads of hot chocolate; Holly Archer and Scarlet Jones for your empowerment, putting up with the tears and bringing me back in the room; Geraldine McKelvie for the support you have not only provided to myself but also to the many survivors of CSE in Telford; Gaye Dalton for helping me piece together the truth, your kindness and support; Ms Bennett for everything that you have done for myself and others; my lawyers for helping me to challenge the systemic failings; A.S. for your knowledge, amazing support and for being so super cool; Andy Wallis OBE, for the Modern Slavery Helpline and helping me access the NRM; my writer Shannon Kyle, agent Eve White and my publisher Mirror Books for believing in me and putting this book together. And, of course, my children for giving me the strength and love to keep fighting.

Joanne Phillips